# BUSINESS PROFITABILITY DATA–1980

John B. Walton, M.S., M.B.A.

WEYBRIDGE PUBLISHING COMPANY  Dallas, Texas  75248

ISBN 0-939356-01-5

# INDEX

Please note that each business is also described by its category; Retail - Rtl, Whole-sale - Wsle, Manufacturer - Mfg, Service - Sve.

Page

**A**

## V



## W

# DATA METHEDOLOGY

## 1.0  INTRODUCTION

The purpose of this data compilation, which is a unique computer analysis of published data, is to help you compare different kinds of small businesses that you might acquire or start.

It is impossible to rely on any data with 100% certainly, but the data used (Robert Morris Associates) is probably the most recent, accurate and comprehensive data available.  Robert Morris data is, in fact, used by bankers in assessing the validity of balance sheets and income statements of businesses that apply for loans and so forth.  The data itself is the latest available; the statements used cover the three years ending in mid 1980.  Thus, the data is current, but the reader must judge for himself whether or not any unusual influences might have affected a particular business during the past year.  The recent severe downturn in the economy has, of course, affected all businesses and some, such as home building, more than others. The reader is advised to go through the past year's back issues of journals such as Business Week, Dun's Review, and Fortune to pick up such recent trends.  In addition, the reader should look up the references given in our companion book "Small Business Start Up Manual" in seeking information on a particular business.

## 1.1  Profitability

The primary purpose of this compilation is to list the various businesses (retail, wholesale, service and manufacturing) in order of decreasing profitability.  The most profitable business, Physicians (Service) is denoted #1, the next #2, and so on.

A special definition of profitability has been used.  This definition is somewhat different from that used by almost all financial analysts, but it is the most appropriate for small business evaluation.

In order to understand the new definition of profitability, the layout of a typical balance sheet must be discussed.  You will remember from Small Business Start Up Manual that the typical balance sheet has the following format:

<u>XYZ Corp.     Balance Sheet</u>
Dec. 31, 19XX

| <u>Assets</u> | <u>Equities</u> |
|---|---|
| Current Assets | Current Liabilities |
| Fixed Assets | Long Term Debt |
| <u>Miscellaneous</u> | <u>Owner's Equity</u> |
| Total Assets | Total Equity |

Since Total Assets must always be equal to Total Equity, then the following is also true:

Current Assets + Fixed Asset + Miscellaneous = Current Liabilities + Long Term Debt + Owner's Equity.

Rearranging we have:

Current Assets - Current Liabililites + Long Term Assets = Long Term Debt + Owner's Equity, where Long Term Assets = Fixed Assets + Miscellaneous

Also since (Current Assets - Current Liabilities) = Working Capital, we have, finally:

Working Capital + Long Term Assets = Long Term Debt + Owner's Equity.

This equation means that the total amount of funds required by the business, which equals the amount invested by the owner (Owner's Equity) plus the amount borrowed (Long Term Debt), is used to finance the day to day running of the business (Working Capital) plus the purchase of furniture, equipment and buildings

(Long Term Assets).  So, the total amount of Capital invested in the business is the combined amount of Capital that is borrowed and owner financed.

We have defined, therefore, how much funding a business requires.  In order to complete the definition of profitability, the amount of funds generated by the business needs to be described.  In order to do this let us consider a typical Income Statement.

<u>XYZ Corp.      Income Statement</u>
Year Ending Dec. 31, 19XX

Revenues
<u>Cost Of Goods</u>
Gross Margin

Expenses:
    Officers' Salary (before taxes)*
    Insurance
    Travel
    Heat, Water, Light
    Rent
    Wages
    Legal
    Office Expense
    Repairs & Maintenance
    <u>Etc.</u>

Total Expenses
<u>Profit Before Taxes*</u>

You will observe that the two items denoted by *, namely Officers' Salary and Profit Before Taxes, are <u>almost</u> interchangeable.  The reason is that after paying for the various expenses out of the gross margin you can decide how to allocate the remainder between Officers' Salary and Profit Before Taxes.  Sometimes, as will be discussed later, you will be forced into a certain apportionment, but these two items - salary and profit - represent the funds generated by the business that come back to the owner(s) either as salary or as increased Owner's Equity via retained earnings.

Thus, Profitability (%) = $\dfrac{\text{Funds generated by business}}{\text{Funds required by business}} \times 100$

or,

Profitability (%) = $\dfrac{\text{Officers' Salary + Profit Before Taxes}}{\text{Long Term Debt + Owner's Equity}} \times 100$

## 2.0 BUSINESS DATA SHEET

Now that profitability has been defined, the full data sheet can be discussed in detail.

## 2.1 #XX

The number given in the top left hand corner is the profitability ranking, #1 being the most profitable and #261 being the least profitable.

## 2.2 Name/SIC

The type of business is named together with its SIC number. The SIC number, or Standard Industrial Code, was developed for U.S. Government statistical purposes. A detailed description of the meaning of each code number can be found in the publication "Standard Industrial Classification Manual", which can be found in your local library or from Superindendent of Documents, U.S. Government Printing Office, Washington, D.C. 20402.

## 2.3 Total Assets

You will notice that each business is listed as having total assets of $250,000. A standard value, such as $250,000, has to be chosen in order to make a fair comparison between different businesses. This is because profitability varies markedly with asset size.  In general, profitability decreases as asset size increases.  The implications of this are discussed later under "Conclusions".

The asset value $250,000 was chosen for several reasons:

- It is the smallest asset size for which complete data is available.

- It was felt that the comparison of very small businesses would not be valid because of the extremely wide variation in their profitability.

- $250,000 is the value that a small business of $100,000 in total assets can, on average, grow to over a five years period.  Taking a Typesetting Business (SIC 2791) as an example; $100,000 in total assets corresponds to an Owners' Equity of $26,000, a Long Term Debt of $28,300 and Retained Earnings of $12,500 a year (before taxes). You will see on page  46   that a Typesetting Business of $250,000 in total assets has an Owners' Equity of $95,000, a Long Term Debt of $75,000 and Retained Earnings of $25,250 per year (before taxes).  It is clear, therefore, that a business man can invest $26,000 of his own money in a small business, and can easily have a total of  $95,000 invested after five years by retaining an average of about $14,000 (after taxes) every year.

Thus, by using a $250,000 total assets figure we are comparing the profitability of relatively mature businesses that the average purchaser could expect to have in five years, after starting from a modest investment of $25,000 - $30,000.  It is felt that most readers would be more interested in the profitability and income available from a mature business rather than first year results.  Naturally, a business can stop growing at any point by not retaining any earnings, but business profitability is usually such that retaining earnings probably represents the best investment a businessman can make.

You will note, however, that where the data is available the profitabilities of businesses having assets in the $0 – $250,000 range is also provided.

## 2.3 Profitability

The meaning of profitability was discussed in Section 1.1 and you will remember it is for businesses with total assets of $250,000.

## 2.4 Trend

The profitability trend, upwards indicated by + and downwards by –, is the average yearly percentage change over the past three years.  This was calculated by the computer using a method known as "linear least – squares fit".

Any change below $\pm$ 1% may be regarded as not very significant. However, changes above that value should be investigated and their cause determined.

The meaning of profitability trend can be seen in the following example.  If a business has a profitability of 40% and a trend of +2.0%, this means that the profitability was 36% in 1978, 38% in 1979 and 40% in 1980.

## 2.5 Downside Risk/Upside Potential

In order to understand the terms Downside Risk and Upside Potential, you must first understand the terms Median, Upper Quartile and Lower Quartile. Suppose, for example, there are 100 businesses of a given type and they are ranked from 1 to 100 in order of their increasing total income (officers' compensation plus net profit).  The business ranked in the 50th position is called the Median, and, therefore, 50% of businesses have less income than the Median and 50% have more income. Note, averages are not used because they can be misleading.

The business ranked in the 75th place is called the Upper Quartile point since only one quarter or 25 of the businesses have more income, whereas 75 have less income.

<u>NOTE</u> The values calculated for Profitability and Trend are for the Median business in each category.

The Downside Risk is calculated for each type of business and reflects how far, in percentage terms, the total income of the Lower Quartile business is away from the total income of the Median business. As an example, suppose the Median total income and Lower Quartile total income of a business are, respectively, $70,000 and $20,000. The Downside Risk (DR) is:

$$DR \; = \; \frac{70,000 - 20,000}{70,000} \; X100 = \quad 71.4\%$$

Obviously, the greater the DR percentage, the lower is the total income of the Lower Quartile business and the more risky is that given type of business.

The Upside Potential is the reverse calculation and indicates the total income of the Upper Quartile business in relation to that of the Median business. If, for example, the Median total income and Upper Quartile total income of a business are, respectively, $70,000 and $125,000 the Upside Potential (UP) is:

$$UP \; = \; \frac{125,000 - 70,000}{70,000} \; x100 = \quad 78.6\%$$

Obviously, the greater the UP percentage the greater is the profit potential in that business category.

## 2.6 Space Required

The space required figure was derived from the dollar value of the rent paid by the Median business. A value of $5 per square foot per year was assumed in order to calculate the space required. However, the $5 value is merely an average figure; warehouse space probably rents for a little less than this whereas retail space, if new, is at least double this. In order to calculate the space required in your area more exactly, do the following:

- Contact a local realtor and obtain the average cost of space in your area for your particular type of business.

- If the local value per square foot per year is \$X, then multiply the space required figure provided in the text by 5 divided by X.

- For example, the local figure may be \$4 per square foot per year and the space required figure may be 2000 sq. ft. In this case, the space actually required in your area is:

$$\frac{2000 \times 5}{4} = 2{,}500 \text{ sq. ft.}$$

## 2.7  Source And Use Of Capital

The source and use of Capital section is again based on Median businesses having total assets of \$250,000. You will immediately notice that the total Capital used and required falls far short of the total assets figure of \$250,000. This is because total equities, which equals total assets, includes short-term liabilities. Short-term liabilities are the average ongoing outstanding liabilities that are never paid for out of Capital.

The table shown is structured around the equation derived in Section 1.1:

Working Capital + Long Term Assets = Long Term Debt + Owners' Equity.

This table is interesting because it shows the Debt/Equity Mix, that is how much Long Term Debt is carried by the business in relation to owner funds. It reflects how much the business wants or needs to borrow and how much banks permit it to borrow. Generally, banks do not like to lend more than the amount of Owner Equity.

The Capital use side of the table reflects, somewhat, the nature of the business. For example, a Dry Cleaners has a large proportion of Long Term Assets in relation to Working Capital because, being essentially a quick turn around cash business, it does not need a large amount of Working Capital. On the other hand, many service businesses, Lawyers for example, have little in the way of fixed assets and need a higher proportion of working capital.

## 2.8 Sales And Income ($)

Sales, Officers' Compensation, Net Profit and Total Income are listed for Upper Quartile, Median and Lower Quartile businesses all having total assets of $250,000.

## 2.9 Profitability Versus Asset Size

Where the data is available profitability is listed against asset size range.  N/A reflects data Not Available.

## 3.0 CONCLUSIONS

## 3.1 Profitability Range

You can see from the data listings that there is, approximately, a 15:1 range in the Median profitabilities of the 261 businesses listed.  The Median profitability amongst all the businesses, i.e., #131, has a profitability of about 33%, the Upper quartile point at  66 a profitability of 39%, and the Lower Quartile point a profitability of 27%.  Thus, 50% of all businesses lie in the relatively narrow range of profitability between 27% and 39%.

You will see under "comments" for each business a pertinent remark about that business.  You will observe that as the business becomes increasing less profitable the concern for Downside Risk grows and a statement is always made reflecting it.  In the less profitable businesses you will see a tendency for Lower Quartile Net Profits to far exceed Officers' Salaries; for example, #246, where Net Profit is $8,500 and Officer's Salary is $2,800.  This happens because of the debt repayment requirement, which forces lower salaries and, obviously, increases the risk.  You will note that in this case even the Upper Quartile business has relatively poor profitability; that is about 50%.  In situations such as #246 it is clearly best to avoid acquiring such a business.

## 3.2 Business Category

As you have probably already noted, there are four business categories: Service, Manufacturing, Wholesale and Retail. The profitability curve of all business categories is shown in Figure 1. You will see that most business fall within the peak from 25% - 40% profitability. Figure 2 shows the same plot, but broken out for each business category. They each have the same general shaped curve. The cures for Manufacturing, Wholesale and Retail were tested using a statistical test known as the Chi-Square test and found to be bell shaped curves having what is called a normal distribution (or shape). They were then tested using a "t distribution" test and found to have the same average values, with a 95% confident limit. All this mathematical jargon means that as a general classification Wholesale, Retail and Manufacturing businesses have about the same profitability.

Service businesses form a different category, however. Once the professional type of Service businesses were excluded, that is Architects through Physicians, it was found, using statistical tests, that Service businesses were significantly less profitable than other business categories. This is probably because they require less skill to operate and, therefore, command less revenue in the marketplace.

Returning to Wholesale, Retail and Manufacturing businesses, you will note that some show strong uptrends whilst others down trends. It is probable that businesses show cyclical variations in profitability. It would be helpful to make sure your type of business is in an uptrend.

You may want to know whether or not it is better to be a re-tailer, a manufacturer or a wholesaler in a particular type of business. A few businesses, which have each type of category are examined below:

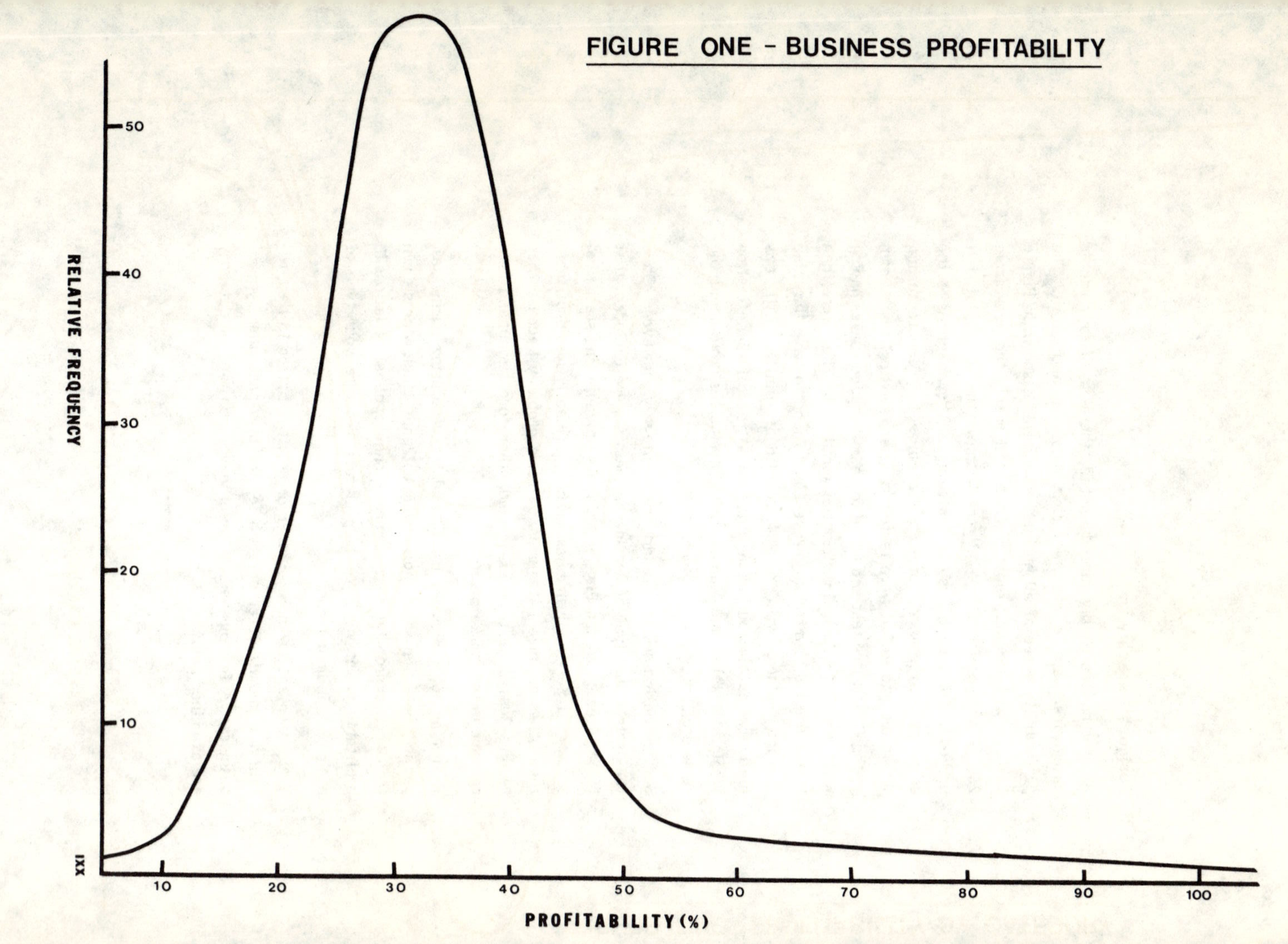

FIGURE ONE - BUSINESS PROFITABILITY
RELATIVE FREQUENCY
50
40
30
20
10
IXX
PROFITABILITY (%)
10
20
30
40
50
60
70
80
90
100

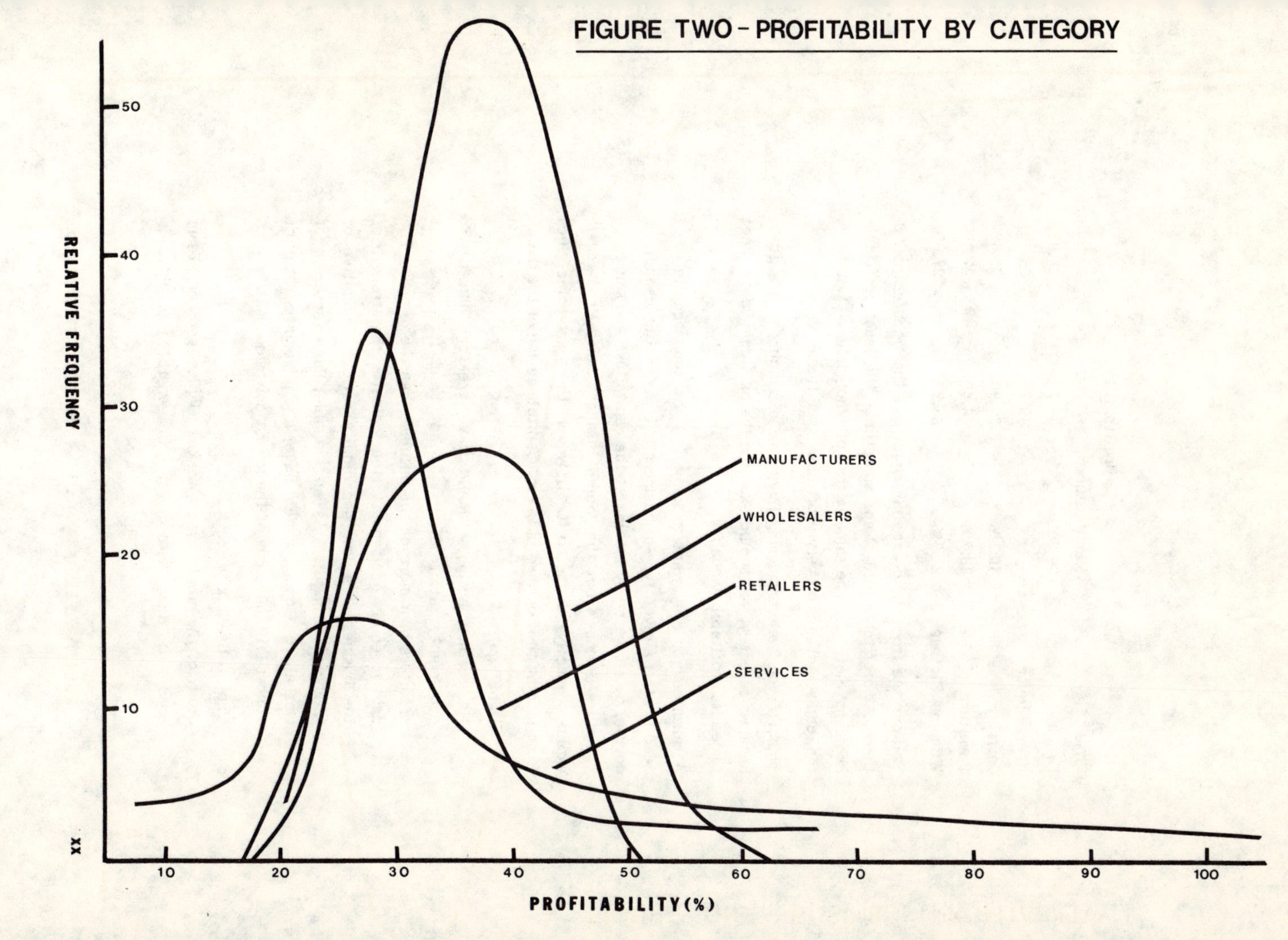

FIGURE TWO - PROFITABILITY BY CATEGORY
RELATIVE FREQUENCY
PROFITABILITY (%)
MANUFACTURERS
WHOLESALERS
RETAILERS
SERVICES
XX

|                 | Profitability |            |          |
|-----------------|---------------|------------|----------|
| Business        | Manufacturer  | Wholesaler | Retailer |
| Drugs           | 39.7%         | 34.7%      | 36.0%    |
| Beer, Liquor    | —             | 40.2%      | 26.5%    |
| Jewelry         | 40.1%         | 29.9%      | 35.6%    |
| Furniture       | 38.2%         | 48.4%      | 27.3%    |
| Womens' Clothes | 24.7%         | 38.2%      | 27.6%    |

You can see from the chart that sometimes the Manufacturer is the most profitable (drugs) and sometimes the least profitable (womens' clothes). The same is true of Wholesalers. Retailers, too, can sometimes be very profitable - see furs.

Thus, if you are considering buying or expanding into a given business category, you should examine the particular data sheet to see its profitability quality.

A question you may want to know is ' how much capital do I need to start a given type of business'? This question cannot, of course, be answered by looking at the capital use and source of a mature business, but the "Small Business Start Up Manual" explains exactly how to do it. However, there are some clues from looking the Source and Use of Capital section of the data.

- Debt/Equity Mix

  No mature business should have greater than a 1:1 debt/equity ratio. If this is not true, it means that creditors own more of the business than the owners. The debt to equity need most often indicates the strength of the business - a low debt/equity ratio is indicative of financial strength. As an example, Manufacturers of Opthalmic Goods, Which have a debt/equity ratio of almost 1:10, have one of the lowest downside risks.

- Capital Use Mix

  Study of the mix between Working Capital and Long Term Assets is also instructive. In general this ratio is

reflective of business category. For example, Wholesalers
have relatively low fixed assets, relying as they do on
rented space and, if they wish, rented fork lift trucks, etc.
Businesses requiring large Working Capital are more prone
to the accumulation of bad debts and are, therefore,
somewhat more risky than low Working Capital businesses.
Certain businesses, such as Dry Cleaners and Restaurants
have very little need for Working Capital, and, indeed,
some businesses, such as the Refuse Collection service,
have large negative Working Capital balances. In this
case, the negative Working Capital is used, in fact, as a
source of Capital to finance the business.

## 3.3   Asset Size

In almost every case business profitability decreases with
increasing assets. There are two reasons for this:

1.   The proportion of Officers' Salaries obviously declines
     since larger businesses have a higher proportion of em-
     ployees who are non officers.

2.   The actual percentage figure for net profits declines with
     increasing assets. Clearly, small businesses are more
     efficient than large businesses. The reason may be that
     small business owners work harder, keep a stricter control
     on costs and can respond more quickly to market
     conditions. Does this mean that a businessman should
     expand his business enterprise by buying several small
     related or unrelated businesses, rather than expanding a
     given location? Is is doubtful whether this strategy would
     work, since the businessman would have to employ well
     paid managers to oversee the various operations.
     However, no real data exists to prove the matter one way
     or the other. In any event, you need to expand to a
     reasonable size to gain a satisfactory income. Once you
     are profitable, a bank will lend you more and more so that

it becomes easier to expand.

## 3.4  Value Of A Business

This book is intended to provide you with several benchmarks
to enable you to make a wise choice concerning a given business.  In order to decide how much to pay for a business, you
should use the valuation technique described in Section 8.9 in
"Small Business Start Up Manual".

## 3.5  Business Failure Rate

The primary purpose of the data compiled in this book is to
guide the entrepreneur to the most profitable business oppor-
tunities.  Another interesting piece of information is the failure rate of various businesses.  Such a compilation does exist
and is readily available from Dun and Bradstreet, 99 Church
Street, New York, N.Y. 10007.  Four publications are available:

I.  Business Failure Record

This annual publication provides a wealth of statistical
data:

- Annual failure rate since 1920.  For example, the
  average business failure rate was 43 per thousand
  in 1975 and 24 per thousand in 1978.  Thus, failure
  rate undergoes significant changes over the years
  and the failure rate of a particular business must
  be studied in the light of the overall business failure rate for that year.

- A detailed discussion of the years' business conditions is provided.

- Number of business failures by businesses in 25
  U.S. cities over the last three years.

- The failure trend by state over several years since
  1940.

- The failure rate in specific retail and manufacturing lines.

- The failure rate by size of business liability.

- The number of failures in 43 commercial and industrial lines.

- The age of failed businesses.

- The age trend of failed businesses.

- The reason for business failure.

This publication is available free of charge by writing to Dun and Bradstreet.

II.    Quarterly Analysis Of Failures

This publication provides the number of business failures in 43 business lines.

III.   Monthly Business Failures

This publication provides the number and liabilities in 43 business lines. A concise discussion on business conditions and the business most influenced by those conditions is also discussed.

IV.   Business Failures

This is a weekly publication with comment and analysis. The last three publications can be found, usually on microfiche, in the business section of your central library.

The Dun and Bradstreet publications can be used to determine how risky a given business is and to determine its trend in relation to other business lines. For example, Laundries can be compared with other service businesses.

As you can see in the chart below, failures have shown a steady decrease over the last six years and have also shown a steady decrease as a percentage of service business failures

LAUNDRY FAILURES (By Number)

| Year<br>Quarter | 1974 | 1975 | 1976 | 1977 | 1978<br>I  II  III  IV | 1979<br>I  II  III  IV |
|---|---|---|---|---|---|---|
| Laundries | 42 | 46 | 33 | 18 | 2  7  2  3 | 4  4  2  3 |
| Total for Service Businesses | 1320 | 1637 | 1331 | 1041 | 205  215  171  182 | 206  252  257  215 |
| Laundry failures as a % of all Services | 3.2 | 2.8 | 2.5 | 1.7 | 0.9  3.2  1.2  1.6<br>for year – 1.8% | 1.9  1.6  0.8  1.4<br>for year – 1.4% |

# PHYSICIANS (SVE)                    SIC:8011

| | |
|---|---|
| **Total Assets** | $250,000 |
| **Profitability** | 122.2% |
| **Trend** | N/A |
| **Downside Risk** | 51.4% |
| **Upside Potential** | 74.2% |
| **Space Required** | 2760 Sq. Ft. |

### SOURCE AND USE OF CAPITAL

| Capital Source | | Capital Use | |
|---|---|---|---|
| Owner's Equity | $113,500 | Working Capital | $ 44,250 |
| Long Term Debt | $ 55,750 | Long Term Assets | $125,000 |
| Total Capital Requ'd | $169,250 | Total Capital Used | $169,250 |

### SALES AND INCOME

| | Upper Quartile | Median | Lower Quartile |
|---|---|---|---|
| Sales | 750,000 | 600,000 | 350,000 |
| Officer's Salary* | 313,500 | 184,800 | 92,050 |
| Net Profit* | 46,750 | 22,000 | 8,500 |
| Total Income* | 360,250 | 206,800 | 100,550 |

*Before Tax

### PROFITABILITY VS ASSETS

| Assets | 0-250$K | 250-1,000$K | 1-10$M |
|---|---|---|---|
| Profitability | 340.1% | 122.2% | 86.9% |

**COMMENTS:** *No surprises here. An excellent business, although AMA complains of a coming Physicians' glut that will reduce profitability.*



# LEGAL SERVICES (SVE)                    SIC:8111

| | |
|---|---|
| **Total Assets** | $250,000 |
| **Profitability** | 118.8% |
| **Trend** | -71.1% |
| **Downside Risk** | 54.6% |
| **Upside Potential** | 254.5% |
| **Space Required** | 4140 Sq. Ft. |

### SOURCE AND USE OF CAPITAL

| Capital Source | | Capital Use | |
|---|---|---|---|
| Owner's Equity | $109,750 | Working Capital | $ 69,500 |
| Long Term Debt | $ 60,000 | Long Term Assets | $100,250 |
| Total Capital Requ'd | $169,750 | Total Capital Used | $169,750 |

### SALES AND INCOME

| | Upper Quartile | Median | Lower Quartile |
|---|---|---|---|
| Sales | 1,000,000 | 575,000 | 400,000 |
| Officer's Salary* | 410,000 | 150,650 | 64,000 |
| Net Profit* | 304,750 | 51,000 | 27,500 |
| Total Income* | 714,750 | 201,650 | 91,500 |

*Before Tax

### PROFITABILITY VS ASSETS

| Assets | 0-250$K | 250-1,000$K | 1-10$M |
|---|---|---|---|
| Profitability | 377.5% | 118.8% | 258.0% |

**COMMENTS:** *Another excellent business. Far better upside potential than Physicians! Perhaps explained by multi-officer partnership.*

# #3   COMPUTER PROGRAMMING/SOFTWARE SERVICES SIC:7372

| | |
|---|---|
| **Total Assets** | $250,000 |
| **Profitability** | 96.3% |
| **Trend** | N/A |
| **Downside Risk** | 76.5% |
| **Upside Potential** | 66.6% |
| **Space Required** | 3875 Sq. Ft. |

## SOURCE AND USE OF CAPITAL

| Capital Source | | Capital Use | |
|---|---|---|---|
| Owner's Equity | $ 93,250 | Working Capital | $ 45,750 |
| Long Term Debt | $ 42,750 | Long Term Assets | $ 90,250 |
| Total Capital Requ'd | $136,000 | Total Capital Used | $136,000 |

## SALES AND INCOME

| | Upper Quartile | Median | Lower Quartile |
|---|---|---|---|
| Sales | 750,000 | 625,000 | 400,000 |
| Officer's Salary* | 150,000 | 92,500 | 17,600 |
| Net Profit* | 68,250 | 38,500 | 13,250 |
| Total Income* | 218,250 | 131,000 | 30,850 |

*Before Tax

## PROFITABILITY VS ASSETS

| Assets | 0-250$K | 250-1,000$K | 1-10$M |
|---|---|---|---|
| Profitability | N/A | 96.3% | N/A |

**COMMENTS:** *Very high downside risk. Good business for the successful in an area of growing demand.*


# #4   ACCOUNTING,AUDITING&BOOKKEEPING   SIC:8931

| | |
|---|---|
| **Total Assets** | $250,000 |
| **Profitability** | 95.0% |
| **Trend** | -8.0% |
| **Downside Risk** | 46.5% |
| **Upside Potential** | 82.1% |
| **Space Required** | 4085 Sq. Ft. |

## SOURCE AND USE OF CAPITAL

| Capital Source | | Capital Use | |
|---|---|---|---|
| Owner's Equity | $144,250 | Working Capital | $117,250 |
| Long Term Debt | $ 47,250 | Long Term Assets | $ 74,250 |
| Total Capital Requ'd | $191,500 | Total Capital Used | $191,500 |

## SALES AND INCOME

| | Upper Quartile | Median | Lower Quartile |
|---|---|---|---|
| Sales | 625,000 | 475,000 | 375,000 |
| Officer's Salary* | 195,625 | 115,425 | 74,250 |
| Net Profit* | 135,750 | 66,500 | 23,000 |
| Total Income* | 331,375 | 181,925 | 97,250 |

*Before Tax

## PROFITABILITY VS ASSETS

| Assets | 0-250$K | 250-1,000$K | 1-10$M |
|---|---|---|---|
| Profitability | 161.2% | 95.0% | 76.2% |

**COMMENTS:** *Excellent return, low downside risk in a profession of relatively low professional skill demands – CPA. Small business computers may be causing the downtrend.*

# #5 MANAGEMENT CONSULTING & PUBLIC RELATIONS SIC:7392

| | |
|---|---|
| Total Assets | $250,000 |
| Profitability | 84.0% |
| Trend | +2.4% |
| Downside Risk | 60.7% |
| Upside Potential | 244.2% |
| Space Required | 4725 Sq. Ft. |

## SOURCE AND USE OF CAPITAL

| Capital Source | | Capital Use | |
|---|---|---|---|
| Owner's Equity | $102,500 | Working Capital | $ 50,750 |
| Long Term Debt | $ 22,500 | Long Term Assets | $ 74,250 |
| Total Capital Requ'd | $125,000 | Total Capital Used | $125,000 |

## SALES AND INCOME

| | Upper Quartile | Median | Lower Quartile |
|---|---|---|---|
| Sales | 950,000 | 675,000 | 500,000 |
| Officer's Salary* | 311,600 | 71,550 | 24,500 |
| Net Profit* | 50,000 | 33,500 | 16,750 |
| Total Income* | 361,600 | 105,050 | 41,250 |

*Before Tax

## PROFITABILITY VS ASSETS

| Assets | 0-250$K | 250-1,000$K | 1-10$M |
|---|---|---|---|
| Profitability | 171.0% | 84.0% | N/A |

**COMMENTS:** *Good returns for degreed individual prepared to slowly build up clientel. Fairly high downside risk. Excellent upside potential. Lot of away from home travel.*

# #6     FURS(RTL)     SIC:5681

| | |
|---|---|
| Total Assets | $250,000 |
| Profitability | 68.8% |
| Trend | +14.4% |
| Downside Risk | 56.2% |
| Upside Potential | 66.6% |
| Space Required | 2470 Sq. Ft. |

## SOURCE AND USE OF CAPITAL

| Capital Source | | Capital Use | |
|---|---|---|---|
| Owner's Equity | $ 88,250 | Working Capital | $ 64,250 |
| Long Term Debt | $ 3,000 | Long Term Assets | $ 27,000 |
| Total Capital Requ'd | $ 91,250 | Total Capital Used | $ 91,250 |

## SALES AND INCOME

| | Upper Quartile | Median | Lower Quartile |
|---|---|---|---|
| Sales | 550,000 | 475,000 | 325,000 |
| Officer's Salary* | 75,350 | 41,800 | 16,250 |
| Net Profit* | 29,250 | 21,000 | 11,250 |
| Total Income* | 104,600 | 62,800 | 27,500 |

*Before Tax

## PROFITABILITY VS ASSETS

| Assets | 0-250$K | 250-1,000$K | 1-10$M |
|---|---|---|---|
| Profitability | N/A | 68.8% | N/A |

**COMMENTS:** *The most profitable retail business by far! Perhaps the recent cold winters in the North and East helped the upward trend.*

| | |
|---|---|
| Total Assets | $250,000 |
| Profitability | 65.6% |
| Trend | +3.4% |
| Downside Risk | 55.0% |
| Upside Potential | 92.2% |
| Space Required | 1120 Sq. Ft. |

### SOURCE AND USE OF CAPITAL

| Capital Source | | Capital Use | |
|---|---|---|---|
| Owner's Equity | $ 65,750 | Working Capital | $ 12,000 |
| Long Term Debt | $ 29,000 | Long Term Assets | $ 82,750 |
| Total Capital Requ'd | $ 94,750 | Total Capital Used | $ 94,750 |

### SALES AND INCOME

| | Upper Quartile | Median | Lower Quartile |
|---|---|---|---|
| Sales | 275,000 | 200,000 | 150,000 |
| Officer's Salary* | 94,875 | 48,600 | 21,900 |
| Net Profit* | 24,500 | 13,500 | 6,000 |
| Total Income* | 119,375 | 62,100 | 27,900 |

*Before Tax

### PROFITABILITY VS ASSETS

| Assets | 0-250$K | 250-1,000$K | 1-10$M |
|---|---|---|---|
| Profitability | 140.8% | 65.5% | 57.1% |

**COMMENTS:** *Reasonable profits for the relatively unskilled! Good upside potential.*



| | |
|---|---|
| Total Assets | $250,000 |
| Profitability | 64.4% |
| Trend | -15.9% |
| Downside Risk | 57.6% |
| Upside Potential | 111.5% |
| Space Required | 3960 Sq. Ft. |

### SOURCE AND USE OF CAPITAL

| Capital Source | | Capital Use | |
|---|---|---|---|
| Owner's Equity | $ 90,250 | Working Capital | $ 25,250 |
| Long Term Debt | $ 45,000 | Long Term Assets | $110,000 |
| Total Capital Requ'd | $135,250 | Total Capital Used | $135,250 |

### SALES AND INCOME

| | Upper Quartile | Median | Lower Quartile |
|---|---|---|---|
| Sales | 725,000 | 550,000 | 450,000 |
| Officer's Salary* | 132,675 | 53,350 | 21,150 |
| Net Profit* | 51,500 | 33,750 | 15,750 |
| Total Income* | 184,175 | 87,100 | 36,900 |

*Before Tax

### PROFITABILITY VS ASSETS

| Assets | 0-250$K | 250-1,000$K | 1-10$M |
|---|---|---|---|
| Profitability | 72.9% | 64.4% | N/A |

**COMMENTS:** *The downward trend should be investigated - may be small business computers again (see "Accounting Services").*

# #9 COMMERCIAL RESEARCH & DEVELOPMENT LABS (SVE) SIC:7391

| | |
|---|---|
| **Total Assets** | $250,000 |
| **Profitability** | 63.3% |
| **Trend** | +4.5% |
| **Downside Risk** | 58.1% |
| **Upside Potential** | 69.3% |
| **Space Required** | 3500 Sq. Ft. |

## SOURCE AND USE OF CAPITAL

| Capital Source | | Capital Use | |
|---|---|---|---|
| Owner's Equity | $105,250 | Working Capital | $ 55,000 |
| Long Term Debt | $ 51,750 | Long Term Assets | $102,000 |
| Total Capital Requ'd | $157,000 | Total Capital Used | $157,000 |

## SALES AND INCOME

| | Upper Quartile | Median | Lower Quartile |
|---|---|---|---|
| Sales | 650,000 | 500,000 | 375,000 |
| Officer's Salary* | 120,250 | 66,000 | 20,625 |
| Net Profit* | 48,250 | 33,500 | 21,000 |
| Total Income* | 168,500 | 99,500 | 41,625 |

*Before Tax

## PROFITABILITY VS ASSETS

| Assets | 0-250$K | 250-1,000$K | 1-10$M |
|---|---|---|---|
| Profitability | N/A | 63.3% | N/A |

**COMMENTS:** *Specialised skills needed here - good upside potential. High initial asset investment.*

# #10 ENGINEERING & ARCHITECTURAL CO (SVE) SIC:8911

| | |
|---|---|
| **Total Assets** | $250,000 |
| **Profitability** | 60.3% |
| **Trend** | -1.4% |
| **Downside Risk** | 58.9% |
| **Upside Potential** | 111.7% |
| **Space Required** | 2880 Sq. Ft. |

## SOURCE AND USE OF CAPITAL

| Capital Source | | Capital Use | |
|---|---|---|---|
| Owner's Equity | $100,500 | Working Capital | $ 63,250 |
| Long Term Debt | $ 38,000 | Long Term Assets | $ 75,250 |
| Total Capital Requ'd | $138,500 | Total Capital Used | $138,500 |

## SALES AND INCOME

| | Upper Quartile | Median | Lower Quartile |
|---|---|---|---|
| Sales | 800,000 | 600,000 | 425,000 |
| Officer's Salary* | 117,600 | 52,800 | 20,825 |
| Net Profit* | 59,250 | 30,750 | 13,500 |
| Total Income* | 176,850 | 83,550 | 34,325 |

*Before Tax

## PROFITABILITY VS ASSETS

| Assets | 0-250$K | 250-1,000$K | 1-10$M |
|---|---|---|---|
| Profitability | 180.0% | 60.3% | 33.6% |

**COMMENTS:** *Professional qualifications required - moderate downside risk.*

### #11  JANITORIAL CO (SVE)  SIC:7349

| | |
|---|---|
| Total Assets | $250,000 |
| Profitability | 59.5% |
| Trend | +0.6% |
| Downside Risk | 59.3% |
| Upside Potential | 62.6% |
| Space Required | 1200 Sq. Ft. |

#### SOURCE AND USE OF CAPITAL

| Capital Source | | Capital Use | |
|---|---|---|---|
| Owner's Equity | $100,500 | Working Capital | $ 53,750 |
| Long Term Debt | $ 40,250 | Long Term Assets | $ 87,000 |
| Total Capital Requ'd | $140,750 | Total Capital Used | $140,750 |

#### SALES AND INCOME

| | Upper Quartile | Median | Lower Quartile |
|---|---|---|---|
| Sales | 1,275,000 | 1,000,000 | 600,000 |
| Officer's Salary* | 71,400 | 42,000 | 19,800 |
| Net Profit* | 64,750 | 41,750 | 14,250 |
| Total Income* | 136,150 | 83,750 | 34,050 |

*Before Tax

#### PROFITABILITY VS ASSETS

| Assets | 0-250$K | 250-1,000$K | 1-10$M |
|---|---|---|---|
| Profitability | 86.0% | 59.5% | N/A |

**COMMENTS:** *Big surprise! Excellent opportunity for minority who can organize unskilled, reliable workers (or anyone else).*

### #12  ADVERTISING AGENCIES (SVE)  SIC:7311

| | |
|---|---|
| Total Assets | $250,000 |
| Profitability | 59.0% |
| Trend | +0.3% |
| Downside Risk | 52.8% |
| Upside Potential | 109.8% |
| Space Required | 3255 Sq. Ft. |

#### SOURCE AND USE OF CAPITAL

| Capital Source | | Capital Use | |
|---|---|---|---|
| Owner's Equity | $ 75,250 | Working Capital | $ 25,500 |
| Long Term Debt | $ 28,250 | Long Term Assets | $ 78,000 |
| Total Capital Requ'd | $103,500 | Total Capital Used | $103,500 |

#### SALES AND INCOME

| | Upper Quartile | Median | Lower Quartile |
|---|---|---|---|
| Sales | 1,100,000 | 775,000 | 475,000 |
| Officer's Salary* | 95,700 | 41,850 | 17,575 |
| Net Profit* | 32,500 | 19,250 | 11,250 |
| Total Income* | 128,200 | 61,100 | 28,825 |

*Before Tax

#### PROFITABILITY VS ASSETS

| Assets | 0-250$K | 250-1,000$K | 1-10$M |
|---|---|---|---|
| Profitability | 123.6% | 59.0% | N/A |

**COMMENTS:** *Stable industrial; good return even in bad economic climate. Good upside potential.*

# OPTHALMIC GOODS (MFG)   SIC:3851

| Total Assets | $250,000 |
|---|---|
| Profitability | 57.0% |
| Trend | +0.1% |
| Downside Risk | 37.3% |
| Upside Potential | 102.2% |
| Space Required | 1560 Sq. Ft. |

## SOURCE AND USE OF CAPITAL

| Capital Source | | Capital Use | |
|---|---|---|---|
| Owner's Equity | $134,750 | Working Capital | $ 79,250 |
| Long Term Debt | $ 14,000 | Long Term Assets | $ 69,500 |
| Total Capital Requ'd | $148,750 | Total Capital Used | $148,750 |

## SALES AND INCOME

| | Upper Quartile | Median | Lower Quartile |
|---|---|---|---|
| Sales | 950,000 | 650,000 | 550,000 |
| Officer's Salary* | 114,000 | 50,050 | 34,650 |
| Net Profit* | 57,500 | 34,750 | 18,500 |
| Total Income* | 171,500 | 84,800 | 53,150 |

*Before Tax

## PROFITABILITY VS ASSETS

| Assets | 0-250$K | 250-1,000$K | 1-10$M |
|---|---|---|---|
| Profitability | N/A | 57.0% | N/A |

**COMMENTS:** *Excellent return, low downside risk. Large working capital required. Pandering to eye wear vanity pays!*




# PLASTIC MATERIALS, RESINS (MFG)   SIC:2821

| Total Assets | $250,000 |
|---|---|
| Profitability | 52.7% |
| Trend | -1.7% |
| Downside Risk | 56.1% |
| Upside Potential | 125.3% |
| Space Required | 2070 Sq. Ft. |

## SOURCE AND USE OF CAPITAL

| Capital Source | | Capital Use | |
|---|---|---|---|
| Owner's Equity | $ 99,000 | Working Capital | $ 47,750 |
| Long Term Debt | $ 28,250 | Long Term Assets | $ 79,500 |
| Total Capital Requ'd | $127,250 | Total Capital Used | $127,250 |

## SALES AND INCOME

| | Upper Quartile | Median | Lower Quartile |
|---|---|---|---|
| Sales | 825,000 | 575,000 | 350,000 |
| Officer's Salary* | 97,350 | 40,825 | 12,950 |
| Net Profit* | 53,750 | 26,250 | 16,500 |
| Total Income* | 151,100 | 67,075 | 29,450 |

*Before Tax

## PROFITABILITY VS ASSETS

| Assets | 0-250$K | 250-1,000$K | 1-10$M |
|---|---|---|---|
| Profitability | N/A | 52.7% | 28.0% |

**COMMENTS:** *Demand is high for plastic products - oil price increase may be causing some drop in profitability.*

| | |
|---|---|
| Total Assets | $250,000 |
| Profitability | 52.1% |
| Trend | -9.9% |
| Downside Risk | 64.1% |
| Upside Potential | 92.1% |
| Space Required | 1804 Sq. Ft. |

## SOURCE AND USE OF CAPITAL

| Capital Source | | Capital Use | |
|---|---|---|---|
| Owner's Equity | $ 80,250 | Working Capital | $ 79,500 |
| Long Term Debt | $ 35,500 | Long Term Assets | $ 36,250 |
| Total Capital Requ'd | $115,750 | Total Capital Used | $115,750 |

## SALES AND INCOME

| | Upper Quartile | Median | Lower Quartile |
|---|---|---|---|
| Sales | 1,375,000 | 1,150,000 | 900,000 |
| Officer's Salary* | 63,250 | 34,500 | 14,400 |
| Net Profit* | 52,500 | 25,750 | 7,250 |
| Total Income* | 115,750 | 60,250 | 21,650 |

*Before Tax

## PROFITABILITY VS ASSETS

| Assets | 0-250$K | 250-1,000$K | 1-10$M |
|---|---|---|---|
| Profitability | 62.2% | 52.1% | N/A |

**COMMENTS:** *Even after a significant downtrend, the used car salesman still makes good money. Relatively small long term assets needed.*

# #16    SURGICAL, MEDICAL & DENTAL INSTRUMENTS (MFG)

| | | |
|---|---|---|
| Total Assets | $250,000 | SIC:3841,43 |
| Profitability | 51.3% | |
| Trend | -1.8% | |
| Downside Risk | 68.8% | |
| Upside Potential | 102.9% | |
| Space Required | 2600 Sq. Ft. | |

## SOURCE AND USE OF CAPITAL

| Capital Source | | Capital Use | |
|---|---|---|---|
| Owner's Equity | $107,000 | Working Capital | $ 78,750 |
| Long Term Debt | $ 31,000 | Long Term Assets | $ 59,250 |
| Total Capital Requ'd | $138,000 | Total Capital Used | $138,000 |

## SALES AND INCOME

| | Upper Quartile | Median | Lower Quartile |
|---|---|---|---|
| Sales | 700,000 | 500,000 | 400,000 |
| Officer's Salary* | 86,100 | 35,000 | 12,800 |
| Net Profit* | 57,500 | 35,750 | 9,250 |
| Total Income* | 143,600 | 70,750 | 22,050 |

*Before Tax

## PROFITABILITY VS ASSETS

| Assets | 0-250$K | 250-1,000$K | 1-10$M |
|---|---|---|---|
| Profitability | N/A | 51.3% | 19.0% |

**COMMENTS:** *Profitable, specialty manufacturing skill.*

| | |
|---|---|
| Total Assets | $250,000 |
| Profitability | 50.2% |
| Trend | +5.0% |
| Downside Risk | 50.9% |
| Upside Potential | 51.2% |
| Space Required | 2415 Sq. Ft. |

## SOURCE AND USE OF CAPITAL

| Capital Source | | Capital Use | |
|---|---|---|---|
| Owner's Equity | $ 79,500 | Working Capital | $ 49,500 |
| Long Term Debt | $ 47,750 | Long Term Assets | $ 77,750 |
| Total Capital Requ'd | $127,250 | Total Capital Used | $127,250 |

## SALES AND INCOME

| | Upper Quartile | Median | Lower Quartile |
|---|---|---|---|
| Sales | 675,000 | 525,000 | 350,000 |
| Officer's Salary* | 43,200 | 25,200 | 11,900 |
| Net Profit* | 53,500 | 38,750 | 19,500 |
| Total Income* | 96,700 | 63,950 | 31,400 |

*Before Tax

## PROFITABILITY VS ASSETS

| Assets | 0-250$K | 250-1,000$K | 1-10$M |
|---|---|---|---|
| Profitability | N/A | 50.2% | N/A |

**COMMENTS:** *Demand continues to grow, specialist skills needed,  Heavy initial (probably venture) capital required.*



| | |
|---|---|
| Total Assets | $250,000 |
| Profitability | 48.4% |
| Trend | +3.2% |
| Downside Risk | 46.9% |
| Upside Potential | 80.5% |
| Space Required | 2400 Sq. Ft. |

## SOURCE AND USE OF CAPITAL

| Capital Source | | Capital Use | |
|---|---|---|---|
| Owner's Equity | $ 96,250 | Working Capital | $ 82,500 |
| Long Term Debt | $ 18,500 | Long Term Assets | $ 32,250 |
| Total Capital Requ'd | $114,750 | Total Capital Used | $114,750 |

## SALES AND INCOME

| | Upper Quartile | Median | Lower Quartile |
|---|---|---|---|
| Sales | 925,000 | 800,000 | 650,000 |
| Officer's Salary* | 64,750 | 32,800 | 19,500 |
| Net Profit* | 35,500 | 22,750 | 10,000 |
| Total Income* | 100,250 | 55,550 | 29,500 |

*Before Tax

## PROFITABILITY VS ASSETS

| Assets | 0-250$K | 250-1,000$K | 1-10$M |
|---|---|---|---|
| Profitability | N/A | 48.4% | 26.4% |

**COMMENTS:** *The most profitable wholesaling business.  Low downside risk, good upside potential.*

# #19 ELECTRICAL COMPONENTS & ACCESSORIES (MFG)

| | | |
|---|---|---|
| Total Assets | $250,000 | |
| Profitability | 47.7% | SIC:3671,72,74,76,77 |
| Trend | -1.7% | |
| Downside Risk | 59.1% | |
| Upside Potential | 105.2% | |
| Space Required | 1840 Sq. Ft. | |

## SOURCE AND USE OF CAPITAL

| Capital Source | | Capital Use | |
|---|---|---|---|
| Owner's Equity | $ 82,250 | Working Capital | $ 55,000 |
| Long Term Debt | $ 43,750 | Long Term Assets | $ 71,000 |
| Total Capital Requ'd | $126,000 | Total Capital Used | $126,000 |

## SALES AND INCOME

| | Upper Quartile | Median | Lower Quartile |
|---|---|---|---|
| Sales | 700,000 | 575,000 | 400,000 |
| Officer's Salary* | 76,300 | 32,200 | 15,600 |
| Net Profit* | 47,250 | 28,000 | 9,000 |
| Total Income* | 123,550 | 60,200 | 24,600 |

*Before Tax

## PROFITABILITY VS ASSETS

| Assets | 0-250$K | 250-1,000$K | 1-10$M |
|---|---|---|---|
| Profitability | N/A | 47.7% | 31.9% |

**COMMENTS:** *Specialty manufacturing - good upside potential.*


# #20 VALVE & PIPE FITTINGS (EXCEPT BRASS) (MFG)

| | | |
|---|---|---|
| Total Assets | $250,000 | |
| Profitability | 47.1% | SIC:3494 |
| Trend | -2.0% | |
| Downside Risk | 33.3% | |
| Upside Potential | 73.5% | |
| Space Required | 1155 Sq. Ft. | |

## SOURCE AND USE OF CAPITAL

| Capital Source | | Capital Use | |
|---|---|---|---|
| Owner's Equity | $122,500 | Working Capital | $ 81,000 |
| Long Term Debt | $ 33,500 | Long Term Assets | $ 75,000 |
| Total Capital Requ'd | $156,000 | Total Capital Used | $156,000 |

## SALES AND INCOME

| | Upper Quartile | Median | Lower Quartile |
|---|---|---|---|
| Sales | 750,000 | 525,000 | 325,000 |
| Officer's Salary* | 66,000 | 34,000 | 24,100 |
| Net Profit* | 61,500 | 39,500 | 25,500 |
| Total Income* | 127,500 | 73,500 | 49,600 |

*Before Tax

## PROFITABILITY VS ASSETS

| Assets | 0-250$K | 250-1,000$K | 1-10$M |
|---|---|---|---|
| Profitability | N/A | 47.1% | 21.5% |

**COMMENTS:** *Large initial capital outlay, but low downside risk.*

## PHOTOFINISHING LABS (SVE) - SIC:7394

| | |
|---|---|
| Total Assets | $250,000 |
| Profitability | 46.8% |
| Trend | +2.7% |
| Downside Risk | 51.3% |
| Upside Potential | 129.5% |
| Space Required | 2420 Sq. Ft. |

### SOURCE AND USE OF CAPITAL

| Capital Source | | Capital Use | |
|---|---|---|---|
| Owner's Equity | $103,250 | Working Capital | $ 37,500 |
| Long Term Debt | $ 56,500 | Long Term Assets | $122,250 |
| Total Capital Requ'd | $159,750 | Total Capital Used | $159,750 |

### SALES AND INCOME

| | Upper Quartile | Median | Lower Quartile |
|---|---|---|---|
| Sales | 725,000 | 550,000 | 400,000 |
| Officer's Salary* | 121,800 | 41,250 | 18,400 |
| Net Profit* | 49,750 | 33,500 | 18,000 |
| Total Income* | 171,550 | 74,750 | 36,400 |

*Before Tax

### PROFITABILITY VS ASSETS

| Assets | 0-250$K | 250-1,000$K | 1-10$M |
|---|---|---|---|
| Profitability | 89.0% | 46.8% | N/A |

**COMMENTS:** *Very large capital outlay, average risk excellent upside potential.*


## #22 PUBLIC UTILITY & INDUSTRIAL EQUIPMENT (MFG)

| | |
|---|---|
| Total Assets | $250,000 |
| Profitability | 46.5% |
| Trend | +5.4% |
| Downside Risk | 50.8% |
| Upside Potential | 89.5% |
| Space Required | 1495 Sq. Ft. |

SIC:3612,13,1421

### SOURCE AND USE OF CAPITAL

| Capital Source | | Capital Use | |
|---|---|---|---|
| Owner's Equity | $ 91,250 | Working Capital | $ 69,250 |
| Long Term Debt | $ 36,750 | Long Term Assets | $ 58,750 |
| Total Capital Requ'd | $128,000 | Total Capital Used | $128,000 |

### SALES AND INCOME

| | Upper Quartile | Median | Lower Quartile |
|---|---|---|---|
| Sales | 750,000 | 575,000 | 500,000 |
| Officer's Salary* | 70,500 | 34,500 | 20,000 |
| Net Profit* | 42,250 | 25,000 | 9,250 |
| Total Income* | 112,750 | 59,500 | 29,250 |

*Before Tax

### PROFITABILITY VS ASSETS

| Assets | 0-250$K | 250-1,000$K | 1-10$M |
|---|---|---|---|
| Profitability | N/A | 46.5% | 37.6% |

**COMMENTS:** *Better than average manufacturing business. Excellent upward trend.*

# #23  GENERAL MACHINERY & EQUIPMENT (MFG)

| | |
|---|---|
| Total Assets | $250,000 |
| Profitability | 45.5% |
| Trend | +0.6% |
| Downside Risk | 55.4% |
| Upside Potential | 104.1% |
| Space Required | 1440 Sq. Ft. |

SIC:3561,64,66,67,69

### SOURCE AND USE OF CAPITAL

| Capital Source | | Capital Use | |
|---|---|---|---|
| Owner's Equity | $101,500 | Working Capital | $ 50,750 |
| Long Term Debt | $ 30,250 | Long Term Assets | $ 81,000 |
| Total Capital Requ'd | $131,750 | Total Capital Used | $131,750 |

### SALES AND INCOME

| | Upper Quartile | Median | Lower Quartile |
|---|---|---|---|
| Sales | 775,000 | 600,000 | 450,000 |
| Officer's Salary* | 80,600 | 34,200 | 13,500 |
| Net Profit* | 41,750 | 25,750 | 13,250 |
| Total Income* | 122,350 | 59,950 | 26,750 |

*Before Tax

### PROFITABILITY VS ASSETS

| Assets | 0-250$K | 250-1,000$K | 1-10$M |
|---|---|---|---|
| Profitability | 44.3% | 45.5% | 26.6% |

**COMMENTS:** *Better than average manufacturing business. Stable profitability.*


# #24  ELECTRONIC PARTS & EQUIPMENT (WSLE) SIC:5065

| | |
|---|---|
| Total Assets | $250,000 |
| Profitability | 45.4% |
| Trend | +0.6% |
| Downside Risk | 55.7% |
| Upside Potential | 57.7% |
| Space Required | 1450 Sq. Ft. |

### SOURCE AND USE OF CAPITAL

| Capital Source | | Capital Use | |
|---|---|---|---|
| Owner's Equity | $ 91,500 | Working Capital | $ 87,750 |
| Long Term Debt | $ 31,250 | Long Term Assets | $ 35,000 |
| Total Capital Requ'd | $122,750 | Total Capital Used | $122,750 |

### SALES AND INCOME

| | Upper Quartile | Median | Lower Quartile |
|---|---|---|---|
| Sales | 850,000 | 725,000 | 550,000 |
| Officer's Salary* | 47,600 | 30,450 | 15,400 |
| Net Profit* | 40,250 | 25,250 | 9,250 |
| Total Income* | 87,850 | 55,700 | 24,650 |

*Before Tax

### PROFITABILITY VS ASSETS

| Assets | 0-250$K | 250-1,000$K | 1-10$M |
|---|---|---|---|
| Profitability | 76.5% | 45.4% | 32.3% |

**COMMENTS:** *Sound business - average risk and potential. Relatively low long term assets required.*

# #25 HEAVY COMMERCIAL & INDUSTRIAL MACHINERY (WSLE)

| | |
|---|---|
| Total Assets | $250,000 |
| Profitability | 43.9% |
| Trend | +3.6% |
| Downside Risk | 48.6% |
| Upside Potential | 88.0% |
| Space Required | 1260 Sq. Ft. |

SIC:5084

## SOURCE AND USE OF CAPITAL

| Capital Source | | Capital Use | |
|---|---|---|---|
| Owner's Equity | $ 91,000 | Working Capital | $ 69,250 |
| Long Term Debt | $ 24,500 | Long Term Assets | $ 46,250 |
| Total Capital Requ'd | $115,500 | Total Capital Used | $115,500 |

## SALES AND INCOME

| | Upper Quartile | Median | Lower Quartile |
|---|---|---|---|
| Sales | 900,000 | 700,000 | 575,000 |
| Officer's Salary* | 61,200 | 29,400 | 15,525 |
| Net Profit* | 34,000 | 21,250 | 10,500 |
| Total Income* | 95,200 | 50,650 | 26,025 |

*Before Tax

## PROFITABILITY VS ASSETS

| Assets | 0-250$K | 250-1,000$K | 1-10$M |
|---|---|---|---|
| Profitability | 50.8% | 43.9% | 32.4% |

**COMMENTS:** *Sound business - average risk, good potential. Improving trend.*


# #26 AIR CONDITIONING & HEATING EQUIPMENT (MFG)

| | |
|---|---|
| Total Assets | $250,000 |
| Profitability | 43.9% |
| Trend | +1.6% |
| Downside Risk | 57.4% |
| Upside Potential | 51.4% |
| Space Required | 1725 Sq. Ft. |

SIC:3581

## SOURCE AND USE OF CAPITAL

| Capital Source | | Capital Use | |
|---|---|---|---|
| Owner's Equity | $103,750 | Working Capital | $ 71,500 |
| Long Term Debt | $ 31,750 | Long Term Assets | $ 64,000 |
| Total Capital Requ'd | $135,500 | Total Capital Used | $135,500 |

## SALES AND INCOME

| | Upper Quartile | Median | Lower Quartile |
|---|---|---|---|
| Sales | 675,000 | 575,000 | 475,000 |
| Officer's Salary* | 45,225 | 29,325 | 11,875 |
| Net Profit* | 45,000 | 30,250 | 13,500 |
| Total Income* | 90,225 | 59,575 | 25,375 |

*Before Tax

## PROFITABILITY VS ASSETS

| Assets | 0-250$K | 250-1,000$K | 1-10$M |
|---|---|---|---|
| Profitability | N/A | 43.9% | 22.2% |

**COMMENTS:** *Sound business average risk and potential.*

| | |
|---|---|
| Total Assets | $250,000 |
| Profitability | 43.6% |
| Trend | -0.8% |
| Downside Risk | 64.4% |
| Upside Potential | 85.6% |
| Space Required | 1850 Sq. Ft. |

### SOURCE AND USE OF CAPITAL

| Capital Source | | Capital Use | |
|---|---|---|---|
| Owner's Equity | $ 78,000 | Working Capital | $ 51,500 |
| Long Term Debt | $ 36,750 | Long Term Assets | $ 63,250 |
| Total Capital Requ'd | $114,750 | Total Capital Used | $114,750 |

### SALES AND INCOME

| | Upper Quartile | Median | Lower Quartile |
|---|---|---|---|
| Sales | 2,575,000 | 1,850,000 | 1,300,000 |
| Officer's Salary* | 69,525 | 37,000 | 14,300 |
| Net Profit* | 23,250 | 13,000 | 3,500 |
| Total Income* | 92,775 | 50,000 | 17,800 |

*Before Tax

### PROFITABILITY VS ASSETS

| Assets | 0-250$K | 250-1,000$K | 1-10$M |
|---|---|---|---|
| Profitability | 51.1% | 43.9% | 22.9% |

**COMMENTS:** *One of the most profitable sections of the food industry. Fairly high risk, good potential.*


## #28   AIRCRAFT PARTS (EXCEPT ENGINES) (MFG)   SIC:3728

| | |
|---|---|
| Total Assets | $250,00 |
| Profitability | 43.7% |
| Trend | -0.2% |
| Downside Risk | 50.3% |
| Upside Potential | 97.8% |
| Space Required | 1540 Sq. Ft. |

### SOURCE AND USE OF CAPITAL

| Capital Source | | Capital Use | |
|---|---|---|---|
| Owner's Equity | $108,250 | Working Capital | $ 76,250 |
| Long Term Debt | $ 40,000 | Long Term Assets | $ 72,000 |
| Total Capital Requ'd | $148,250 | Total Capital Used | $148,250 |

### SALES AND INCOME

| | Upper Quartile | Median | Lower Quartile |
|---|---|---|---|
| Sales | 625,000 | 550,000 | 500,000 |
| Officer's Salary* | 69,375 | 40,150 | 22,000 |
| Net Profit* | 59,000 | 24,750 | 10,250 |
| Total Income* | 128,375 | 64,900 | 32,250 |

*Before Tax

### PROFITABILITY VS ASSETS

| Assets | 0-250$K | 250-1,000$K | 1-10$M |
|---|---|---|---|
| Profitability | N/A | 43.7% | 19.2% |

**COMMENTS:** *Average risk - good potential.*

## #29 COMMERCIAL MACHINES & EQUIPMENT (WSLE)

| | |
|---|---|
| Total Assets | $250,000 |
| Profitability | 43.7% |
| Trend | -3.1% |
| Downside Risk | 45.8% |
| Upside Potential | 76.7% |
| Space Required | 1485 Sq. Ft. |

**SIC:5081**

### SOURCE AND USE OF CAPITAL

| Capital Source | | Capital Use | |
|---|---|---|---|
| Owner's Equity | $ 99,000 | Working Capital | $ 82,250 |
| Long Term Debt | $ 30,750 | Long Term Assets | $ 47,500 |
| Total Capital Requ'd | $129,750 | Total Capital Used | $129,750 |

### SALES AND INCOME

| | Upper Quartile | Median | Lower Quartile |
|---|---|---|---|
| Sales | 875,000 | 675,000 | 500,000 |
| Officer's Salary* | 59,000 | 33,750 | 17,000 |
| Net Profit* | 40,750 | 23,000 | 13,750 |
| Total Income* | 100,250 | 56,750 | 30,750 |

*Before Tax

### PROFITABILITY VS ASSETS

| Assets | 0-250$K | 250-1,000$K | 1-10$M |
|---|---|---|---|
| Profitability | N/A | 43.7% | N/A |

**COMMENTS:** *Significant downtrend?  Average risk and potential.*


## #30 INDUSTRIAL MEASURING & CONTROL INSTRUMENTS (MFG)

| | |
|---|---|
| Total Assets | $250,000 |
| Profitability | 43.7% |
| Trend | +2.6% |
| Downside Risk | 47.0% |
| Upside Potential | 67.9% |
| Space Required | 2160 Sq. Ft. |

**SIC:3823**

### SOURCE AND USE OF CAPITAL

| Capital Source | | Capital Use | |
|---|---|---|---|
| Owner's Equity | $ 80,250 | Working Capital | $ 52,750 |
| Long Term Debt | $ 33,000 | Long Term Assets | $ 60,500 |
| Total Capital Requ'd | $113,250 | Total Capital Used | $113,250 |

### SALES AND INCOME

| | Upper Quartile | Median | Lower Quartile |
|---|---|---|---|
| Sales | 700,000 | 600,000 | 400,000 |
| Officer's Salary* | 37,100 | 24,000 | 8,000 |
| Net Profit* | 46,000 | 25,500 | 18,250 |
| Total Income* | 83,100 | 49,500 | 26,250 |

*Before Tax

### PROFITABILITY VS ASSETS

| Assets | 0-250$K | 250-1,000$K | 1-10$M |
|---|---|---|---|
| Profitability | N/A | 43.7% | N/A |

**COMMENTS:** *Average risk, good potential, good trend.*

# STATIONERY SUPPLIES (WSLE)     SIC:5112

| | |
|---|---|
| Total Assets | $250,000 |
| Profitability | 43.4% |
| Trend | N/A |
| Downside Risk | 53.9% |
| Upside Potential | 117.8% |
| Space Required | 2325 Sq. Ft. |

## SOURCE AND USE OF CAPITAL

| Capital Source | | Capital Use | |
|---|---|---|---|
| Owner's Equity | $106,000 | Working Capital | $106,250 |
| Long Term Debt | $ 25,250 | Long Term Assets | $ 25,000 |
| Total Capital Requ'd | $131,250 | Total Capital Used | >131,250 |

## SALES AND INCOME

| | Upper Quartile | Median | Lower Quartile |
|---|---|---|---|
| Sales | 900,000 | 775,000 | 500,000 |
| Officer's Salary* | 77,400 | 31,000 | 13,000 |
| Net Profit* | 46,750 | 26,000 | 13,250 |
| Total Income* | 124,150 | 57,000 | 26,250 |

*Before Tax

## PROFITABILITY VS ASSETS

| Assets | 0-250$K | 250-1,000$K | 1-10$M |
|---|---|---|---|
| Profitability | N/A | 43.4 | N/A |

**COMMENTS:** *Average risk, good upside potential with low capital assets.*




# MOBILE HOME (RTL)     SIC:5271

| | |
|---|---|
| Total Assets | $250,000 |
| Profitability | 43.4% |
| Trend | +2.4% |
| Downside Risk | 54.9% |
| Upside Potential | 80.5% |
| Space Required | 140 Sq. Ft. |

## SOURCE AND USE OF CAPITAL

| Capital Source | | Capital Use | |
|---|---|---|---|
| Owner's Equity | $ 58,500 | Working Capital | $ 25,000 |
| Long Term Debt | $ 26,750 | Long Term Assets | $ 60,250 |
| Total Capital Requ'd | $ 85,250 | Total Capital Used | $ 85,250 |

## SALES AND INCOME

| | Upper Quartile | Median | Lower Quartile |
|---|---|---|---|
| Sales | 875,000 | 700,000 | 525,000 |
| Officer's Salary* | 35,875 | 20,300 | 9,450 |
| Net Profit* | 31,000 | 16,750 | 7,250 |
| Total Income* | 66,875 | 37,050 | 16,700 |

*Before Tax

## PROFITABILITY VS ASSETS

| Assets | 0-250$K | 250-1,000$K | 1-10$M |
|---|---|---|---|
| Profitability | N/A | 43.4% | 24.9% |

**COMMENTS:** *Average risk, good potential. Good upward trend as more people cannot afford regular housing.*

# ELECTRIC LIGHTING FIXTURES (MFG) SIC:3645,46

| | |
|---|---|
| Total Assets | $250,000 |
| Profitability | 43.4% |
| Trend | +3.4% |
| Downside Risk | 81.9% |
| Upside Potential | 78.1% |
| Space Required | 2625 Sq. Ft. |

## SOURCE AND USE OF CAPITAL

| Capital Source | | Capital Use | |
|---|---|---|---|
| Owner's Equity | $100,750 | Working Capital | $ 97,000 |
| Long Term Debt | $ 38,750 | Long Term Assets | $ 42,500 |
| Total Capital Requ'd | $139,500 | Total Capital Used | $139,500 |

## SALES AND INCOME

| | Upper Quartile | Median | Lower Quartile |
|---|---|---|---|
| Sales | 700,000 | 625,000 | 425,000 |
| Officer's Salary* | 63,000 | 45,000 | 15,725 |
| Net Profit* | 44,750 | 15,500 | (4,750) |
| Total Income* | 107,750 | 60,500 | 10,975 |

*Before Tax

## PROFITABILITY VS ASSETS

| Assets | 0-250$K | 250-1,000$K | 1-10$M |
|---|---|---|---|
| Profitability | N/A | 43.4% | N/A |

**COMMENTS:** *High risk! But good potential with good upward trend.*




# CURTAINS & DRAPERIES (MFG) SIC2391

| | |
|---|---|
| Total Assets | $250,000 |
| Profitability | 43.4% |
| Trend | +5.7% |
| Downside Risk | 59.7% |
| Upside Potential | 64.2% |
| Space Required | 2100 Sq. Ft. |

## SOURCE AND USE OF CAPITAL

| Capital Source | | Capital Use | |
|---|---|---|---|
| Owner's Equity | $101,000 | Working Capital | $ 81,500 |
| Long Term Debt | $ 21,250 | Long Term Assets | $ 40,750 |
| Total Capital Requ'd | $122,250 | Total Capital Used | $122,250 |

## SALES AND INCOME

| | Upper Quartile | Median | Lower Quartile |
|---|---|---|---|
| Sales | 875,000 | 700,000 | 625,000 |
| Officer's Salary* | 56,875 | 34,300 | 14,375 |
| Net Profit* | 30,250 | 18,750 | 7,000 |
| Total Income* | 87,125 | 53,050 | 21,375 |

*Before Tax

## PROFITABILITY VS ASSETS

| Assets | 0-250$K | 250-1,000$K | 1-10$M |
|---|---|---|---|
| Profitability | N/A | 43.4 | N/A |

**COMMENTS:** *Excellent upward trend. Average risk with good potential.*

## #35  STORE,OFFICE,BAR,RESTAURANT FIXTURES (MFG)

| | |
|---|---|
| Total Assets | $250,000 |
| Profitability | 43.1% |
| Trend | 3.7% |
| Downside Risk | 64.5% |
| Upside Potential | 77.5% |
| Space Required | 2610 Sq. Ft. |

SIC:2541,42,99

### SOURCE AND USE OF CAPITAL

| Capital Source | | Capital Use | |
|---|---|---|---|
| Owner's Equity | $100,500 | Working Capital | $ 66,250 |
| Long Term Debt | $ 27,500 | Long Term Assets | $ 61,750 |
| Total Capital Requ'd | $128,000 | Total Capital Used | $128,000 |

### SALES AND INCOME

| | Upper Quartile | Median | Lower Quartile |
|---|---|---|---|
| Sales | 850,000 | 725,000 | 525,000 |
| Officer's Salary* | 54,400 | 31,900 | 12,075 |
| Net Profit* | 43,500 | 23,250 | 7,500 |
| Total Income* | 97,900 | 55,150 | 19,575 |

*Before Tax

### PROFITABILITY VS ASSETS

| Assets | 0-250$K | 250-1,000$K | 1-10$M |
|---|---|---|---|
| Profitability | N/A | 43.1% | 28.2% |

**COMMENTS:** *Good upward trend, but higher than average risk, good potential.*


## #36  PROFESSIONAL EQUIPMENT (WSLE)  SIC:5086

| | |
|---|---|
| Total Assets | $250,000 |
| Profitability | 43.0% |
| Trend | +1.0% |
| Downside Risk | 51.9% |
| Upside Potential | 76.9% |
| Space Required | 1885 Sq. Ft. |

### SOURCE AND USE OF CAPITAL

| Capital Source | | Capital Use | |
|---|---|---|---|
| Owner's Equity | $ 82,750 | Working Capital | $ 68,750 |
| Long Term Debt | $ 31,000 | Long Term Assets | $ 45,000 |
| Total Capital Requ'd | $113,750 | Total Capital Used | $113,750 |

### SALES AND INCOME

| | Upper Quartile | Median | Lower Quartile |
|---|---|---|---|
| Sales | 900,000 | 725,000 | 550,000 |
| Officer's Salary* | 56,700 | 32,625 | 16,500 |
| Net Profit* | 29,750 | 16,250 | 7,000 |
| Total Income* | 86,450 | 48,875 | 23,500 |

*Before Tax

### PROFITABILITY VS ASSETS

| Assets | 0-250$K | 250-1,000$K | 1-10$M |
|---|---|---|---|
| Profitability | 69.7% | 43.0% | 29.3% |

**COMMENTS:** *Average risk, good potential.*

# #37 NON-FERROUS FABRICATED PRODUCTS (MFG)

| | | |
|---|---|---|
| Total Assets | $250,000 | |
| Profitability | 42.9% | SIC:3499 |
| Trend | +1.0% | |
| Downside Risk | 59.9% | |
| Upside Potential | 64.1% | |
| Space Required | 2530 Sq. Ft. | |

## SOURCE AND USE OF CAPITAL

| Capital Source | | Capital Use | |
|---|---|---|---|
| Owner's Equity | $112,000 | Working Capital | $ 69,250 |
| Long Term Debt | $ 45,250 | Long Term Assets | $ 88,000 |
| Total Capital Requ'd | $157,250 | Total Capital Used | $157,250 |

## SALES AND INCOME

| | Upper Quartile | Median | Lower Quartile |
|---|---|---|---|
| Sales | 675,000 | 575,000 | 450,000 |
| Officer's Salary* | 64,800 | 40,250 | 17,550 |
| Net Profit* | 46,000 | 27,250 | 9,500 |
| Total Income* | 110,800 | 67,500 | 27,050 |

*Before Tax

## PROFITABILITY VS ASSETS

| Assets | 0-250$K | 250-1,000$K | 1-10$M |
|---|---|---|---|
| Profitability | 90.8% | 42.9% | 22.2% |

**COMMENTS:** *Slightly higher than average risk, good potential.*


# #38 PREFABRICATED WOOD BUILDINGS & COMPONENTS (MFG)

| | | |
|---|---|---|
| Total Assets | $250,000 | |
| Profitability | 42.6% | SIC:2452 |
| Trend | +5.6% | |
| Downside Risk | 56.8% | |
| Upside Potential | 118.4% | |
| Space Required | 1350 Sq. Ft. | |

## SOURCE AND USE OF CAPITAL

| Capital Source | | Capital Use | |
|---|---|---|---|
| Owner's Equity | $113,250 | Working Capital | $ 78,000 |
| Long Term Debt | $ 36,250 | Long Term Assets | $ 71,500 |
| Total Capital Requ'd | $149,500 | Total Capital Used | $149,500 |

## SALES AND INCOME

| | Upper Quartile | Median | Lower Quartile |
|---|---|---|---|
| Sales | 1,000,000 | 750,000 | 575,000 |
| Officer's Salary* | 77,000 | 36,000 | 15,525 |
| Net Profit* | 62,250 | 27,750 | 12,000 |
| Total Income* | 139,250 | 63,750 | 27,525 |

*Before Tax

## PROFITABILITY VS ASSETS

| Assets | 0-250$K | 250-1,000$K | 1-10$M |
|---|---|---|---|
| Profitability | N/A | 42.6% | 28/5% |

**COMMENTS:** *Excellent upward trend. Average risk, excellent potential.*

     **PIECE GOODS (WSLE)**     **SIC:5133**

| | |
|---|---|
| **Total Assets** | $250,000 |
| **Profitability** | 42.3% |
| **Trend** | -1.4% |
| **Downside Risk** | 42.0% |
| **Upside Potential** | 92.1% |
| **Space Required** | 1500 Sq. Ft. |

### SOURCE AND USE OF CAPITAL

| Capital Source | | Capital Use | |
|---|---|---|---|
| Owner's Equity | $ 99,250 | Working Capital | $ 96,750 |
| Long Term Debt | $ 20,250 | Long Term Assets | $ 22,750 |
| Total Capital Requ'd | $119,500 | Total Capital Used | $119,500 |

### SALES AND INCOME

| | Upper Quartile | Median | Lower Quartile |
|---|---|---|---|
| Sales | 900,000 | 750,000 | 625,000 |
| Officer's Salary* | 67,500 | 36,750 | 20,000 |
| Net Profit* | 29,500 | 13,750 | 9,250 |
| Total Income* | 97,000 | 50,500 | 29,250 |

*Before Tax

### PROFITABILITY VS ASSETS

| Assets | 0-250$K | 250-1,000$K | 1-10$M |
|---|---|---|---|
| Profitability | N/A | 42.3% | 23.8% |

**COMMENTS:** *Fabric distribution has low risk, good potential, some downtrend. Very low capital assets required.*


     **OIL FIELD MACHINERY (MFG)**     **SIC:3533**

| | |
|---|---|
| **Total Assets** | $250,000 |
| **Profitability** | 42.2% |
| **Trend** | -0.8% |
| **Downside Risk** | 53.5% |
| **Upside Potential** | 173.9% |
| **Space Required** | 2000 Sq. Ft. |

### SOURCE AND USE OF CAPITAL

| Capital Source | | Capital Use | |
|---|---|---|---|
| Owner's Equity | $ 96,750 | Working Capital | $ 50,500 |
| Long Term Debt | $ 22,250 | Long Term Assets | $ 68,500 |
| Total Capital Requ'd | $119,000 | Total Capital Used | $119,000 |

### SALES AND INCOME

| | Upper Quartile | Median | Lower Quartile |
|---|---|---|---|
| Sales | 800,000 | 625,000 | 400,000 |
| Officer's Salary* | 70,400 | 20,000 | 7,600 |
| Net Profit* | 67,250 | 30,250 | 15,750 |
| Total Income* | 137,650 | 50,250 | 23,350 |

*Before Tax

### PROFITABILITY VS ASSETS

| Assets | 0-250$K | 250-1,000$K | 1-10$M |
|---|---|---|---|
| Profitability | N/A | 42.2 | N/A |

**COMMENTS:** *Surprising slight downtrend? Average risk with excellent upside potential.*

# TRAVEL AGENCIES (SVE)             SIC:4722

| | |
|---|---|
| Total Assets | $250,000 |
| Profitability | 42.0% |
| Trend | -1.8% |
| Downside Risk | 81.9% |
| Upside Potential | 1,427.0% |
| Space Required | 3060 Sq. Ft. |

## SOURCE AND USE OF CAPITAL

| Capital Source | | Capital Use | |
|---|---|---|---|
| Owner's Equity | $ 67,000 | Working Capital | $ 18,250 |
| Long Term Debt | $ 17,000 | Long Term Assets | $ 65,750 |
| Total Capital Requ'd | $ 84,000 | Total Capital Used | $ 84,000 |

## SALES AND INCOME

| | Upper Quartile | Median | Lower Quartile |
|---|---|---|---|
| Sales | 1,925,000 | 425,000 | 225,000 |
| Officer's Salary* | 513,975 | 22,525 | 1,350 |
| Net Profit* | 25,000 | 12,750 | 5,000 |
| Total Income* | 538,975 | 35,275 | 6,350 |

*Before Tax

## PROFITABILITY VS ASSETS

| Assets | 0-250$K | 250-1,000$K | 1-10$M |
|---|---|---|---|
| Profitability | 56.5% | 42.0% | N/A |

**COMMENTS:**  *Significant downtrend.  Need to have computerised equipment to be really profitable.  High risk, but super excellent potential!*



# LUMBER & MILLWORK (WSLE)             SIC:5031

| | |
|---|---|
| Total Assets | $250,000 |
| Profitability | 41.6% |
| Trend | +2.8% |
| Downside Risk | 52.5% |
| Upside Potential | 117.9% |
| Space Required | 720 Sq. Ft. |

## SOURCE AND USE OF CAPITAL

| Capital Source | | Capital Use | |
|---|---|---|---|
| Owner's Equity | $ 98,250 | Working Capital | $ 78,500 |
| Long Term Debt | $ 23,000 | Long Term Assets | $ 42,750 |
| Total Capital Requ'd | $121,250 | Total Capital Used | $121,250 |

## SALES AND INCOME

| | Upper Quartile | Median | Lower Quartile |
|---|---|---|---|
| Sales | 1,325,000 | 900,000 | 625,000 |
| Officer's Salary* | 71,550 | 27,000 | 10,000 |
| Net Profit* | 38,500 | 23,500 | 14,000 |
| Total Income* | 110,050 | 50,500 | 24,000 |

*Before Tax

## PROFITABILITY VS ASSETS

| Assets | 0-250$K | 250-1,000$K | 1-10$M |
|---|---|---|---|
| Profitability | 55.7% | 41.6% | 31.1% |

**COMMENTS:**  *Good trend, average risk, excellent potential.*

# HARDWARE & PAINTS (WSLE)   SIC:5072,5198

| | |
|---|---|
| Total Assets | $250,000 |
| Profitability | 41.4% |
| Trend | +0.4% |
| Downside Risk | 43.4% |
| Upside Potential | 68.4% |
| Space Required | 1485 Sq. Ft. |

## SOURCE AND USE OF CAPITAL

| Capital Source | | Capital Use | |
|---|---|---|---|
| Owner's Equity | $106,750 | Working Capital | $ 94,500 |
| Long Term Debt | $ 22,250 | Long Term Assets | $ 34,500 |
| Total Capital Requ'd | $129,000 | Total Capital Used | $129,000 |

## SALES AND INCOME

| | Upper Quartile | Median | Lower Quartile |
|---|---|---|---|
| Sales | 825,000 | 675,000 | 575,000 |
| Officer's Salary* | 51,150 | 32,400 | 18,975 |
| Net Profit* | 38,750 | 21,000 | 11,250 |
| Total Income* | 89,900 | 53,400 | 30,225 |

*Before Tax

## PROFITABILITY VS ASSETS

| Assets | 0-250$K | 250-1,000$K | 1-10$M |
|---|---|---|---|
| Profitability | 66.4% | 41.4% | 25.1% |

**COMMENTS:** *Stable profitability, low risk good potential.*


# #44   RADIO & TV TRANSMITTING EQUIPMENT (MFG)

SIC:3662

| | |
|---|---|
| Total Assets | $250,000 |
| Profitability | 41.2% |
| Trend | -3.1% |
| Downside Risk | 75.8% |
| Upside Potential | 100.4% |
| Space Required | 1800 Sq. Ft. |

## SOURCE AND USE OF CAPITAL

| Capital Source | | Capital Use | |
|---|---|---|---|
| Owner's Equity | $ 71,750 | Working Capital | $ 50,250 |
| Long Term Debt | $ 48,500 | Long Term Assets | $ 70,000 |
| Total Capital Requ'd | $120,250 | Total Capital Used | $120,250 |

## SALES AND INCOME

| | Upper Quartile | Median | Lower Quartile |
|---|---|---|---|
| Sales | 600,000 | 500,000 | 350,000 |
| Officer's Salary* | 49,200 | 27,500 | 10,500 |
| Net Profit* | 50,000 | 22,000 | 1,500 |
| Total Income* | 99,200 | 49,500 | 12,000 |

*Before Tax

## PROFITABILITY VS ASSETS

| Assets | 0-250$K | 250-1,000$K | 1-10$M |
|---|---|---|---|
| Profitability | N/A | 41.2% | N/A |

**COMMENTS:** *Significant downtrend, high risk, excellent potential.*

# HEAT TREATING OF STEEL (SVE)     SIC:3398

| | |
|---|---|
| Total Assets | $250,000 |
| Profitability | 41.1% |
| Trend | +4.4% |
| Downside Risk | 47.2% |
| Upside Potential | 80.2% |
| Space Required | 4200 Sq. Ft. |

## SOURCE AND USE OF CAPITAL

| Capital Source | | Capital Use | |
|---|---|---|---|
| Owner's Equity | $109,000 | Working Capital | $ 35,750 |
| Long Term Debt | $ 49,750 | Long Term Assets | $123,000 |
| Total Capital Requ'd | $158,750 | Total Capital Used | $158,750 |

## SALES AND INCOME

| | Upper Quartile | Median | Lower Quartile |
|---|---|---|---|
| Sales | 625,000 | 525,000 | 350,000 |
| Officer's Salary* | 52,500 | 35,700 | 17,150 |
| Net Profit* | 65,000 | 29,500 | 17,250 |
| Total Income* | 117,500 | 65,200 | 34,400 |

*Before Tax

## PROFITABILITY VS ASSETS

| Assets | 0-250$K | 250-1,000$K | 1-10$M |
|---|---|---|---|
| Profitability | N/A | 41.4% | N/A |

**COMMENTS:** *Excellent uptrend, average risk, good potential, Very high initial fixed assets needed.*



# SAWMILLS & PLANING MILLS (MFG)     SIC:2421

| | |
|---|---|
| Total Assets | $250,000 |
| Profitability | 41.1% |
| Trend | +3.0% |
| Downside Risk | 60.9% |
| Upside Potential | 63.1% |
| Space Required | 675 Sq. Ft. |

## SOURCE AND USE OF CAPITAL

| Capital Source | | Capital Use | |
|---|---|---|---|
| Owner's Equity | $109,000 | Working Capital | $ 33,750 |
| Long Term Debt | $ 45,000 | Long Term Assets | $120,250 |
| Total Capital Requ'd | $154,000 | Total Capital Used | $154,000 |

## SALES AND INCOME

| | Upper Quartile | Median | Lower Quartile |
|---|---|---|---|
| Sales | 900,000 | 675,000 | 425,000 |
| Officer's Salary* | 57,600 | 28,350 | 8,500 |
| Net Profit* | 45,750 | 35,000 | 16,250 |
| Total Income* | 103,350 | 63,350 | 24,750 |

*Before Tax

## PROFITABILITY VS ASSETS

| Assets | 0-250$K | 250-1,000$K | 1-10$M |
|---|---|---|---|
| Profitability | N/A | 41.1% | 26.1% |

**COMMENTS:** *Good uptrend, higher than average risk and potential. High fixed asset outlay required.*

     **FABRICATED WIRE PRODUCTS (MFG)**     SIC:3496

| | |
|---|---|
| Total Assets | $250,000 |
| Profitability | 40.9% |
| Trend | +2.0% |
| Downside Risk | 37.3% |
| Upside Potential | 93.5% |
| Space Required | 1800 Sq. Ft. |

## SOURCE AND USE OF CAPITAL

| Capital Source | | Capital Use | |
|---|---|---|---|
| Owner's Equity | $113,500 | Working Capital | $ 72,500 |
| Long Term Debt | $ 33,500 | Long Term Assets | $ 74,500 |
| Total Capital Requ'd | $147,000 | Total Capital Used | $147,000 |

## SALES AND INCOME

| | Upper Quartile | Median | Lower Quartile |
|---|---|---|---|
| Sales | 775,000 | 600,000 | 475,000 |
| Officer's Salary* | 65,100 | 33,000 | 20,900 |
| Net Profit* | 51,500 | 27,250 | 16,750 |
| Total Income* | 116,600 | 60,250 | 37,650 |

*Before Tax

## PROFITABILITY VS ASSETS

| Assets | 0-250$K | 250-1,000$K | 1-10$M |
|---|---|---|---|
| Profitability | N/A | 40.9% | 24.0% |

**COMMENTS:** Good trend. Low risk, good - excellent potential. Moderate fixed asset outlay.

---

     **FURS (MFG)**     SIC:2371

| | |
|---|---|
| Total Assets | $250,000 |
| Profitability | 40.9% |
| Trend | +1.8% |
| Downside Risk | 49.5% |
| Upside Potential | 77.1% |
| Space Required | --- Sq. Ft. |

## SOURCE AND USE OF CAPITAL

| Capital Source | | Capital Use | |
|---|---|---|---|
| Owner's Equity | $ 89,500 | Working Capital | $ 93,000 |
| Long Term Debt | $ 21,250 | Long Term Assets | $ 17,750 |
| Total Capital Requ'd | $110,750 | Total Capital Used | $110,750 |

## SALES AND INCOME

| | Upper Quartile | Median | Lower Quartile |
|---|---|---|---|
| Sales | 650,000 | 550,000 | 350,000 |
| Officer's Salary* | 53,300 | 34,100 | 15,400 |
| Net Profit* | 27,000 | 11,250 | 7,500 |
| Total Income* | 80,300 | 45,350 | 22,900 |

*Before Tax

## PROFITABILITY VS ASSETS

| Assets | 0-250$K | 250-1,000$K | 1-10$M |
|---|---|---|---|
| Profitability | N/A | 40.9% | N/A |

**COMMENTS:** Good uptrend, average risk, good potential. Very high proportion of working capital needed.

**#49    PRESSED & BLOWN GLASS ( MFG )     SIC:3229**

| Total Assets | $250,000 |
|---|---|
| Profitability | 40.8% |
| Trend | N/A |
| Downside Risk | 54.3% |
| Upside Potential | 104.6% |
| Space Required | 1320 Sq. Ft. |

### SOURCE AND USE OF CAPITAL

| Capital Source | | Capital Use | |
|---|---|---|---|
| Owner's Equity | $112,250 | Working Capital | $ 62,250 |
| Long Term Debt | $ 33,750 | Long Term Assets | $ 83,750 |
| Total Capital Requ'd | $146,000 | Total Capital Used | $146,000 |

### SALES AND INCOME

| | Upper Quartile | Median | Lower Quartile |
|---|---|---|---|
| Sales | 775,000 | 600,000 | 500,000 |
| Officer's Salary* | 67,425 | 33,600 | 15,500 |
| Net Profit* | 54,500 | 26,000 | 11,750 |
| Total Income* | 121,925 | 59,600 | 27,250 |

*Before Tax

### PROFITABILITY VS ASSETS

| Assets | 0-250$K | 250-1,000$K | 1-10$M |
|---|---|---|---|
| Profitability | N/A | 40.8% | N/A |

**COMMENTS:**   *Average risk, excellent potential.*


**#50    METAL STAMPINGS (MFG)     SIC:3465,66,69**

| Total Assets | $250,000 |
|---|---|
| Profitability | 40.8% |
| Trend | -2.8% |
| Downside Risk | 59.0% |
| Upside Potential | 59.3% |
| Space Required | 2500 Sq. Ft. |

### SOURCE AND USE OF CAPITAL

| Capital Source | | Capital Use | |
|---|---|---|---|
| Owner's Equity | $106,500 | Working Capital | $ 44,000 |
| Long Term Debt | $ 40,000 | Long Term Assets | $102,500 |
| Total Capital Requ'd | $146,500 | Total Capital Used | $146,500 |

### SALES AND INCOME

| | Upper Quartile | Median | Lower Quartile |
|---|---|---|---|
| Sales | 725,000 | 625,000 | 425,000 |
| Officer's Salary* | 52,200 | 35,000 | 14,450 |
| Net Profit* | 43,000 | 24,750 | 10,000 |
| Total Income* | 95,200 | 59,750 | 24,450 |

*Before Tax

### PROFITABILITY VS ASSETS

| Assets | 0-250$K | 250-1,000$K | 1-10$M |
|---|---|---|---|
| Profitability | N/A | 40.8% | 24.3% |

**COMMENTS:**   *Significant downtrend? Average risk and potential.*

# #51   METALS SERVICE CENTER OFFICES (WSLE) SIC:5051

| | |
|---|---|
| Total Assets | $250,000 |
| Profitability | 40.8% |
| Trend | +1.6% |
| Downside Risk | 45.0% |
| Upside Potential | 71.8% |
| Space Required | 1820 Sq. Ft. |

## SOURCE AND USE OF CAPITAL

| Capital Source | | Capital Use | |
|---|---|---|---|
| Owner's Equity | $ 86,750 | Working Capital | $ 71,500 |
| Long Term Debt | $ 32,000 | Long Term Assets | $ 47,250 |
| Total Capital Requ'd | $118,750 | Total Capital Used | $118,750 |

## SALES AND INCOME

| | Upper Quartile | Median | Lower Quartile |
|---|---|---|---|
| Sales | 850,000 | 700,000 | 575,000 |
| Officer's Salary* | 56,100 | 31,500 | 16,675 |
| Net Profit* | 27,250 | 17,000 | 10,000 |
| Total Income* | 83,350 | 48,500 | 26,675 |

*Before Tax

## PROFITABILITY VS ASSETS

| Assets | 0-250$K | 250-1,000$K | 1-10$M |
|---|---|---|---|
| Profitability | N/A | 40.8% | 27.3% |

COMMENTS: *Good trend, lower than average risk, good potential.*


# #52   CUT FLOWERS & GROWING PLANTS (RTL) SIC:5992

| | |
|---|---|
| Total Assets | $250,000 |
| Profitability | 40.5% |
| Trend | -5.2% |
| Downside Risk | 81.3% |
| Upside Potential | 91.3% |
| Space Required | 3250 Sq. Ft. |

## SOURCE AND USE OF CAPITAL

| Capital Source | | Capital Use | |
|---|---|---|---|
| Owner's Equity | $ 97,250 | Working Capital | $ 53,000 |
| Long Term Debt | $ 57,750 | Long Term Assets | $102,000 |
| Total Capital Requ'd | $155,000 | Total Capital Used | $155,000 |

## SALES AND INCOME

| | Upper Quartile | Median | Lower Quartile |
|---|---|---|---|
| Sales | 825,000 | 650,000 | 525,000 |
| Officer's Salary* | 94,050 | 52,000 | 26,250 |
| Net Profit* | 26,000 | 10,750 | (14,500) |
| Total Income* | 120,050 | 62,750 | 11,750 |

*Before Tax

## PROFITABILITY VS ASSETS

| Assets | 0-250$K | 250-1,000$K | 1-10$M |
|---|---|---|---|
| Profitability | 53.4% | 40.5% | N/A |

COMMENTS: *High downtrend? Competition or changing tastes? Very high risk, good - excellent potential.*

| | |
|---|---|
| Total Assets | $250,000 |
| Profitability | 40.3% |
| Trend | +2.7% |
| Downside Risk | 58.9% |
| Upside Potential | 139.1% |
| Space Required | 1295 Sq. Ft. |

### SOURCE AND USE OF CAPITAL

| Capital Source | | Capital Use | |
|---|---|---|---|
| Owner's Equity | $ 79,500 | Working Capital | $ 29,250 |
| Long Term Debt | $ 50,000 | Long Term Assets | $100,250 |
| Total Capital Requ'd | $129,500 | Total Capital Used | $129,500 |

### SALES AND INCOME

| | Upper Quartile | Median | Lower Quartile |
|---|---|---|---|
| Sales | 1,425,000 | 925,000 | 575,000 |
| Officer's Salary* | 76,950 | 27,750 | 10,900 |
| Net Profit* | 48,000 | 24,500 | 10,500 |
| Total Income* | 124,950 | 52,250 | 21,425 |

*Before Tax

### PROFITABILITY VS ASSETS

| Assets | 0-250$K | 250-1,000$K | 1-10$M |
|---|---|---|---|
| Profitability | N/A | 40.3% | N/A |

**COMMENTS:**  *Good trend (unhappier social scene?)  Slightly above average risk. Excellent potential.  High fixed assets (guard dogs, patrol cars?)*

---

**#54**          **WINE,LIQUOR,BEER (WSLE)**          **SIC:5181,82**

| | |
|---|---|
| Total Assets | $250,000 |
| Profitability | 40.2% |
| Trend | -0.3% |
| Downside Risk | 57.8% |
| Upside Potential | 83.5% |
| Space Required | 1960 Sq. Ft. |

### SOURCE AND USE OF CAPITAL

| Capital Source | | Capital Use | |
|---|---|---|---|
| Owner's Equity | $105,500 | Working Capital | $ 60,750 |
| Long Term Debt | $ 42,000 | Long Term Assets | $ 86,750 |
| Total Capital Requ'd | $147,500 | Total Capital Used | $147,500 |

### SALES AND INCOME

| | Upper Quartile | Median | Lower Quartile |
|---|---|---|---|
| Sales | 1,650,000 | 1,400,000 | 1,000,000 |
| Officer's Salary* | 57,750 | 35,000 | 15,000 |
| Net Profit* | 51,000 | 24,250 | 10,000 |
| Total Income* | 108,750 | 59,250 | 25,000 |

*Before Tax

### PROFITABILITY VS ASSETS

| Assets | 0-250$K | 250-1,000$K | 1-10$M |
|---|---|---|---|
| Profitability | 48.2% | 40.2% | 31.7% |

**COMMENTS:**  *Stable profitability.  Slightly above average risk, good potential.*

| | |
|---|---|
| Total Assets | $250,000 |
| Profitability | 40.1% |
| Trend | +2.9% |
| Downside Risk | 51.6% |
| Upside Potential | 56.8% |
| Space Required | 880 Sq. Ft. |

## SOURCE AND USE OF CAPITAL

| Capital Source | | Capital Use | |
|---|---|---|---|
| Owner's Equity | $ 94,000 | Working Capital | $ 96,250 |
| Long Term Debt | $ 27,500 | Long Term Assets | $ 25,250 |
| Total Capital Requ'd | $121,500 | Total Capital Used | $121,500 |

## SALES AND INCOME

| | Upper Quartile | Median | Lower Quartile |
|---|---|---|---|
| Sales | 675,000 | 550,000 | 400,000 |
| Officer's Salary* | 50,625 | 29,700 | 14,800 |
| Net Profit* | 25,750 | 19,000 | 8,750 |
| Total Income* | 76,375 | 48,700 | 23,550 |

*Before Tax

## PROFITABILITY VS ASSETS

| Assets | 0-250$K | 250-1,000$K | 1-10$M |
|---|---|---|---|
| Profitability | 45.4% | 40.1% | 25.8% |

**COMMENTS:**   *Good uptrend.  Average risk and potential.  High working capital content.*

#56        **CHEMICALS & ALLIED PRODUCTS (WSLE) SIC:5161**

| | |
|---|---|
| Total Assets | $250,000 |
| Profitability | 40.0% |
| Trend | -1.7% |
| Downside Risk | 51.2% |
| Upside Potential | 112.0% |
| Space Required | 1440 Sq. Ft. |

## SOURCE AND USE OF CAPITAL

| Capital Source | | Capital Use | |
|---|---|---|---|
| Owner's Equity | $ 89,750 | Working Capital | $ 54,750 |
| Long Term Debt | $ 24,000 | Long Term Assets | $ 59,000 |
| Total Capital Requ'd | $113,750 | Total Capital Used | $113,750 |

## SALES AND INCOME

| | Upper Quartile | Median | Lower Quartile |
|---|---|---|---|
| Sales | 1,025,000 | 800,000 | 650,000 |
| Officer's Salary* | 64,575 | 27,200 | 10,400 |
| Net Profit* | 31,750 | 18,250 | 11,750 |
| Total Income* | 96,325 | 45,450 | 22,150 |

*Before Tax

## PROFITABILITY VS ASSETS

| Assets | 0-250$K | 250-1,000$K | 1-10$M |
|---|---|---|---|
| Profitability | 47.1% | 40.0% | 25.5% |

**COMMENTS:**   *Downtrend.  Average risk, excellent potential.*

# #57 AIR CONDITIONING,HEATING EQUIPMENT (WSLE)

SIC:5075,78

| | |
|---|---|
| Total Assets | $250,000 |
| Profitability | 40.0% |
| Trend | +1.9% |
| Downside Risk | 44.9% |
| Upside Potential | 86.2% |
| Space Required | 1170 Sq. Ft. |

## SOURCE AND USE OF CAPITAL

| Capital Source | | Capital Use | |
|---|---|---|---|
| Owner's Equity | $ 87,250 | Working Capital | $ 74,500 |
| Long Term Debt | $ 26,250 | Long Term Assets | $ 39,000 |
| Total Capital Requ'd | $113,500 | Total Capital Used | $113,500 |

## SALES AND INCOME

| | Upper Quartile | Median | Lower Quartile |
|---|---|---|---|
| Sales | 825,000 | 650,000 | 525,000 |
| Officer's Salary* | 54,450 | 28,600 | 15,750 |
| Net Profit* | 30,000 | 16,750 | 9,250 |
| Total Income* | 84,450 | 45,350 | 25,000 |

*Before Tax

## PROFITABILITY VS ASSETS

| Assets | 0-250$K | 250-1,000$K | 1-10$M |
|---|---|---|---|
| Profitability | 69.0% | 40.0% | 39.9% |

**COMMENTS:** *Good uptrend. Below average risk, good potential.*


# #58 MILL SUPPLY (WSLE)

SIC:5085

| | |
|---|---|
| Total Assets | $250,000 |
| Profitability | 40.0% |
| Trend | -0.6% |
| Downside Risk | 52.0% |
| Upside Potential | 72.2% |
| Space Required | 1705 Sq. Ft. |

## SOURCE AND USE OF CAPITAL

| Capital Source | | Capital Use | |
|---|---|---|---|
| Owner's Equity | $103,500 | Working Capital | $ 85,000 |
| Long Term Debt | $ 23,750 | Long Term Assets | $ 42,250 |
| Total Capital Requ'd | $127,250 | Total Capital Used | $127,250 |

## SALES AND INCOME

| | Upper Quartile | Median | Lower Quartile |
|---|---|---|---|
| Sales | 950,000 | 775,000 | 600,000 |
| Officer's Salary* | 53,200 | 28,675 | 13,200 |
| Net Profit* | 34,500 | 22,250 | 11,250 |
| Total Income* | 87,700 | 50,925 | 24,450 |

*Before Tax

## PROFITABILITY VS ASSETS

| Assets | 0-250$K | 250-1,000$K | 1-10$M |
|---|---|---|---|
| Profitability | N/A | 40.0% | 31.0% |

**COMMENTS:** *Stable profitability. Average risk, good potential.*

| | |
|---|---|
| Total Assets | $250,000 |
| Profitability | 39.8% |
| Trend | +4.3% |
| Downside Risk | 69.2% |
| Upside Potential | 71.8% |
| Space Required | 5510 Sq. Ft. |

### SOURCE AND USE OF CAPITAL

| Capital Source | | Capital Use | |
|---|---|---|---|
| Owner's Equity | $106,750 | Working Capital | $ 24,500 |
| Long Term Debt | $ 66,250 | Long Term Assets | $148,500 |
| Total Capital Requ'd | $173,000 | Total Capital Used | $173,000 |

### SALES AND INCOME

| | Upper Quartile | Median | Lower Quartile |
|---|---|---|---|
| Sales | 675,000 | 475,000 | 300,000 |
| Officer's Salary* | 82,350 | 45,600 | 8,700 |
| Net Profit* | 36,000 | 23,250 | 12,500 |
| Total Income* | 118,350 | 68,850 | 21,200 |

*Before Tax

### PROFITABILITY VS ASSETS

| Assets | 0-250$K | 250-1,000$K | 1-10$M |
|---|---|---|---|
| Profitability | N/A | 39.8% | N/A |

COMMENTS:    *Excellent uptrend.  High risk and potential.*


## #60 COMMERCIAL PRINTING (LETTERPRESS&SCREEN) (MFG)

| | | |
|---|---|---|
| Total Assets | $250,000 | SIC:2751 |
| Profitability | 39.8% | |
| Trend | +2.3% | |
| Downside Risk | 50.5% | |
| Upside Potential | 66.9% | |
| Space Required | 2160 Sq. Ft. | |

### SOURCE AND USE OF CAPITAL

| Capital Source | | Capital Use | |
|---|---|---|---|
| Owner's Equity | $101,750 | Working Capital | $ 39,000 |
| Long Term Debt | $ 48,250 | Long Term Assets | $111,000 |
| Total Capital Requ'd | $150,000 | Total Capital Used | $150,000 |

### SALES AND INCOME

| | Upper Quartile | Median | Lower Quartile |
|---|---|---|---|
| Sales | 700,000 | 600,000 | 500,000 |
| Officer's Salary* | 59,000 | 38,400 | 18,000 |
| Net Profit* | 40,000 | 21,250 | 11,000 |
| Total Income* | 99,000 | 59,650 | 29,500 |

*Before Tax

### PROFITABILITY VS ASSETS

| Assets | 0-250$K | 250-1,000$K | 1-10$M |
|---|---|---|---|
| Profitability | 47.1% | 39.8% | 24.2% |

COMMENTS:    *Good uptrend, average risk and good potential.*

# DRUGS & MEDICINES (MFG)　　SIC:2831,33,34

| | |
|---|---|
| Total Assets | $250,000 |
| Profitability | 39.7% |
| Trend | +2.0% |
| Downside Risk | 37.9% |
| Upside Potential | 119.0% |
| Space Required | 1265 Sq. Ft. |

## SOURCE AND USE OF CAPITAL

| Capital Source | | Capital Use | |
|---|---|---|---|
| Owner's Equity | $115,500 | Working Capital | $ 54,000 |
| Long Term Debt | $ 21,250 | Long Term Assets | $ 82,750 |
| Total Capital Requ'd | $136,750 | Total Capital Used | $136,750 |

## SALES AND INCOME

| | Upper Quartile | Median | Lower Quartile |
|---|---|---|---|
| Sales | 750,000 | 575,000 | 425,000 |
| Officer's Salary* | 74,250 | 27,600 | 15,725 |
| Net Profit* | 44,750 | 26,750 | 18,000 |
| Total Income* | 119,000 | 54,350 | 33,725 |

*Before Tax

## PROFITABILITY VS ASSETS

| Assets | 0-250$K | 250-1,000$K | 1-10$M |
|---|---|---|---|
| Profitability | N/A | 39.7% | 30.6% |

**COMMENTS:**　Good uptrend.  Low risk, excellent potential.




# MACHINE TOOLS (MFG)　　SIC:3541,42,45

| | |
|---|---|
| Total Assets | $250,000 |
| Profitability | 39.7% |
| Trend | +4.0% |
| Downside Risk | 39.6% |
| Upside Potential | 73.3% |
| Space Required | 1430 Sq. Ft. |

## SOURCE AND USE OF CAPITAL

| Capital Source | | Capital Use | |
|---|---|---|---|
| Owner's Equity | $115,750 | Working Capital | $ 64,000 |
| Long Term Debt | $ 38,250 | Long Term Assets | $ 90,000 |
| Total Capital Requ'd | $154,000 | Total Capital Used | $154,000 |

## SALES AND INCOME

| | Upper Quartile | Median | Lower Quartile |
|---|---|---|---|
| Sales | 675,000 | 550,000 | 450,000 |
| Officer's Salary* | 57,375 | 33,000 | 18,450 |
| Net Profit* | 48,750 | 28,250 | 18,500 |
| Total Income* | 106,125 | 61,250 | 36,950 |

*Before Tax

## PROFITABILITY VS ASSETS

| Assets | 0-250$K | 250-1,00)$K | 1-10$M |
|---|---|---|---|
| Profitability | 63.4% | 39.7% | 32.3% |

**COMMENTS:**　Excellent uptrend, low risk and good potential.

# #63  MOBILE HOMES,CAMPERS (MFG)  SIC:3451,3792

| | |
|---|---|
| Total Assets | $250,000 |
| Profitability | 39.3% |
| Trend | +0.1% |
| Downside Risk | 37.2% |
| Upside Potential | 179.4% |
| Space Required | 1665 Sq. Ft. |

### SOURCE AND USE OF CAPITAL

| Capital Source | | Capital Use | |
|---|---|---|---|
| Owner's Equity | $ 82,500 | Working Capital | $ 54,250 |
| Long Term Debt | $ 40,750 | Long Term Assets | $ 69,000 |
| Total Capital Requ'd | $123,250 | Total Capital Used | $123,250 |

### SALES AND INCOME

| | Upper Quartile | Median | Lower Quartile |
|---|---|---|---|
| Sales | 1,375,000 | 925,000 | 625,000 |
| Officer's Salary* | 79,750 | 25,900 | 11,875 |
| Net Profit* | 55,500 | 22,500 | 18,500 |
| Total Income* | 135,250 | 48,400 | 30,375 |

*Before Tax

### PROFITABILITY VS ASSETS

| Assets | 0-250$K | 250-1,000$K | 1-10$M |
|---|---|---|---|
| Profitability | N/A | 39.3% | 40.7% |

**COMMENTS:**  *Low risk, excellent potential.*


# #64  COMMERCIAL PRINTING (LITHOGRAPHIC) (MFG)

SIC:2752

| | |
|---|---|
| Total Assets | $250,000 |
| Profitability | 39.3% |
| Trend | +1.0% |
| Downside Risk | 45.3% |
| Upside Potential | 70.9% |
| Space Required | 2040 Sq. Ft. |

### SOURCE AND USE OF CAPITAL

| Capital Source | | Capital Use | |
|---|---|---|---|
| Owner's Equity | $100,250 | Working Capital | $ 43,250 |
| Long Term Debt | $ 49,750 | Long Term Assets | $106,750 |
| Total Capital Requ'd | $150,000 | Total Capital Used | $150,000 |

### SALES AND INCOME

| | Upper Quartile | Median | Lower Quartile |
|---|---|---|---|
| Sales | 750,000 | 600,000 | 500,000 |
| Officer's Salary* | 63,000 | 34,200 | 18,000 |
| Net Profit* | 37,750 | 24,750 | 14,250 |
| Total Income* | 100,750 | 58,950 | 32,250 |

*Before Tax

### PROFITABILITY VS ASSETS

| Assets | 0-250$K | 250-1,000$K | 1-10$M |
|---|---|---|---|
| Profitability | 47.4% | 39.3% | 22.9% |

**COMMENTS:**  *Lower than average risk, good potential, but high fixed asset investment.*

# FISH–SEA FOODS (WSLE)

SIC:5146

| | |
|---|---|
| Total Assets | $250,000 |
| Profitability | 39.2% |
| Trend | -0.8% |
| Downside Risk | 54.9% |
| Upside Potential | 114.2% |
| Space Required | 735 Sq. Ft. |

## SOURCE AND USE OF CAPITAL

| Capital Source | | Capital Use | |
|---|---|---|---|
| Owner's Equity | $ 81,750 | Working Capital | $ 53,000 |
| Long Term Debt | $ 41,000 | Long Term Assets | $ 69,750 |
| Total Capital Requ'd | $122,750 | Total Capital Used | $122,750 |

## SALES AND INCOME

| Sales | Upper Quartile | Median | Lower Quartile |
|---|---|---|---|
| Sales | 1,725,000 | 1,225,000 | 775,000 |
| Officer's Salary* | 72,450 | 28,175 | 13,950 |
| Net Profit* | 30,750 | 20,000 | 7,750 |
| Total Income* | 103,200 | 48,175 | 21,700 |

*Before Tax

## PROFITABILITY VS ASSETS

| Assets | 0-250$K | 250-1,000$K | 1-10$M |
|---|---|---|---|
| Profitability | N/A | 39.2% | 30.1% |

**COMMENTS:** *Average risk, excellent potential.*



# SCIENTIFIC INSTRUMENTS (MFG)

SIC:3811

| | |
|---|---|
| Total Assets | $250,000 |
| Profitability | 39.1% |
| Trend | +3.8% |
| Downside Risk | 48.9% |
| Upside Potential | 62.4% |
| Space Required | 1890 Sq. Ft. |

## SOURCE AND USE OF CAPITAL

| Capital Source | | Capital Use | |
|---|---|---|---|
| Owner's Equity | $103,500 | Working Capital | $ 92,750 |
| Long Term Debt | $ 41,500 | Long Term Assets | $ 52,250 |
| Total Capital Requ'd | $145,000 | Total Capital Used | $145,000 |

## SALES AND INCOME

| Sales | Upper Quartile | Median | Lower Quartile |
|---|---|---|---|
| Sales | 600,000 | 450,000 | 375,000 |
| Officer's Salary* | 50,400 | 29,250 | 12,000 |
| Net Profit* | 41,750 | 27,500 | 17,000 |
| Total Income* | 92,150 | 56,750 | 29,000 |

*Before Tax

## PROFITABILITY VS ASSETS

| Assets | 0-250$K | 250-1,000$K | 1-10$M |
|---|---|---|---|
| Profitability | N/A | 39.1% | N/A |

**COMMENTS:** *Good trend, average risk, good potential.*

| | |
|---|---|
| **Total Assets** | $250,000 |
| **Profitability** | 38.9% |
| **Trend** | +1.7% |
| **Downside Risk** | 48.7% |
| **Upside Potential** | 72.5% |
| **Space Required** | 1800 Sq. Ft. |

### SOURCE AND USE OF CAPITAL

| Capital Source | | Capital Use | |
|---|---|---|---|
| **Owner's Equity** | $109,750 | **Working Capital** | $ 48,250 |
| **Long Term Debt** | $ 45,750 | **Long Term Assets** | $107,250 |
| **Total Capital Requ'd** | $155,500 | **Total Capital Used** | $155,500 |

### SALES AND INCOME

| | Upper Quartile | Median | Lower Quartile |
|---|---|---|---|
| **Sales** | 625,000 | 500,000 | 400,000 |
| **Officer's Salary*** | 59,375 | 31,000 | 14,800 |
| **Net Profit*** | 45,000 | 29,500 | 16,250 |
| **Total Income*** | 104,375 | 60,500 | 31,050 |

*Before Tax

### PROFITABILITY VS ASSETS

| Assets | 0-250$K | 250-1,000$K | 1-10$M |
|---|---|---|---|
| **Profitability** | 50.7% | 38.9% | 30.9% |

**COMMENTS:** *Good trend, average risk, good potential.  High initial fixed asset investment.*




| | |
|---|---|
| **Total Assets** | $250,000 |
| **Profitability** | 38.7% |
| **Trend** | -2.4% |
| **Downside Risk** | 54.2% |
| **Upside Potential** | 89.9% |
| **Space Required** | 4050 Sq. Ft. |

### SOURCE AND USE OF CAPITAL

| Capital Source | | Capital Use | |
|---|---|---|---|
| **Owner's Equity** | $119,750 | **Working Capital** | $ 66,000 |
| **Long Term Debt** | $ 34,000 | **Long Term Assets** | $ 87,750 |
| **Total Capital Requ'd** | $153,750 | **Total Capital Used** | $153,750 |

### SALES AND INCOME

| | Upper Quartile | Median | Lower Quartile |
|---|---|---|---|
| **Sales** | 925,000 | 750,000 | 600,000 |
| **Officer's Salary*** | 71,225 | 36,750 | 18,000 |
| **Net Profit*** | 41,750 | 22,750 | 9,250 |
| **Total Income*** | 112,975 | 59,500 | 27,250 |

*Before Tax

### PROFITABILITY VS ASSETS

| Assets | 0-250$K | 250-1,000$K | 1-10$M |
|---|---|---|---|
| **Profitability** | N/A | 38.7% | 18.7% |

**COMMENTS:** *Downtrend?  Average risk, good potential.*

## #69 CUTLERY, HAND TOOLS GENERAL HARDWARE (MFG)

SIC:3421,23,25,2

| | |
|---|---|
| Total Assets | $250,000 |
| Profitability | 38.5% |
| Trend | +2.8% |
| Downside Risk | 59.2% |
| Upside Potential | 70.6% |
| Space Required | 1540 Sq. Ft. |

### SOURCE AND USE OF CAPITAL

| Capital Source | | Capital Use | |
|---|---|---|---|
| Owner's Equity | $114,750 | Working Capital | $ 85,500 |
| Long Term Debt | $ 36,000 | Long Term Assets | $ 65,250 |
| Total Capital Requ'd | $150,750 | Total Capital Used | $150,750 |

### SALES AND INCOME

| | Upper Quartile | Median | Lower Quartile |
|---|---|---|---|
| Sales | 725,000 | 550,000 | 425,000 |
| Officer's Salary* | 60,175 | 30,250 | 17,425 |
| Net Profit* | 38,750 | 27,750 | 6,250 |
| Total Income* | 98,925 | 58,000 | 23,675 |

*Before Tax

### PROFITABILITY VS ASSETS

| Assets | 0-250$K | 250-1,000$K | 1-10$M |
|---|---|---|---|
| Profitability | N/A | 38.5% | 23.0% |

**COMMENTS:** *Good trend. Higher than average risk and potential.*


## #70 MOTOR VEHICLE PARTS (MFG)

SIC:3714

| | |
|---|---|
| Total Assets | $250,000 |
| Profitability | 38.5% |
| Trend | +1.3% |
| Downside Risk | 45.9% |
| Upside Potential | 63.8% |
| Space Required | 1080 Sq. Ft. |

### SOURCE AND USE OF CAPITAL

| Capital Source | | Capital Use | |
|---|---|---|---|
| Owner's Equity | $106,250 | Working Capital | $ 66,750 |
| Long Term Debt | $ 30,000 | Long Term Assets | $ 69,500 |
| Total Capital Requ'd | $136,250 | Total Capital Used | $136,250 |

### SALES AND INCOME

| | Upper Quartile | Median | Lower Quartile |
|---|---|---|---|
| Sales | 850,000 | 675,000 | 555,000 |
| Officer's Salary* | 43,350 | 27,675 | 14,850 |
| Net Profit* | 42,500 | 24,750 | 13,500 |
| Total Income* | 85,850 | 52,425 | 28,350 |

*Before Tax

### PROFITABILITY VS ASSETS

| Assets | 0-250$K | 250-1,000$K | 1-10$M |
|---|---|---|---|
| Profitability | 47.1% | 38.5% | 29.0% |

**COMMENTS:** *Trend? Average risk, good potential*

## #71   RUBBER & PLASTIC FOOTWEAR & PRODUCTS (MFG)

SIC:3021,69

| Total Assets | $250,000 |
|---|---|
| Profitability | 38.4% |
| Trend | -1.1% |
| Downside Risk | 46.9% |
| Upside Potential | 142.2% |
| Space Required | 1200 Sq. Ft. |

### SOURCE AND USE OF CAPITAL

| Capital Source | | Capital Use | |
|---|---|---|---|
| Owner's Equity | $121,250 | Working Capital | $ 62,000 |
| Long Term Debt | $ 28,750 | Long Term Assets | $ 88,000 |
| Total Capital Requ'd | $150,000 | Total Capital Used | $150,000 |

### SALES AND INCOME

| | Upper Quartile | Median | Lower Quartile |
|---|---|---|---|
| Sales | 750,000 | 600,000 | 525,000 |
| Officer's Salary* | 91,500 | 39,600 | 17,375 |
| Net Profit* | 48,000 | 18,000 | 13,200 |
| Total Income* | 139,500 | 57,600 | 30,575 |

*Before Tax

### PROFITABILITY VS ASSETS

| Assets | 0-250$K | 250-1,000$K | 1-10$M |
|---|---|---|---|
| Profitability | N/A | 38.4% | 23.8% |

**COMMENTS:**  *Average risk, excellent potential.*


## #72   TEXTILE WASTE (WSLE)

SIC:5093

| Total Assets | $250,000 |
|---|---|
| Profitability | 38.4% |
| Trend | -1.2% |
| Downside Risk | 72.4% |
| Upside Potential | 110.2% |
| Space Required | 1035 Sq. Ft. |

### SOURCE AND USE OF CAPITAL

| Capital Source | | Capital Use | |
|---|---|---|---|
| Owner's Equity | $109,500 | Working Capital | $ 41,250 |
| Long Term Debt | $ 38,250 | Long Term Assets | $106,500 |
| Total Capital Requ'd | $147,750 | Total Capital Used | $147,750 |

### SALES AND INCOME

| | Upper Quartile | Median | Lower Quartile |
|---|---|---|---|
| Sales | 925,000 | 575,000 | 275,000 |
| Officer's Salary* | 89,725 | 36,225 | 9,350 |
| Net Profit* | 29,500 | 20,500 | 6,250 |
| Total Income* | 119,225 | 56,725 | 15,600 |

*Before Tax

### PROFITABILITY VS ASSETS

| Assets | 0-250$K | 250-1,000$K | 1-10$M |
|---|---|---|---|
| Profitability | N/A | 38.4% | 21.9% |

**COMMENTS:**  *Slight downtrend?  High risk, excellent potential.*

# #73 SCREW MACHINE PRODUCTS (MFG)  SIC:3451,52

| | |
|---|---|
| Total Assets | $250,000 |
| Profitability | 38.4% |
| Trend | +3.9% |
| Downside Risk | 48.1% |
| Upside Potential | 47.8% |
| Space Required | 1540 Sq. Ft. |

## SOURCE AND USE OF CAPITAL

| Capital Source | | Capital Use | |
|---|---|---|---|
| Owner's Equity | $106,500 | Working Capital | $ 55,750 |
| Long Term Debt | $ 43,750 | Long Term Assets | $ 94,500 |
| Total Capital Requ'd | $150,250 | Total Capital Used | $150,250 |

## SALES AND INCOME

| | Upper Quartile | Median | Lower Quartile |
|---|---|---|---|
| Sales | 650,000 | 550,000 | 45,000 |
| Officer's Salary* | 47,450 | 31,900 | 16,650 |
| Net Profit* | 37,750 | 25,750 | 13,250 |
| Total Income* | 85,200 | 57,650 | 29,900 |

*Before Tax

## PROFITABILITY VS ASSETS

| Assets | 0-250$K | 250-1,000$K | 1-10$M |
|---|---|---|---|
| Profitability | N/A | 38.4% | 28.8% |

COMMENTS: *Good uptrend. Higher than average risk, average potential.*


# #74 FABRICATED PIPES & FITTINGS (MFG)  SIC:3498

| | |
|---|---|
| Total Assets | $250,000 |
| Profitability | 38.3% |
| Trend | N/A |
| Downside Risk | 63.1% |
| Upside Potential | 85.8% |
| Space Required | 1045 Sq. Ft. |

## SOURCE AND USE OF CAPITAL

| Capital Source | | Capital Use | |
|---|---|---|---|
| Owner's Equity | $ 96,250 | Working Capital | $ 62,500 |
| Long Term Debt | $ 48,500 | Long Term Assets | $ 82,250 |
| Total Capital Requ'd | $144,750 | Total Capital Used | $144,750 |

## SALES AND INCOME

| | Upper Quartile | Median | Lower Quartile |
|---|---|---|---|
| Sales | 675,000 | 475,000 | 400,000 |
| Officer's Salary* | 39,825 | 19,475 | 9,200 |
| Net Profit* | 63,250 | 36,000 | 11,250 |
| Total Income* | 103,075 | 55,475 | 20,450 |

*Before Tax

## PROFITABILITY VS ASSETS

| Assets | 0-250$K | 250-1,000$K | 1-10$M |
|---|---|---|---|
| Profitability | N/A | 38.3% | N/A |

COMMENTS: *Higher than average risk and potential.*

| | |
|---|---|
| Total Assets | $250,000 |
| Profitability | 38.3% |
| Trend | +2.2% |
| Downside Risk | 55.7% |
| Upside Potential | 81.7% |
| Space Required | 2030 Sq. Ft. |

## SOURCE AND USE OF CAPITAL

| Capital Source | | Capital Use | |
|---|---|---|---|
| Owner's Equity | $ 85,250 | Working Capital | $ 74,250 |
| Long Term Debt | $ 26,500 | Long Term Assets | $ 37,500 |
| Total Capital Requ'd | $111,750 | Total Capital Used | $111,750 |

## SALES AND INCOME

| | Upper Quartile | Median | Lower Quartile |
|---|---|---|---|
| Sales | 900,000 | 725,000 | 550,000 |
| Officer's Salary* | 49,500 | 27,550 | 13,200 |
| Net Profit* | 28,250 | 15,250 | 5,750 |
| Total Income* | 77,750 | 42,800 | 18,950 |

*Before Tax

## PROFITABILITY VS ASSETS

| Assets | 0-250$K | 250-1,000$K | 1-10$M |
|---|---|---|---|
| Profitability | 53.4% | 38.3% | 27.6% |

**COMMENTS:** *Good trend. Average risk, good potential.*


## #76    WOMEN & CHILDRENS CLOTHING (WSLE) SIC:5137

| | |
|---|---|
| Total Assets | $250,000 |
| Profitability | 38.2% |
| Trend | +0.2% |
| Downside Risk | 58.9% |
| Upside Potential | 79.0% |
| Space Required | 1540 Sq. Ft. |

## SOURCE AND USE OF CAPITAL

| Capital Source | | Capital Use | |
|---|---|---|---|
| Owner's Equity | $119,750 | Working Capital | $108,750 |
| Long Term Debt | $ 22,000 | Long Term Assets | $ 33,000 |
| Total Capital Requ'd | $141,750 | Total Capital Used | $141,750 |

## SALES AND INCOME

| | Upper Quartile | Median | Lower Quartile |
|---|---|---|---|
| Sales | 925,000 | 700,000 | 500,000 |
| Officer's Salary* | 64,750 | 35,700 | 14,000 |
| Net Profit* | 32,250 | 18,500 | 8,250 |
| Total Income* | 97,000 | 54,200 | 22,250 |

*Before Tax

## PROFITABILITY VS ASSETS

| Assets | 0-250$K | 250-1,000$K | 1-10$M |
|---|---|---|---|
| Profitability | N/A | 38.2% | 36.1% |

**COMMENTS:** *Higher than average risk and potential.*

## #77  UPHOLSTERED WOODEN FURNITURE (MFG) SIC:2516

| | |
|---|---|
| Total Assets | $250,000 |
| Profitability | 38.2% |
| Trend | +0.1% |
| Downside Risk | 53.2% |
| Upside Potential | 70.9% |
| Space Required | 2970 Sq. Ft. |

### SOURCE AND USE OF CAPITAL

| Capital Source | | Capital Use | |
|---|---|---|---|
| Owner's Equity | $ 97,500 | Working Capital | $ 72,750 |
| Long Term Debt | $ 35,000 | Long Term Assets | $ 59,750 |
| Total Capital Requ'd | $132,500 | Total Capital Used | $132,500 |

### SALES AND INCOME

| | Upper Quartile | Median | Lower Quartile |
|---|---|---|---|
| Sales | 975,000 | 825,000 | 575,000 |
| Officer's Salary* | 54,600 | 34,650 | 14,950 |
| Net Profit* | 32,000 | 16,000 | 8,750 |
| Total Income* | 86,600 | 50,650 | 23,700 |

*Before Tax

### PROFITABILITY VS ASSETS

| Assets | 0-250$K | 250-1,000$K | 1-10$M |
|---|---|---|---|
| Profitability | N/A | 38.2% | 27.0% |

**COMMENTS:**  *Average risk, good potential.*


## #78  RESTAURANT & HOTEL SUPPLIES (WSLE) SIC:5081

| | |
|---|---|
| Total Assets | $250,000 |
| Profitability | 37.9% |
| Trend | -0.3% |
| Downside Risk | 47.5% |
| Upside Potential | 80.7% |
| Space Required | 1885 Sq. Ft. |

### SOURCE AND USE OF CAPITAL

| Capital Source | | Capital Use | |
|---|---|---|---|
| Owner's Equity | $ 92,250 | Working Capital | $ 84,250 |
| Long Term Debt | $ 41,500 | Long Term Assets | $ 49,500 |
| Total Capital Requ'd | $133,750 | Total Capital Used | $133,750 |

### SALES AND INCOME

| | Upper Quartile | Median | Lower Quartile |
|---|---|---|---|
| Sales | 950,000 | 725,000 | 550,000 |
| Officer's Salary* | 60,800 | 31,175 | 17,600 |
| Net Profit* | 30,750 | 19,500 | 9,000 |
| Total Income* | 91,550 | 50,675 | 26,600 |

*Before Tax

### PROFITABILITY VS ASSETS

| Assets | 0-250$K | 250-1,000$K | 1-10$M |
|---|---|---|---|
| Profitability | 62.8% | 37.9% | 30.4% |

**COMMENTS:**  *Average risk, good potential.*

| | |
|---|---|
| Total Assets | $250,000 |
| Profitability | 37.7% |
| Trend | +1.1% |
| Downside Risk | 61.1% |
| Upside Potential | 84.6% |
| Space Required | 3000 Sq. Ft. |

## SOURCE AND USE OF CAPITAL

| Capital Source | | Capital Use | |
|---|---|---|---|
| Owner's Equity | $ 84,750 | Working Capital | $ 60,000 |
| Long Term Debt | $ 35,000 | Long Term Assets | $ 59,750 |
| Total Capital Requ'd | $119,750 | Total Capital Used | $119,750 |

## SALES AND INCOME

| | Upper Quartile | Median | Lower Quartile |
|---|---|---|---|
| Sales | 775,000 | 600,000 | 450,000 |
| Officer's Salary* | 48,825 | 23,400 | 10,800 |
| Net Profit* | 34,500 | 21,750 | 6,750 |
| Total Income* | 83,325 | 45,150 | 17,550 |

*Before Tax

## PROFITABILITY VS ASSETS

| Assets | 0-250$K | 250-1,000$K | 1-10$M |
|---|---|---|---|
| Profitability | 58.0% | 37.7% | 23.5% |

**COMMENTS:** *Slight uptrend. Higher than average risk and potential.*



| | |
|---|---|
| Total Assets | $250,000 |
| Profitability | 37.5% |
| Trend | +4.9% |
| Downside Risk | 44.6% |
| Upside Potential | 81.2% |
| Space Required | 2560 Sq. Ft. |

## SOURCE AND USE OF CAPITAL

| Capital Source | | Capital Use | |
|---|---|---|---|
| Owner's Equity | $101,250 | Working Capital | $ 76,250 |
| Long Term Debt | $ 25,750 | Long Term Assets | $ 50,750 |
| Total Capital Requ'd | $127,000 | Total Capital Used | $127,000 |

## SALES AND INCOME

| | Upper Quartile | Median | Lower Quartile |
|---|---|---|---|
| Sales | 1,000,000 | 800,000 | 600,000 |
| Officer's Salary* | 56,000 | 29,600 | 15,600 |
| Net Profit* | 30,250 | 18,000 | 10,750 |
| Total Income* | 86,250 | 47,600 | 26,350 |

*Before Tax

## PROFITABILITY VS ASSETS

| Assets | 0-250$K | 250-1,000$K | 1-10$M |
|---|---|---|---|
| Profitability | 63.9% | 37.5% | 26.2% |

**COMMENTS:** *Excellent uptrend. Lower risk and higher potential than average.*

## TIRES & TUBES (WSLE)  SIC:5014

| | |
|---|---|
| Total Assets | $250,000 |
| Profitability | 37.5% |
| Trend | +3.0% |
| Downside Risk | 46.7% |
| Upside Potential | 75.8% |
| Space Required | 1300 Sq. Ft. |

### SOURCE AND USE OF CAPITAL

| Capital Source | | Capital Use | |
|---|---|---|---|
| Owner's Equity | $ 86,000 | Working Capital | $ 62,250 |
| Long Term Debt | $ 22,750 | Long Term Assets | $ 46,500 |
| Total Capital Requ'd | $108,750 | Total Capital Used | $108,750 |

### SALES AND INCOME

| | Upper Quartile | Median | Lower Quartile |
|---|---|---|---|
| Sales | 825,000 | 650,000 | 500,000 |
| Officer's Salary* | 43,725 | 24,050 | 11,500 |
| Net Profit* | 28,000 | 16,750 | 10,250 |
| Total Income* | 71,725 | 40,800 | 21,750 |

*Before Tax

### PROFITABILITY VS ASSETS

| Assets | 0-250$K | 250-1,000$K | 1-10$M |
|---|---|---|---|
| Profitability | N/A | 37.5% | 32.9% |

**COMMENTS:**  *Good uptrend.  Average risk, good potential.*




## STATIONERY & PAPER BAGS (MFG) SIC:2643,42,48

| | |
|---|---|
| Total Assets | $250,000 |
| Profitability | 37.4% |
| Trend | +1.9% |
| Downside Risk | 84.4% |
| Upside Potential | 68.3% |
| Space Required | 2340 Sq. Ft. |

### SOURCE AND USE OF CAPITAL

| Capital Source | | Capital Use | |
|---|---|---|---|
| Owner's Equity | $114,750 | Working Capital | $ 72,250 |
| Long Term Debt | $ 47,250 | Long Term Assets | $ 89,750 |
| Total Capital Requ'd | $162,000 | Total Capital Used | $162,000 |

### SALES AND INCOME

| | Upper Quartile | Median | Lower Quartile |
|---|---|---|---|
| Sales | 800,000 | 650,000 | 475,000 |
| Officer's Salary* | 72,800 | 42,900 | 10,450 |
| Net Profit* | 29,250 | 17,750 | (1,000) |
| Total Income* | 102,050 | 60,650 | 9,450 |

*Before Tax

### PROFITABILITY VS ASSETS

| Assets | 0-250$K | 250-1,000$K | 1-10$M |
|---|---|---|---|
| Profitability | N/A | 37.4% | 24.2% |

**COMMENTS:**  *Good uptrend.  Very high risk, good potential.*

| Total Assets | $250,000 |
|---|---|
| Profitability | 37.2% |
| Trend | +1.8% |
| Downside Risk | 50.9% |
| Upside Potential | 84.9% |
| Space Required | 2160 Sq. Ft. |

## SOURCE AND USE OF CAPITAL

| Capital Source | | Capital Use | |
|---|---|---|---|
| Owner's Equity | $ 97,500 | Working Capital | $ 82,000 |
| Long Term Debt | $ 37,750 | Long Term Assets | $ 53,250 |
| Total Capital Requ'd | $135,250 | Total Capital Used | $135,250 |

## SALES AND INCOME

| | Upper Quartile | Median | Lower Quartile |
|---|---|---|---|
| Sales | 850,000 | 675,000 | 550,000 |
| Officer's Salary* | 59,500 | 31,050 | 15,950 |
| Net Profit* | 33,500 | 19,250 | 8,750 |
| Total Income* | 93,000 | 50,300 | 24,700 |

*Before Tax

## PROFITABILITY VS ASSETS

| Assets | 0-250$K | 250-1,000$K | 1-10$M |
|---|---|---|---|
| Profitability | 55.9% | 37.2% | 26.9% |

**COMMENTS:** *Good trend. Average risk, good potential.*


#84       **BOOK PUBLISHING & PRINTING (MFG)**    SIC:2731

| Total Assets | $250,000 |
|---|---|
| Profitability | 36.9% |
| Trend | -1.2% |
| Downside Risk | 70.7% |
| Upside Potential | 154.9% |
| Space Required | 1440 Sq. Ft. |

## SOURCE AND USE OF CAPITAL

| Capital Source | | Capital Use | |
|---|---|---|---|
| Owner's Equity | $ 72,000 | Working Capital | $ 43,750 |
| Long Term Debt | $ 36,250 | Long Term Assets | $ 64,500 |
| Total Capital Requ'd | $108,250 | Total Capital Used | $108,250 |

## SALES AND INCOME

| | Upper Quartile | Median | Lower Quartile |
|---|---|---|---|
| Sales | 600,000 | 450,000 | 275,000 |
| Officer's Salary* | 67,200 | 31,500 | 7,700 |
| Net Profit* | 34,750 | 8,500 | 4,000 |
| Total Income* | 101,950 | 40,000 | 11,700 |

*Before Tax

## PROFITABILITY VS ASSETS

| Assets | 0-250$K | 250-1,000$K | 1-10$M |
|---|---|---|---|
| Profitability | N/A | 36.9% | N/A |

**COMMENTS:** *Downtrend. Higher than average risk, excellent potential.*

# BROAD WOVEN FABRIC (MFG)    SIC:2211,21

| | |
|---|---|
| Total Assets | $250,000 |
| Profitability | 36.7% |
| Trend | +0.4% |
| Downside Risk | 43.0% |
| Upside Potential | 66.6% |
| Space Required | 1550 Sq. Ft. |

## SOURCE AND USE OF CAPITAL

| Capital Source | | Capital Use | |
|---|---|---|---|
| Owner's Equity | $ 68,250 | Working Capital | $ 52,250 |
| Long Term Debt | $ 70,750 | Long Term Assets | $ 86,750 |
| Total Capital Requ'd | $139,000 | Total Capital Used | $139,000 |

## SALES AND INCOME

| | Upper Quartile | Median | Lower Quartile |
|---|---|---|---|
| Sales | 900,000 | 775,000 | 700,000 |
| Officer's Salary* | 37,800 | 24,800 | 12,600 |
| Net Profit* | 47,250 | 26,250 | 16,500 |
| Total Income* | 85,050 | 51,050 | 29,100 |

*Before Tax

## PROFITABILITY VS ASSETS

| Assets | 0-250$K | 250-1,000$K | 1-10$M |
|---|---|---|---|
| Profitability | N/A | 36.7% | 19.1% |

**COMMENTS:** *Stable profitability. Lower than average risk, good potential. High debt content, but good profit to pay back debt.*



# MEN & BOYS SPORT CLOTHING (MFG)    SIC:2329

| | |
|---|---|
| Total Assets | $250,000 |
| Profitability | 36.5% |
| Trend | +0.8% |
| Downside Risk | 50.6% |
| Upside Potential | 91.5% |
| Space Required | 1470 Sq. Ft. |

## SOURCE AND USE OF CAPITAL

| Capital Source | | Capital Use | |
|---|---|---|---|
| Owner's Equity | $100,250 | Working Capital | $ 95,000 |
| Long Term Debt | $ 36,750 | Long Term Assets | $ 42,000 |
| Total Capital Requ'd | $137,000 | Total Capital Used | $137,000 |

## SALES AND INCOME

| | Upper Quartile | Median | Lower Quartile |
|---|---|---|---|
| Sales | 650,000 | 525,000 | 400,000 |
| Officer's Salary* | 63,050 | 26,775 | 11,200 |
| Net Profit* | 32,750 | 23,250 | 13,500 |
| Total Income* | 95,800 | 50,025 | 24,700 |

*Before Tax

## PROFITABILITY VS ASSETS

| Assets | 0-250$K | 250-1,000$K | 1-10$M |
|---|---|---|---|
| Profitability | N/A | 36.5% | 28.5% |

**COMMENTS:** *Stable profitability. Average risk, good - excellent potential. Fairly large working capital required.*

| | |
|---|---|
| **Total Assets** | $250,000 |
| **Profitability** | 36.5% |
| **Trend** | +5.5% |
| **Downside Risk** | 55.0% |
| **Upside Potential** | 67.6% |
| **Space Required** | 1625 Sq. Ft. |

### SOURCE AND USE OF CAPITAL

| Capital Source | | Capital Use | |
|---|---|---|---|
| **Owner's Equity** | $123,500 | **Working Capital** | $114,750 |
| **Long Term Debt** | $ 31,000 | **Long Term Assets** | $ 39,750 |
| **Total Capital Requ'd** | $154,500 | **Total Capital Used** | $154,500 |

### SALES AND INCOME

| | Upper Quartile | Median | Lower Quartile |
|---|---|---|---|
| **Sales** | 750,000 | 625,000 | 450,000 |
| **Officer's Salary*** | 59,250 | 38,125 | 19,350 |
| **Net Profit*** | 35,250 | 18,250 | 6,000 |
| **Total Income*** | 94,500 | 56,375 | 25,350 |

*Before Tax

### PROFITABILITY VS ASSETS

| **Assets** | 0-250$K | 250-1,000$K | 1-10$M |
|---|---|---|---|
| **Profitability** | N/A | 36.5% | N/A |

**COMMENTS:**    *Excellent uptrend. Average risk and potential. Maybe "Urban Cowboy" fad.*




| | |
|---|---|
| **Total Assets** | $250,000 |
| **Profitability** | 36.5% |
| **Trend** | +3.6% |
| **Downside Risk** | 40.8% |
| **Upside Potential** | 64.6% |
| **Space Required** | 2125 Sq. Ft. |

### SOURCE AND USE OF CAPITAL

| Capital Source | | Capital Use | |
|---|---|---|---|
| **Owner's Equity** | $105,750 | **Working Capital** | $ 63,750 |
| **Long Term Debt** | $ 41,750 | **Long Term Assets** | $ 83,750 |
| **Total Capital Requ'd** | $147,500 | **Total Capital Used** | $147,500 |

### SALES AND INCOME

| | Upper Quartile | Median | Lower Quartile |
|---|---|---|---|
| **Sales** | 700,000 | 625,000 | 525,000 |
| **Officer's Salary*** | 49,700 | 30,625 | 18,900 |
| **Net Profit*** | 38,000 | 23,250 | 13,000 |
| **Total Income*** | 88,700 | 53,875 | 31,900 |

*Before Tax

### PROFITABILITY VS ASSETS

| **Assets** | 0-250$K | 250-1,000$K | 1-10$M |
|---|---|---|---|
| **Profitability** | 43.4% | 36.5% | 33.1% |

**COMMENTS:**    *Good uptrend. Low risk and good potential.*

# BUILDING MATERIALS (WSLE)          SIC:5039

| | |
|---|---|
| Total Assets | $250,000 |
| Profitability | 36.4% |
| Trend | -0.9% |
| Downside Risk | 47.5% |
| Upside Potential | 80.3% |
| Space Required | 1705 Sq. Ft. |

## SOURCE AND USE OF CAPITAL

| Capital Source | | Capital Use | |
|---|---|---|---|
| Owner's Equity | $ 99,000 | Working Capital | $ 76,750 |
| Long Term Debt | $ 33,250 | Long Term Assets | $ 55,500 |
| Total Capital Requ'd | $132,250 | Total Capital Used | $132,250 |

## SALES AND INCOME

| | Upper Quartile | Median | Lower Quartile |
|---|---|---|---|
| Sales | 950,000 | 775,000 | 575,000 |
| Officer's Salary* | 51,300 | 27,900 | 13,800 |
| Net Profit* | 35,500 | 20,250 | 11,500 |
| Total Income* | 86,800 | 48,150 | 25,300 |

*Before Tax

## PROFITABILITY VS ASSETS

| Assets | 0-250$K | 250-1,000$K | 1-10$M |
|---|---|---|---|
| Profitability | 61.3% | 36.4% | 28.2% |

**COMMENTS:**  *Average risk, good potential.  Influenced strongly by economic climate.*


# #90  HEATING & PLUMBING EQUIPMENT (RTL)     SIC:5074

| | |
|---|---|
| Total Assets | $250,000 |
| Profitability | 36.4% |
| Trend | +0.3% |
| Downside Risk | 46.3% |
| Upside Potential | 72.2% |
| Space Required | 1450 Sq. Ft. |

## SOURCE AND USE OF CAPITAL

| Capital Source | | Capital Use | |
|---|---|---|---|
| Owner's Equity | $112,750 | Working Capital | $ 96,750 |
| Long Term Debt | $ 22,250 | Long Term Assets | $ 38,250 |
| Total Capital Requ'd | $135,000 | Total Capital Used | $135,000 |

## SALES AND INCOME

| | Upper Quartile | Median | Lower Quartile |
|---|---|---|---|
| Sales | 875,000 | 725,000 | 600,000 |
| Officer's Salary* | 50,750 | 29,725 | 16,200 |
| Net Profit* | 34,000 | 19,500 | 10,250 |
| Total Income* | 84,750 | 49,225 | 26,450 |

*Before Tax

## PROFITABILITY VS ASSETS

| Assets | 0-250$K | 250-1,000$K | 1-10$M |
|---|---|---|---|
| Profitability | 53.1% | 36.4% | 25.4% |

**COMMENTS:**  *Average risk, good potential.*

| | |
|---|---|
| Total Assets | $250,000 |
| Profitability | 36.4% |
| Trend | +4.2% |
| Downside Risk | 40.7% |
| Upside Potential | 55.1% |
| Space Required | 2420 Sq. Ft. |

### SOURCE AND USE OF CAPITAL

| Capital Source | | Capital Use | |
|---|---|---|---|
| Owner's Equity | $ 95,000 | Working Capital | $ 35,000 |
| Long Term Debt | $ 75,750 | Long Term Assets | $135,750 |
| Total Capital Requ'd | $170,750 | Total Capital Used | $170,750 |

### SALES AND INCOME

| | Upper Quartile | Median | Lower Quartile |
|---|---|---|---|
| Sales | 675,000 | 550,000 | 475,000 |
| Officer's Salary* | 60,075 | 36,850 | 22,325 |
| Net Profit* | 36,250 | 25,250 | 14,500 |
| Total Income* | 96,325 | 62,100 | 36,825 |

*Before Tax

### PROFITABILITY VS ASSETS

| Assets | 0-250$K | 250-1,000$K | 1-10$M |
|---|---|---|---|
| Profitability | 65.2% | 36.4% | N/A |

**COMMENTS:** *Good uptrend. Low risk, average potential. High fixed asset content.*

---



| | |
|---|---|
| Total Assets | $250,000 |
| Profitability | 36.3% |
| Trend | N/A |
| Downside Risk | 50.1% |
| Upside Potential | 98.7% |
| Space Required | 560 Sq. Ft. |

### SOURCE AND USE OF CAPITAL

| Capital Source | | Capital Use | |
|---|---|---|---|
| Owner's Equity | $132,000 | Working Capital | $ 42,500 |
| Long Term Debt | $ 42,000 | Long Term Assets | $131,500 |
| Total Capital Requ'd | $174,000 | Total Capital Used | $174,000 |

### SALES AND INCOME

| | Upper Quartile | Median | Lower Quartile |
|---|---|---|---|
| Sales | 800,000 | 700,000 | 475,000 |
| Officer's Salary* | 49,000 | 25,200 | 8,550 |
| Net Profit* | 76,600 | 38,000 | 23,000 |
| Total Income* | 125,600 | 63,200 | 31,550 |

*Before Tax

### PROFITABILITY VS ASSETS

| Assets | 0-250$K | 250-1,000$K | 1-10$M |
|---|---|---|---|
| Profitability | N/A | 36.3% | N/A |

**COMMENTS:** *Average risk, good - excellent potential.*

# INFANTS' CLOTHING (RTL)

SIC:5641

| | |
|---|---|
| Total Assets | $250,000 |
| Profitability | 36.1% |
| Trend | -2.9% |
| Downside Risk | 53.8% |
| Upside Potential | 78.1% |
| Space Required | 7280 Sq. Ft. |

## SOURCE AND USE OF CAPITAL

| Capital Source | | Capital Use | |
|---|---|---|---|
| Owner's Equity | $100,500 | Working Capital | $ 99,000 |
| Long Term Debt | $ 54,500 | Long Term Assets | $ 56,000 |
| Total Capital Requ'd | $155,000 | Total Capital Used | $155,000 |

## SALES AND INCOME

| | Upper Quartile | Median | Lower Quartile |
|---|---|---|---|
| Sales | 875,000 | 700,000 | 525,000 |
| Officer's Salary* | 71,750 | 42,000 | 23,100 |
| Net Profit* | 28,000 | 14,000 | 2,750 |
| Total Income* | 99,750 | 56,000 | 25,850 |

*Before Tax

## PROFITABILITY VS ASSETS

| Assets | 0-250$K | 250-1,000$K | 1-10$M |
|---|---|---|---|
| Profitability | 38.0% | 36.1% | N/A |

**COMMENTS:** *Significant downturn in profitability?  Average risk, good potential.*



# DRUGS (RTL)

SIC:5912

| | |
|---|---|
| Total Assets | $250,000 |
| Profitability | 36.0% |
| Trend | -0.5% |
| Downside Risk | 49.3% |
| Upside Potential | 55.7% |
| Space Required | 4950 Sq. Ft. |

## SOURCE AND USE OF CAPITAL

| Capital Source | | Capital Use | |
|---|---|---|---|
| Owner's Equity | $113,250 | Working Capital | $ 75,800 |
| Long Term Debt | $ 39,250 | Long Term Assets | $ 56,700 |
| Total Capital Requ'd | $152,500 | Total Capital Used | $152,500 |

## SALES AND INCOME

| | Upper Quartile | Median | Lower Quartile |
|---|---|---|---|
| Sales | 950,000 | 825,000 | 625,000 |
| Officer's Salary* | 50,350 | 35,475 | 18,125 |
| Net Profit* | 35,250 | 19,500 | 9,750 |
| Total Income* | 85,600 | 54,975 | 27,875 |

*Before Tax

## PROFITABILITY VS ASSETS

| Assets | 0-250$K | 250-1,000$K | 1-10$M |
|---|---|---|---|
| Profitability | 60.0% | 36.0% | N/A |

**COMMENTS:** *Average risk and potential.*

| | |
|---|---|
| **Total Assets** | $250,000 |
| **Profitability** | 35.8% |
| **Trend** | -2.5% |
| **Downside Risk** | 62.7% |
| **Upside Potential** | 96.4% |
| **Space Required** | 2500 Sq. Ft. |

### SOURCE AND USE OF CAPITAL

| Capital Source | | Capital Use | |
|---|---|---|---|
| **Owner's Equity** | $101,250 | **Working Capital** | $ 27,250 |
| **Long Term Debt** | $ 47,000 | **Long Term Assets** | $121,000 |
| **Total Capital Requ'd** | $148,250 | **Total Capital Used** | $148,250 |

### SALES AND INCOME

| | Upper Quartile | Median | Lower Quartile |
|---|---|---|---|
| **Sales** | 675,000 | 500,000 | 400,000 |
| **Officer's Salary*** | 62,100 | 31,500 | 18,800 |
| **Net Profit*** | 42,000 | 21,500 | 1,000 |
| **Total Income*** | 104,100 | 53,000 | 19,800 |

*Before Tax

### PROFITABILITY VS ASSETS

| Assets | 0-250$K | 250-1,000$K | 1-10$M |
|---|---|---|---|
| **Profitability** | 93.6% | 35.8% | N/A |

**COMMENTS:** *Significant profitability downtrend. Higher than average risk and good - excellent potential.*



| | |
|---|---|
| **Total Assets** | $250,000 |
| **Profitability** | 35.8% |
| **Trend** | +0.3% |
| **Downside Risk** | 52.7% |
| **Upside Potential** | 87.3% |
| **Space Required** | 1805 Sq. Ft. |

### SOURCE AND USE OF CAPITAL

| Capital Source | | Capital Use | |
|---|---|---|---|
| **Owner's Equity** | $ 98,500 | **Working Capital** | $ 39,500 |
| **Long Term Debt** | $ 58,750 | **Long Term Assets** | $117,750 |
| **Total Capital Requ'd** | $157,250 | **Total Capital Used** | $157,250 |

### SALES AND INCOME

| | Upper Quartile | Median | Lower Quartile |
|---|---|---|---|
| **Sales** | 625,000 | 475,000 | 375,000 |
| **Officer's Salary*** | 63,125 | 32,775 | 15,375 |
| **Net Profit*** | 42,250 | 23,500 | 11,250 |
| **Total Income*** | 105,375 | 56,275 | 26,625 |

*Before Tax

### PROFITABILITY VS ASSETS

| Assets | 0-250$K | 250-1,000$K | 1-10$M |
|---|---|---|---|
| **Profitability** | 57.4% | 35.8% | 25.4% |

**COMMENTS:** *Average risk, good potential.*

| | |
|---|---|
| Total Assets | $250,000 |
| Profitability | 35.6% |
| Trend | +0.4% |
| Downside Risk | 43.5% |
| Upside Potential | 78.6% |
| Space Required | 2475 Sq. Ft. |

## SOURCE AND USE OF CAPITAL

| Capital Source | | Capital Use | |
|---|---|---|---|
| Owner's Equity | $106,250 | Working Capital | $106,500 |
| Long Term Debt | $ 31,500 | Long Term Assets | $ 31,250 |
| Total Capital Requ'd | $137,750 | Total Capital Used | $137,750 |

## SALES AND INCOME

| | Upper Quartile | Median | Lower Quartile |
|---|---|---|---|
| Sales | 450,000 | 375,000 | 275,000 |
| Officer's Salary* | 51,750 | 27,750 | 13,200 |
| Net Profit* | 35,750 | 21,250 | 14,500 |
| Total Income* | 87,500 | 49,000 | 27,700 |

*Before Tax

## PROFITABILITY VS ASSETS

| Assets | 0-250$K | 250-1,000$K | 1-10$M |
|---|---|---|---|
| Profitability | 36.3% | 35.6% | 28.9% |

**COMMENTS:**  *Lower than average risk, good potential.*


#98      ROAD MACHINERY EQUIPMENT (RTL)        SIC:5082

| | |
|---|---|
| Total Assets | $250,000 |
| Profitability | 35.5% |
| Trend | +0.5% |
| Downside Risk | 48.7% |
| Upside Potential | 116.4% |
| Space Required | 1430 Sq. Ft. |

## SOURCE AND USE OF CAPITAL

| Capital Source | | Capital Use | |
|---|---|---|---|
| Owner's Equity | $ 89,500 | Working Capital | $ 68,750 |
| Long Term Debt | $ 29,500 | Long Term Assets | $ 50,250 |
| Total Capital Requ'd | $119,000 | Total Capital Used | $119,000 |

## SALES AND INCOME

| | Upper Quartile | Median | Lower Quartile |
|---|---|---|---|
| Sales | 850,000 | 650,000 | 475,000 |
| Officer's Salary* | 53,550 | 21,450 | 11,400 |
| Net Profit* | 37,750 | 20,750 | 10,250 |
| Total Income* | 91,300 | 42,200 | 21,650 |

*Before Tax

## PROFITABILITY VS ASSETS

| Assets | 0-250$K | 250-1,000$K | 1-10$M |
|---|---|---|---|
| Profitability | N/A | 35.5% | 22.1% |

**COMMENTS:**  *Average risk, excellent potential.*

| | |
|---|---|
| Total Assets | $250,000 |
| Profitability | 35.4% |
| Trend | -0.8% |
| Downside Risk | 56.7% |
| Upside Potential | 144.2% |
| Space Required | 1770 Sq. Ft. |

### SOURCE AND USE OF CAPITAL

| Capital Source | | Capital Use | |
|---|---|---|---|
| Owner's Equity | $ 96,750 | Working Capital | $ 57,750 |
| Long Term Debt | $ 15,500 | Long Term Assets | $ 54,500 |
| Total Capital Requ'd | $112,250 | Total Capital Used | $112,250 |

### SALES AND INCOME

| | Upper Quartile | Median | Lower Quartile |
|---|---|---|---|
| Sales | 2,000,000 | 1,475,000 | 875,000 |
| Officer's Salary* | 70,000 | 25,075 | 10,500 |
| Net Profit* | 27,250 | 14,750 | 6,750 |
| Total Income* | 97,250 | 39,825 | 17,250 |

*Before Tax

### PROFITABILITY VS ASSETS

| Assets | 0-250$K | 250-1,000$K | 1-10$M |
|---|---|---|---|
| Profitability | N/A | 35.4% | 22.6% |

**COMMENTS:**  *Average risk, excellent potential.*


**#100**  **DIRECT MAIL ADVERTISING (SVE)**        **SIC:7331**

| | |
|---|---|
| Total Assets | $250,000 |
| Profitability | 35.4% |
| Trend | +1.8% |
| Downside Risk | 52.8% |
| Upside Potential | 105.6% |
| Space Required | 2860 Sq. Ft. |

### SOURCE AND USE OF CAPITAL

| Capital Source | | Capital Use | |
|---|---|---|---|
| Owner's Equity | $103,250 | Working Capital | $ 38,000 |
| Long Term Debt | $ 47,500 | Long Term Assets | $112,750 |
| Total Capital Requ'd | $150,750 | Total Capital Used | $150,750 |

### SALES AND INCOME

| | Upper Quartile | Median | Lower Quartile |
|---|---|---|---|
| Sales | 700,000 | 550,000 | 475,000 |
| Officer's Salary* | 72,100 | 33,550 | 16,150 |
| Net Profit* | 37,500 | 19,750 | 9,000 |
| Total Income* | 109,600 | 53,300 | 25,150 |

*Before Tax

### PROFITABILITY VS ASSETS

| Assets | 0-250$K | 250-1,000$K | 1-10$M |
|---|---|---|---|
| Profitability | N/A | 35.4% | N/A |

**COMMENTS:**  *Average risk, excellent potential.*

| | |
|---|---|
| Total Assets | $250,000 |
| Profitability | 35.4% |
| Trend | +2.4% |
| Downside Risk | 59.4% |
| Upside Potential | 101.5% |
| Space Required | 980 Sq. Ft. |

## SOURCE AND USE OF CAPITAL

| Capital Source | | Capital Use | |
|---|---|---|---|
| Owner's Equity | $110,250 | Working Capital | $104,250 |
| Long Term Debt | $ 15,750 | Long Term Assets | $ 21,750 |
| Total Capital Requ'd | $126,000 | Total Capital Used | $126,000 |

## SALES AND INCOME

| | Upper Quartile | Median | Lower Quartile |
|---|---|---|---|
| Sales | 925,000 | 700,000 | 550,000 |
| Officer's Salary* | 61,975 | 25,900 | 12,100 |
| Net Profit* | 28,000 | 18,750 | 6,000 |
| Total Income* | 89,975 | 44,650 | 18,100 |

*Before Tax

## PROFITABILITY VS ASSETS

| Assets | 0-250$K | 250-1,000$K | 1-10$M |
|---|---|---|---|
| Profitability | N/A | 35.4% | 33.9% |

**COMMENTS:** *Good uptrend. Higher than average risk, excellent potential.*


# #102 ELECTRICAL SUPPLIES & APPARATUS (WSLE) SIC:5063

| | |
|---|---|
| Total Assets | $250,000 |
| Profitability | 35.4% |
| Trend | +0.1% |
| Downside Risk | 42.9% |
| Upside Potential | 81.9% |
| Space Required | 1400 Sq. Ft. |

## SOURCE AND USE OF CAPITAL

| Capital Source | | Capital Use | |
|---|---|---|---|
| Owner's Equity | $105,750 | Working Capital | $ 87,250 |
| Long Term Debt | $ 25,500 | Long Term Assets | $ 44,000 |
| Total Capital Requ'd | $131,250 | Total Capital Used | $131,250 |

## SALES AND INCOME

| | Upper Quartile | Median | Lower Quartile |
|---|---|---|---|
| Sales | 850,000 | 700,000 | 575,000 |
| Officer's Salary* | 47,600 | 24,500 | 13,800 |
| Net Profit* | 37,000 | 22,000 | 12,750 |
| Total Income* | 84,600 | 46,500 | 26,550 |

*Before Tax

## PROFITABILITY VS ASSETS

| Assets | 0-250$K | 250-1,000$K | 1-10$M |
|---|---|---|---|
| Profitability | 54.0% | 35.4% | 32.3% |

**COMMENTS:** *Lower than average risk, good potential.*

| | |
|---|---|
| Total Assets | $250,000 |
| Profitability | 35.4% |
| Trend | -0.9% |
| Downside Risk | 56.3% |
| Upside Potential | 75.8% |
| Space Required | 1265 Sq. Ft. |

### SOURCE AND USE OF CAPITAL

| Capital Source | | Capital Use | |
|---|---|---|---|
| Owner's Equity | $ 81,750 | Working Capital | $ 26,500 |
| Long Term Debt | $ 35,250 | Long Term Assets | $ 90,500 |
| Total Capital Requ'd | $117,000 | Total Capital Used | $117,000 |

### SALES AND INCOME

| | Upper Quartile | Median | Lower Quartile |
|---|---|---|---|
| Sales | 875,000 | 575,000 | 425,000 |
| Officer's Salary* | 41,125 | 20,700 | 9,350 |
| Net Profit* | 31,750 | 20,750 | 8,750 |
| Total Income* | 72,875 | 41,450 | 18,100 |

*Before Tax

### PROFITABILITY VS ASSETS

| Assets | 0-250$K | 250-1,000$K | 1-10$M |
|---|---|---|---|
| Profitability | N/A | 35.4% | 25.3% |

**COMMENTS:**   *Average risk and potential.*


#104      CHILDREN'S CLOTHING (MFG)      SIC:2369

| | |
|---|---|
| Total Assets | $250,000 |
| Profitability | 35.1% |
| Trend | +0.1% |
| Downside Risk | 82.1% |
| Upside Potential | 120.0% |
| Space Required | 1470 Sq. Ft. |

### SOURCE AND USE OF CAPITAL

| Capital Source | | Capital Use | |
|---|---|---|---|
| Owner's Equity | $120,500 | Working Capital | $ 85,250 |
| Long Term Debt | $ 12,500 | Long Term Assets | $ 47,750 |
| Total Capital Requ'd | $133,000 | Total Capital Used | $133,000 |

### SALES AND INCOME

| | Upper Quartile | Median | Lower Quartile |
|---|---|---|---|
| Sales | 900,000 | 525,000 | 475,000 |
| Officer's Salary* | 73,800 | 30,975 | 7,125 |
| Net Profit* | 29,000 | 15,750 | 1,250 |
| Total Income* | 102,800 | 46,725 | 8,375 |

*Before Tax

### PROFITABILITY VS ASSETS

| Assets | 0-250$K | 250-1,000$K | 1-10$M |
|---|---|---|---|
| Profitability | N/A | 35.1% | 23.3% |

**COMMENTS:**   *High risk, excellent potential.*

# #105    MILLWORK (FOR LUMBER) (MFG)     SIC:2431

| Total Assets | $250,000 |
|---|---|
| Profitability | 35.1% |
| Trend | +1.3% |
| Downside Risk | 60.3% |
| Upside Potential | 98.9% |
| Space Required | 1500 Sq. Ft. |

## SOURCE AND USE OF CAPITAL

| Capital Source | | Capital Use | |
|---|---|---|---|
| Owner's Equity | $ 89,250 | Working Capital | $ 68,500 |
| Long Term Debt | $ 50,500 | Long Term Assets | $ 71,250 |
| Total Capital Requ'd | $139,750 | Total Capital Used | $139,750 |

## SALES AND INCOME

| | Upper Quartile | Median | Lower Quartile |
|---|---|---|---|
| Sales | 800,000 | 625,000 | 500,000 |
| Officer's Salary* | 60,000 | 24,375 | 11,500 |
| Net Profit* | 37,750 | 24,750 | 8,000 |
| Total Income* | 97,750 | 49,125 | 19,500 |

*Before Tax

## PROFITABILITY VS ASSETS

| Assets | 0-250$K | 250-1,000$K | 1-10$M |
|---|---|---|---|
| Profitability | N/A | 35.1% | 29.7% |

**COMMENTS:** *Higher than average risk, good - excellent potential.*


# #106    BOOKS-STATIONERY (RTL)     SIC:5942,43

| Total Assets | $250,000 |
|---|---|
| Profitability | 35.1% |
| Trend | -0.3% |
| Downside Risk | 52.4% |
| Upside Potential | 94.3% |
| Space Required | 2970 Sq. Ft. |

## SOURCE AND USE OF CAPITAL

| Capital Source | | Capital Use | |
|---|---|---|---|
| Owner's Equity | $ 93,750 | Working Capital | $ 66,500 |
| Long Term Debt | $ 40,250 | Long Term Assets | $ 67,500 |
| Total Capital Requ'd | $134,000 | Total Capital Used | $134,000 |

## SALES AND INCOME

| | Upper Quartile | Median | Lower Quartile |
|---|---|---|---|
| Sales | 850,000 | 675,000 | 525,000 |
| Officer's Salary* | 52,700 | 26,325 | 14,175 |
| Net Profit* | 38,750 | 20,750 | 8,250 |
| Total Income* | 91,450 | 47,075 | 22,425 |

*Before Tax

## PROFITABILITY VS ASSETS

| Assets | 0-250$K | 250-1,000$ K | 1-10$M |
|---|---|---|---|
| Profitability | 62.0% | 35.1% | N/A |

**COMMENTS:** *Average risk, good - excellent potential.*

| | |
|---|---|
| Total Assets | $250,000 |
| Profitability | 34.9% |
| Trend | +4.3% |
| Downside Risk | 58.9% |
| Upside Potential | 47.7% |
| Space Required | 1320 Sq. Ft. |

## SOURCE AND USE OF CAPITAL

| Capital Source | | Capital Use | |
|---|---|---|---|
| Owner's Equity | $114,500 | Working Capital | $102,500 |
| Long Term Debt | $ 19,500 | Long Term Assets | $ 31,500 |
| Total Capital Requ'd | $134,000 | Total Capital Used | $134,000 |

## SALES AND INCOME

| | Upper Quartile | Median | Lower Quartile |
|---|---|---|---|
| Sales | 700,000 | 600,000 | 475,000 |
| Officer's Salary* | 44,800 | 30,000 | 15,675 |
| Net Profit* | 24,250 | 16,700 | 3,500 |
| Total Income* | 69,050 | 46,700 | 19,175 |

*Before Tax

## PROFITABILITY VS ASSETS

| Assets | 0-250$K | 250-1,000$K | 1-10$M |
|---|---|---|---|
| Profitability | N/A | 34.9% | 27.7% |

**COMMENTS:**   *Good uptrend.  Average risk and potential.*


# #108 LAUNDRY & DRY CLEANING EQUIPMENT (WSLE) SIC:5087

| | |
|---|---|
| Total Assets | $250,000 |
| Profitability | 34.9% |
| Trend | +4.7% |
| Downside Risk | 62.5% |
| Upside Potential | 43.9% |
| Space Required | 1920 Sq. Ft. |

## SOURCE AND USE OF CAPITAL

| Capital Source | | Capital Use | |
|---|---|---|---|
| Owner's Equity | $123,000 | Working Capital | $106,500 |
| Long Term Debt | $ 26,750 | Long Term Assets | $ 43,250 |
| Total Capital Requ'd | $149,750 | Total Capital Used | $149,750 |

## SALES AND INCOME

| | Upper Quartile | Median | Lower Quartile |
|---|---|---|---|
| Sales | 900,000 | 800,000 | 625,000 |
| Officer's Salary* | 42,300 | 32,800 | 11,875 |
| Net Profit* | 33,000 | 19,500 | 7,750 |
| Total Income* | 75,300 | 52,300 | 19,625 |

*Before Tax

## PROFITABILITY VS ASSETS

| Assets | 0-250$K | 250-1,000$K | 1-10$M |
|---|---|---|---|
| Profitability | N/A | 34.9% | N/A |

**COMMENTS:**   *Excellent uptrend.  Higher than average risk and below average potential.*

## #109 FRESH FRUIT & VEGETABLES (WSLE)                SIC:5148

| | |
|---|---|
| Total Assets | $250,000 |
| Profitability | 34.8% |
| Trend | -0.1% |
| Downside Risk | 48.8% |
| Upside Potential | 171.5% |
| Space Required | 1080 Sq. Ft. |

### SOURCE AND USE OF CAPITAL

| Capital Source | | Capital Use | |
|---|---|---|---|
| Owner's Equity | $105,500 | Working Capital | $ 52,250 |
| Long Term Debt | $ 31,500 | Long Term Assets | $ 84,750 |
| Total Capital Requ'd | $137,000 | Total Capital Used | $137,000 |

### SALES AND INCOME

| | Upper Quartile | Median | Lower Quartile |
|---|---|---|---|
| Sales | 2,1000,000 | 1,350,000 | 1,125,000 |
| Officer's Salary* | 86,100 | 25,650 | 14,625 |
| Net Profit* | 43,250 | 22,000 | 9,750 |
| Total Income* | 129,350 | 47,650 | 24,375 |

*Before Tax

### PROFITABILITY VS ASSETS

| Assets | 0-250$K | 250,1,000$K | 1-10$M |
|---|---|---|---|
| Profitability | N/A | 34.8% | 26.3% |

**COMMENTS:**  *Average risk, excellent potential.*


## #110        HEATING EQUIPMENT (MFG)                SIC:3433

| | |
|---|---|
| Total Assets | $250,000 |
| Profitability | 34.8% |
| Trend | -0.1% |
| Downside Risk | 86.0% |
| Upside Potential | 116.8% |
| Space Required | 1430 Sq. Ft. |

### SOURCE AND USE OF CAPITAL

| Capital Source | | Capital Use | |
|---|---|---|---|
| Owner's Equity | $ 75,000 | Working Capital | $ 74,000 |
| Long Term Debt | $ 43,250 | Long Term Assets | $ 44,250 |
| Total Capital Requ'd | $118,250 | Total Capital Used | $118,250 |

### SALES AND INCOME

| | Upper Quartile | Median | Lower Quartile |
|---|---|---|---|
| Sales | 725,000 | 650,000 | 525,000 |
| Officer's Salary* | 47,125 | 18,850 | 5,250 |
| Net Profit* | 42,000 | 22,250 | 500 |
| Total Income* | 89,125 | 41,100 | 5,750 |

*Before Tax

### PROFITABILITY VS ASSETS

| Assets | 0-250$K | 250-1,000$K | 1-10$M |
|---|---|---|---|
| Profitability | N/A | 34.8% | N/A |

**COMMENTS:**  *High risk, excellent potential.*

<table>
<tr><td>**#111**</td><td align="center"># DRUGS (WSLE)</td><td align="right">**SIC:5122**</td></tr>
</table>

| | |
|---|---|
| **Total Assets** | $250,000 |
| **Profitability** | 34.7% |
| **Trend** | +2.6% |
| **Downside Risk** | 54.7% |
| **Upside Potential** | 114.8% |
| **Space Required** | 1240 Sq. Ft. |

### SOURCE AND USE OF CAPITAL

| Capital Source | | Capital Use | |
|---|---|---|---|
| Owner's Equity | $ 80,250 | Working Capital | $ 66,000 |
| Long Term Debt | $ 29,500 | Long Term Assets | $ 43,750 |
| Total Capital Requ'd | $109,750 | Total Capital Used | $109,750 |

### SALES AND INCOME

| | Upper Quartile | Median | Lower Quartile |
|---|---|---|---|
| Sales | 1,000,000 | 775,000 | 550,000 |
| Officer's Salary* | 57,000 | 24,800 | 13,750 |
| Net Profit* | 24,750 | 13,250 | 3,500 |
| Total Income* | 81,750 | 38,050 | 17,250 |

*Before Tax

### PROFITABILITY VS ASSETS

| Assets | 0-250$K | 250-1,000$K | 1-10$M |
|---|---|---|---|
| Profitability | N/A | 34.7% | 27.3% |

**COMMENTS:** *Average risk, excellent potential.*


<table>
<tr><td>**#112**</td><td align="center"># FURS (WSLE)</td><td align="right">**SIC:5137**</td></tr>
</table>

| | |
|---|---|
| **Total Assets** | $250,000 |
| **Profitability** | 34.6% |
| **Trend** | +3.6% |
| **Downside Risk** | 71.6% |
| **Upside Potential** | 73.9% |
| **Space Required** | 1155 Sq. Ft. |

### SOURCE AND USE OF CAPITAL

| Capital Source | | Capital Use | |
|---|---|---|---|
| Owner's Equity | $114,500 | Working Capital | $109,000 |
| Long Term Debt | $ 12,250 | Long Term Assets | $ 17,750 |
| Total Capital Requ'd | $126,750 | Total Capital Used | $126,750 |

### SALES AND INCOME

| | Upper Quartile | Median | Lower Quartile |
|---|---|---|---|
| Sales | 1,125,000 | 825,000 | 325,000 |
| Officer's Salary* | 36,000 | 19,800 | 3,575 |
| Net Profit* | 39,750 | 23,750 | 8,750 |
| Total Income* | 75,750 | 43,550 | 12,325 |

*Before Tax

### PROFITABILITY VS ASSETS

| Assets | 0-250$K | 250-1,000$K | 1-10$M |
|---|---|---|---|
| Profitability | N/A | 34.6% | N/A |

**COMMENTS:** *Good uptrend, high risk, good potential.*

# ELECTRICAL APPLIANCES (WSLE)    SIC:5064

| | |
|---|---|
| Total Assets | $250,000 |
| Profitability | 34.5% |
| Trend | -1.0% |
| Downside Risk | 73.1% |
| Upside Potential | 86.7% |
| Space Required | 1560 Sq. Ft. |

## SOURCE AND USE OF CAPITAL

| Capital Source | | Capital Use | |
|---|---|---|---|
| Owner's Equity | $ 96,750 | Working Capital | $ 83,000 |
| Long Term Debt | $ 19,250 | Long Term Assets | $ 33,000 |
| Total Capital Requ'd | $116,000 | Total Capital Used | $116,000 |

## SALES AND INCOME

| | Upper Quartile | Median | Lower Quartile |
|---|---|---|---|
| Sales | 875,000 | 650,000 | 550,000 |
| Officer's Salary* | 48,125 | 25,350 | 8,800 |
| Net Profit* | 26,750 | 14,750 | 2,000 |
| Total Income* | 74,875 | 40,100 | 10,800 |

*Before Tax

## PROFITABILITY VS ASSETS

| Assets | 0-250$K | 250-1,000$K | 1-10$M |
|---|---|---|---|
| Profitability | N/A | 34.5% | 24.6% |

**COMMENTS:**    *Downtrend.  High risk and good potential.*




# METAL DOORS, FRAMES & TRIM  MFG)    SIC:3442

| | |
|---|---|
| Total Assets | $250,000 |
| Profitability | 34.4% |
| Trend | +5.2% |
| Downside Risk | 58.7% |
| Upside Potential | 65.1% |
| Space Required | 1920 Sq. Ft. |

## SOURCE AND USE OF CAPITAL

| Capital Source | | Capital Use | |
|---|---|---|---|
| Owner's Equity | $113,250 | Working Capital | $ 95,250 |
| Long Term Debt | $ 33,500 | Long Term Assets | $ 51,500 |
| Total Capital Requ'd | $146,750 | Total Capital Used | $146,750 |

## SALES AND INCOME

| | Upper Quartile | Median | Lower Quartile |
|---|---|---|---|
| Sales | 800,000 | 600,000 | 475,000 |
| Officer's Salary* | 43,200 | 22,800 | 16,150 |
| Net Profit* | 40,250 | 27,750 | 4,750 |
| Total Income* | 83,450 | 50,550 | 20,900 |

*Before Tax

## PROFITABILITY VS ASSETS

| Assets | 0-250$K | 250-1,000$K | 1-10$M |
|---|---|---|---|
| Profitability | N/A | 34.4% | 31.4% |

**COMMENTS:**    *Excellent uptrend.  Above average risk, average potential.*

| | |
|---|---|
| **Total Assets** | $250,000 |
| **Profitability** | 34.0% |
| **Trend** | -3.8% |
| **Downside Risk** | 59.9% |
| **Upside Potential** | 85.2% |
| **Space Required** | 1375 Sq. Ft. |

## SOURCE AND USE OF CAPITAL

| Capital Source | | Capital Use | |
|---|---|---|---|
| Owner's Equity | $108,250 | Working Capital | $ 63,500 |
| Long Term Debt | $ 36,750 | Long Term Assets | $ 81,500 |
| Total Capital Requ'd | $145,000 | Total Capital Used | $145,000 |

## SALES AND INCOME

| | Upper Quartile | Median | Lower Quartile |
|---|---|---|---|
| Sales | 775,000 | 625,000 | 475,000 |
| Officer's Salary* | 61,225 | 31,250 | 14,725 |
| Net Profit* | 30,000 | 18,000 | 5,000 |
| Total Income* | 91,225 | 49,250 | 19,725 |

*Before Tax

## PROFITABILITY VS ASSETS

| Assets | 0-250$K | 250-1,000$K | 1-10$M |
|---|---|---|---|
| Profitability | N/A | 34.0% | 20.0% |

**COMMENTS:** *Strong down trend. Above average risk but good potential.*


#116     **IRON & STEEL FOUNDRIES (MFG) SIC:3321,22,24,25**

| | |
|---|---|
| **Total Assets** | $250,000 |
| **Profitability** | 34.0% |
| **Trend** | -0.1% |
| **Downside Risk** | 52.1% |
| **Upside Potential** | 67.5% |
| **Space Required** | 1080 Sq. Ft. |

## SOURCE AND USE OF CAPITAL

| Capital Source | | Capital Use | |
|---|---|---|---|
| Owner's Equity | $109,750 | Working Capital | $ 44,250 |
| Long Term Debt | $ 28,500 | Long Term Assets | $ 94,000 |
| Total Capital Requ'd | $138,250 | Total Capital Used | $138,250 |

## SALES AND INCOME

| | Upper Quartile | Median | Lower Quartile |
|---|---|---|---|
| Sales | 725,000 | 625,000 | 500,000 |
| Officer's Salary* | 38,425 | 24,975 | 10,500 |
| Net Profit* | 40,250 | 22,000 | 12,000 |
| Total Income* | 78,675 | 46,975 | 22,500 |

*Before Tax

## PROFITABILITY VS ASSETS

| Assets | 0-250$K | 250-1,000$K | 1-10$M |
|---|---|---|---|
| Profitability | N/A | 34.0% | 23.5% |

**COMMENTS:** *Average risk and good potential.*

## CAR WASH (SVE)     SIC:7542

| | |
|---|---|
| Total Assets | $250,000 |
| Profitability | 33.8% |
| Trend | 0.5% |
| Downside Risk | 64.4% |
| Upside Potential | 144.1% |
| Space Required | 2860 Sq. Ft. |

### SOURCE AND USE OF CAPITAL

| Capital Source | | Capital Use | |
|---|---|---|---|
| Owner's Equity | $ 72,750 | Working Capital | $ 82,750 |
| Long Term Debt | $ 97,000 | Long Term Assets | $ 87,000 |
| Total Capital Requ'd | $169,750 | Total Capital Used | $169,750 |

### SALES AND INCOME

| | Upper Quartile | Median | Lower Quartile |
|---|---|---|---|
| Sales | 900,000 | 550,000 | 325,000 |
| Officer's Salary* | 99,000 | 37,950 | 11,700 |
| Net Profit* | 41,250 | 19,500 | 8,750 |
| Total Income* | 140,250 | 57,450 | 20,450 |

*Before Tax

### PROFITABILITY VS ASSETS

| Assets | 0-250$K | 250-1,000$K | 1-10$M |
|---|---|---|---|
| Profitability | N/A | 33.8% | N/A |

**COMMENTS:** *Above average risk, excellent potential.*


## #118 WRAPPING, COARSE PAPER PRODUCTS (WSLE) SIC:5113

| | |
|---|---|
| Total Assets | $250,000 |
| Profitability | 33.7% |
| Trend | -3.2% |
| Downside Risk | 47.3% |
| Upside Potential | 127.5% |
| Space Required | 1900 Sq. Ft. |

### SOURCE AND USE OF CAPITAL

| Capital Source | | Capital Use | |
|---|---|---|---|
| Owner's Equity | $113,250 | Working Capital | $ 94,500 |
| Long Term Debt | $ 20,500 | Long Term Assets | $ 39,250 |
| Total Capital Requ'd | $133,750 | Total Capital Used | $133,750 |

### SALES AND INCOME

| | Upper Quartile | Median | Lower Quartile |
|---|---|---|---|
| Sales | 1,200,000 | 950,000 | 750,000 |
| Officer's Salary* | 66,000 | 27,550 | 15,000 |
| Net Profit* | 36,500 | 17,500 | 8,750 |
| Total Income* | 102,500 | 45,050 | 23,750 |

*Before Tax

### PROFITABILITY VS ASSETS

| Assets | 0-250$K | 250-1,000$K | 1-10$M |
|---|---|---|---|
| Profitability | 53.9% | 33.7% | 29.1% |

**COMMENTS:** *Significant down trend. Average risk and excellent potential.*

| Total Assets | $250,000 |
|---|---|
| Profitability | 33.7% |
| Trend | -0.8% |
| Downside Risk | 65.9% |
| Upside Potential | 112.0% |
| Space Required | 1690 Sq. Ft. |

## SOURCE AND USE OF CAPITAL

| Capital Source | | Capital Use | |
|---|---|---|---|
| Owner's Equity | $ 97,250 | Working Capital | $ 81,500 |
| Long Term Debt | $ 27,500 | Long Term Assets | $ 48,250 |
| Total Capital Requ'd | $129,750 | Total Capital Used | $129,750 |

## SALES AND INCOME

| | Upper Quartile | Median | Lower Quartile |
|---|---|---|---|
| Sales | 900,000 | 650,000 | 450,000 |
| Officer's Salary* | 62,100 | 27,300 | 11,700 |
| Net Profit* | 30,750 | 16,500 | 3,250 |
| Total Income* | 92,850 | 43,800 | 14,950 |

*Before Tax

## PROFITABILITY VS ASSETS

| Assets | 0-250$K | 250-1,000$K | 1-10$M |
|---|---|---|---|
| Profitability | 50.9% | 33.7% | 28.8% |

**COMMENTS:**   *High risk, but excellent potential.*


#120   **TIRE, BATTERY & ACCESSORIES (RTL)**   SIC:5531

| Total Assets | $250,000 |
|---|---|
| Profitability | 33.5% |
| Trend | -2.3% |
| Downside Risk | 52.9% |
| Upside Potential | 89.4% |
| Space Required | 1920 Sq. Ft. |

## SOURCE AND USE OF CAPITAL

| Capital Source | | Capital Use | |
|---|---|---|---|
| Owner's Equity | $ 85,000 | Working Capital | $ 58,500 |
| Long Term Debt | $ 40,500 | Long Term Assets | $ 67,000 |
| Total Capital Requ'd | $125,500 | Total Capital Used | $125,500 |

## SALES AND INCOME

| | Upper Quartile | Median | Lower Quartile |
|---|---|---|---|
| Sales | 750,000 | 600,000 | 475,000 |
| Officer's Salary* | 49,500 | 24,600 | 12,350 |
| Net Profit* | 30,250 | 17,500 | 7,500 |
| Total Income* | 79,750 | 42,100 | 19,850 |

*Before Tax

## PROFITABILITY VS ASSETS

| Assets | 0-250$K | 250-1,000$K | 1-10$M |
|---|---|---|---|
| Profitability | 45.9% | 33.5% | 21.7% |

**COMMENTS:**   *Down trend, average risk and good potential.*

| | |
|---|---|
| Total Assets | $250,000 |
| Profitability | 33.4% |
| Trend | +0.5% |
| Downside Risk | 63.7% |
| Upside Potential | 63.2% |
| Space Required | 1320 Sq. Ft. |

### SOURCE AND USE OF CAPITAL

| Capital Source | | Capital Use | |
|---|---|---|---|
| Owner's Equity | $104,500 | Working Capital | $ 79,250 |
| Long Term Debt | $ 35,750 | Long Term Assets | $ 61,000 |
| Total Capital Requ'd | $140,250 | Total Capital Used | $140,250 |

### SALES AND INCOME

| | Upper Quartile | Median | Lower Quartile |
|---|---|---|---|
| Sales | 1,425,000 | 1,100,000 | 875,000 |
| Officer's Salary* | 49,875 | 30,800 | 10,500 |
| Net Profit* | 26,500 | 16,000 | 6,500 |
| Total Income* | 76,375 | 46,800 | 17,000 |

*Before Tax

### PROFITABILITY VS ASSETS

| Assets | 0-250$K | 250-1,000$K | 1-10$M |
|---|---|---|---|
| Profitability | 53.3% | 33.4% | 21.9% |

**COMMENTS:** *Above average risk and good potential.*


## #122 HOUSEFURNISHINGS (EXCEPT DRAPERIES) (MFG) SIC:2392

| | |
|---|---|
| Total Assets | $250,000 |
| Profitability | 33.2% |
| Trend | +4.2% |
| Downside Risk | 48.1% |
| Upside Potential | 113.6% |
| Space Required | 1820 Sq. Ft. |

### SOURCE AND USE OF CAPITAL

| Capital Source | | Capital Use | |
|---|---|---|---|
| Owner's Equity | $ 87,250 | Working Capital | $ 61,750 |
| Long Term Debt | $ 37,250 | Long Term Assets | $ 62,750 |
| Total Capital Requ'd | $124,500 | Total Capital Used | $124,500 |

### SALES AND INCOME

| | Upper Quartile | Median | Lower Quartile |
|---|---|---|---|
| Sales | 700,000 | 650,000 | 550,000 |
| Officer's Salary* | 49,700 | 20,800 | 10,450 |
| Net Profit* | 38,500 | 20,500 | 11,000 |
| Total Income* | 88,200 | 41,300 | 21,450 |

*Before Tax

### PROFITABILITY VS ASSETS

| Assets | 0-250$K | 250-1,000$K | 1-10$M |
|---|---|---|---|
| Profitability | N/A | 33.2% | N/A |

**COMMENTS:** *Excellent uptrend. Average risk and excellent potential.*

# RADIO, TV, HI-FI (MFG)                SIC:3651

| | |
|---|---|
| Total Assets | $250,000 |
| Profitability | 33.1% |
| Trend | -1.0% |
| Downside Risk | 54.9% |
| Upside Potential | 137.3% |
| Space Required | 1530 Sq. Ft. |

## SOURCE AND USE OF CAPITAL

| Capital Source | | Capital Use | |
|---|---|---|---|
| Owner's Equity | $106,500 | Working Capital | $ 86,000 |
| Long Term Debt | $ 34,000 | Long Term Assets | $ 54,500 |
| Total Capital Requ'd | $140,500 | Total Capital Used | $140,500 |

## SALES AND INCOME

| | Upper Quartile | Median | Lower Quartile |
|---|---|---|---|
| Sales | 625,000 | 450,000 | 350,000 |
| Officer's Salary* | 48,750 | 15,300 | 8,750 |
| Net Profit* | 61,750 | 31,250 | 12,250 |
| Total Income* | 110,500 | 46,550 | 21,000 |

*Before Tax

## PROFITABILITY VS ASSETS

| Assets | 0-250$K | 250-1,000$K | 1-10$M |
|---|---|---|---|
| Profitability | N/A | 33.1% | N/A |

**COMMENTS:**   *Some down trend.  Average risk, excellent potential.*




# INDUSTRIAL CHEMICALS (MFG)       SIC:2861,65,69

| | |
|---|---|
| Total Assets | $250,000 |
| Profitability | 33.1% |
| Trend | -2.3% |
| Downside Risk | 42.8% |
| Upside Potential | 73.2% |
| Space Required | 1320 Sq. Ft. |

## SOURCE AND USE OF CAPITAL

| Capital Source | | Capital Use | |
|---|---|---|---|
| Owner's Equity | $ 99,250 | Working Capital | $ 65,750 |
| Long Term Debt | $ 43,750 | Long Term Assets | $ 77,250 |
| Total Capital Requ'd | $143,000 | Total Capital Used | $143,000 |

## SALES AND INCOME

| | Upper Quartile | Median | Lower Quartile |
|---|---|---|---|
| Sales | 800,000 | 600,000 | 450,000 |
| Officer's Salary* | 45,600 | 23,400 | 12,600 |
| Net Profit* | 36,500 | 24,000 | 14,500 |
| Total Income* | 82,100 | 47,400 | 27,100 |

*Before Tax

## PROFITABILITY VS ASSETS

| Assets | 0-250$K | 250-1,000$K | 1-10$M |
|---|---|---|---|
| Profitability | N/A | 33.1% | 27.0% |

**COMMENTS:**   *Down trend.  Below average risk and good potential.*

# HORTICULTURAL SERVICES (SVE)   SIC:0781-83

| | |
|---|---|
| Total Assets | $250,000 |
| Profitability | 33.0% |
| Trend | -2.6% |
| Downside Risk | 43.9% |
| Upside Potential | 76.6% |
| Space Required | 1320 Sq. Ft. |

## SOURCE AND USE OF CAPITAL

| Capital Source | | Capital Use | |
|---|---|---|---|
| Owner's Equity | $118,000 | Working Capital | $ 52,000 |
| Long Term Debt | $ 43,000 | Long Term Assets | $109,000 |
| Total Capital Requ'd | $161,000 | Total Capital Used | $161,000 |

## SALES AND INCOME

| | Upper Quartile | Median | Lower Quartile |
|---|---|---|---|
| Sales | 725,000 | 550,000 | 475,000 |
| Officer's Salary* | 49,300 | 23,100 | 13,775 |
| Net Profit* | 44,500 | 30,000 | 16,000 |
| Total Income* | 93,800 | 53,100 | 29,775 |

*Before Tax

## PROFITABILITY VS ASSETS

| Assets | 0-250$K | 250-1,000$K | 1-10$M |
|---|---|---|---|
| Profitability | 45.6% | 33.0% | N/A |

**COMMENTS:**   *Down trend.  Below average risk and good potential.*




# FERTILIZERS (MFG)                SIC:2873,74

| | |
|---|---|
| Total Assets | $250,000 |
| Profitability | 32.9% |
| Trend | -5.3% |
| Downside Risk | 62.1% |
| Upside Potential | 124.1% |
| Space Required | 1690 Sq. Ft. |

## SOURCE AND USE OF CAPITAL

| Capital Source | | Capital Use | |
|---|---|---|---|
| Owner's Equity | $ 76,500 | Working Capital | $ 14,500 |
| Long Term Debt | $ 40,750 | Long Term Assets | $102,750 |
| Total Capital Requ'd | $117,250 | Total Capital Used | $117,250 |

## SALES AND INCOME

| | Upper Quartile | Median | Lower Quartile |
|---|---|---|---|
| Sales | 825,000 | 650,000 | 400,000 |
| Officer's Salary* | 64,350 | 26,650 | 10,400 |
| Net Profit* | 22,250 | 12,000 | 4,250 |
| Total Income* | 86,600 | 38,650 | 14,650 |

*Before Tax

## PROFITABILITY VS ASSETS

| Assets | 0-250$K | 250-1,000$K | 1-10$M |
|---|---|---|---|
| Profitability | N/A | 32.9% | 16.1% |

**COMMENTS:**   *Strong down trend.  Above average risk and excellent potential.*

| | |
|---|---|
| Total Assets | $250,000 |
| Profitability | 32.9% |
| Trend | +0.1% |
| Downside Risk | 45.7% |
| Upside Potential | 73.9% |
| Space Required | 1690 Sq. Ft. |

## SOURCE AND USE OF CAPITAL

| Capital Source | | Capital Use | |
|---|---|---|---|
| Owner's Equity | $102,000 | Working Capital | $ 93,250 |
| Long Term Debt | $ 33,500 | Long Term Assets | $ 42,250 |
| Total Capital Requ'd | $135,500 | Total Capital Used | $135,500 |

## SALES AND INCOME

| | Upper Quartile | Median | Lower Quartile |
|---|---|---|---|
| Sales | 800,000 | 650,000 | 550,000 |
| Officer's Salary* | 45,600 | 25,350 | 13,200 |
| Net Profit* | 32,000 | 19,250 | 11,000 |
| Total Income* | 77,600 | 44,600 | 24,200 |

*Before Tax

## PROFITABILITY VS ASSETS

| Assets | 0-250$K | 250-1,000$K | 1-10$M |
|---|---|---|---|
| Profitability | 51.7% | 32.9% | 25.1% |

**COMMENTS:** *Below average risk, good potential.*




| | |
|---|---|
| Total Assets | $250,000 |
| Profitability | 32.7% |
| Trend | -2.5% |
| Downside Risk | 66.6% |
| Upside Potential | 103.6% |
| Space Required | 960 Sq. Ft. |

## SOURCE AND USE OF CAPITAL

| Capital Source | | Capital Use | |
|---|---|---|---|
| Owner's Equity | $ 83,000 | Working Capital | $ 35,250 |
| Long Term Debt | $ 55,250 | Long Term Assets | $103,000 |
| Total Capital Requ'd | $138,250 | Total Capital Used | $138,250 |

## SALES AND INCOME

| | Upper Quartile | Median | Lower Quartile |
|---|---|---|---|
| Sales | 800,000 | 600,000 | 425,000 |
| Officer's Salary* | 54,400 | 27,000 | 10,625 |
| Net Profit* | 37,750 | 18,250 | 4,500 |
| Total Income* | 92,150 | 45,250 | 15,125 |

*Before Tax

## PROFITABILITY VS ASSETS

| Assets | 0-250$K | 250-1,000$K | 1-10$M |
|---|---|---|---|
| Profitability | N/A | 32.7% | 30.0% |

**COMMENTS:** *Strong down trend and risk. Excellent potential.*

# #129 FOOTWARE (MFG)                                  SIC:3143,44

| | |
|---|---|
| Total Assets | $250,000 |
| Profitability | 32.7% |
| Trend | -4.4% |
| Downside Risk | 100.8% |
| Upside Potential | 98.1% |
| Space Required | 1200 Sq. Ft. |

## SOURCE AND USE OF CAPITAL

| Capital Source | | Capital Use | |
|---|---|---|---|
| Owner's Equity | $ 85,000 | Working Capital | $ 75,000 |
| Long Term Debt | $ 27,500 | Long Term Assets | $ 37,500 |
| Total Capital Requ'd | $112,500 | Total Capital Used | $112,500 |

## SALES AND INCOME

| | Upper Quartile | Median | Lower Quartile |
|---|---|---|---|
| Sales | 825,000 | 600,000 | 450,000 |
| Officer's Salary* | 33,000 | 15,600 | 7,200 |
| Net Profit* | 40,000 | 21,250 | (7,500) |
| Total Income* | 73,000 | 36,850 | (300) |

*Before Tax

## PROFITABILITY VS ASSETS

| Assets | 0-250$K | 250-1,000$K | 1-10$M |
|---|---|---|---|
| Profitability | N/A | 32.7% | 16.9% |

**COMMENTS:** *Strong down trend and very high risk, good - excellent potential.*


# #130 PLASTIC PRODUCTS (MFG)                          SIC:3079

| | |
|---|---|
| Total Assets | $250,000 |
| Profitability | 32.6% |
| Trend | -0.1% |
| Downside Risk | 53.1% |
| Upside Potential | 88.0% |
| Space Required | 4680 Sq. Ft. |

## SOURCE AND USE OF CAPITAL

| Capital Source | | Capital Use | |
|---|---|---|---|
| Owner's Equity | $ 98,250 | Working Capital | $ 47,500 |
| Long Term Debt | $ 49,250 | Long Term Assets | $100,000 |
| Total Capital Requ'd | $147,500 | Total Capital Used | $147,500 |

## SALES AND INCOME

| | Upper Quartile | Median | Lower Quartile |
|---|---|---|---|
| Sales | 750,000 | 600,000 | 450,000 |
| Officer's Salary* | 48,000 | 23,400 | 12,600 |
| Net Profit* | 42,500 | 24,750 | 10,000 |
| Total Income* | 90,500 | 48,150 | 22,600 |

*Before Tax

## PROFITABILITY VS ASSETS

| Assets | 0-250$K | 250-1,000$K | 1-10$M |
|---|---|---|---|
| Profitability | 66.9% | 32.6% | 26.7% |

**COMMENTS:** *Average risk and good potential.  High initial fixed asset investment.*

# #131 ADVERTISING DISPLAYS & DEVICES (MFG)    SIC:3993

| | |
|---|---|
| Total Assets | $250,000 |
| Profitability | 32.4% |
| Trend | -4.8% |
| Downside Risk | 50.9% |
| Upside Potential | 102.3% |
| Space Required | 2070 Sq. Ft. |

## SOURCE AND USE OF CAPITAL

| Capital Source | | Capital Use | |
|---|---|---|---|
| Owner's Equity | $ 92,000 | Working Capital | $ 50,000 |
| Long Term Debt | $ 43,250 | Long Term Assets | $ 85,250 |
| Total Capital Requ'd | $135,250 | Total Capital Used | $135,250 |

## SALES AND INCOME

| | Upper Quartile | Median | Lower Quartile |
|---|---|---|---|
| Sales | 700,000 | 575,000 | 475,000 |
| Officer's Salary* | 51,800 | 24,150 | 13,775 |
| Net Profit* | 37,000 | 19,750 | 7,750 |
| Total Income* | 88,800 | 43,900 | 21,525 |

*Before Tax

## PROFITABILITY VS ASSETS

| Assets | 0-250$K | 250-1,000$K | 1-10$M |
|---|---|---|---|
| Profitability | N/A | 32.4% | 24.2% |

**COMMENTS:** *Strong down trend, average risk and excellent potential.*


# #132    PAINT, VARNISH & LACQUER (MFG)    SIC:2851

| | |
|---|---|
| Total Assets | $250,000 |
| Profitability | 32.3% |
| Trend | +1.9% |
| Downside Risk | 56.3% |
| Upside Potential | 79.9% |
| Space Required | 1560 Sq. Ft. |

## SOURCE AND USE OF CAPITAL

| Capital Source | | Capital Use | |
|---|---|---|---|
| Owner's Equity | $105,000 | Working Capital | $ 76,750 |
| Long Term Debt | $ 37,500 | Long Term Assets | $ 65,750 |
| Total Capital Requ'd | $142,500 | Total Capital Used | $142,500 |

## SALES AND INCOME

| | Upper Quartile | Median | Lower Quartile |
|---|---|---|---|
| Sales | 800,000 | 650,000 | 575,000 |
| Officer's Salary* | 53,600 | 30,550 | 14,375 |
| Net Profit* | 29,250 | 15,500 | 5,750 |
| Total Income* | 82,850 | 46,050 | 20,125 |

*Before Tax

## PROFITABILITY VS ASSETS

| Assets | 0-250$K | 250-1,000$K | 1-10$M |
|---|---|---|---|
| Profitability | N/A | 32.3% | 23.3% |

**COMMENTS:** *Good uptrend, average risk and good potential.*

| | |
|---|---|
| **Total Assets** | $250,000 |
| **Profitability** | 32.2% |
| **Trend** | -4.8% |
| **Downside Risk** | 84.0% |
| **Upside Potential** | 155.9% |
| **Space Required** | 1705 Sq. Ft. |

### SOURCE AND USE OF CAPITAL

| Capital Source | | Capital Use | |
|---|---|---|---|
| **Owner's Equity** | $106,250 | **Working Capital** | $ 9,750 |
| **Long Term Debt** | $ 50,250 | **Long Term Assets** | $146,750 |
| **Total Capital Requ'd** | $156,500 | **Total Capital Used** | $156,500 |

### SALES AND INCOME

| | Upper Quartile | Median | Lower Quartile |
|---|---|---|---|
| **Sales** | 900,000 | 775,000 | 575,000 |
| **Officer's Salary*** | 92,700 | 34,875 | 13,800 |
| **Net Profit*** | 36,250 | 15,500 | (5,750) |
| **Total Income*** | 128,950 | 50,375 | 8,050 |

*Before Tax

### PROFITABILITY VS ASSETS

| **Assets** | 0-250$K | 250-1,000$K | 1-10$M |
|---|---|---|---|
| **Profitability** | N/A | 32.2% | 14.5% |

**COMMENTS:**   *Strong down trend, high risk and excellent potential.*


#134     **SPORTING GOODS & BICYCLES (RTL)**     SIC:5941

| | |
|---|---|
| **Total Assets** | $250,000 |
| **Profitability** | 32.2% |
| **Trend** | -0.6% |
| **Downside Risk** | 55.6% |
| **Upside Potential** | 81.9% |
| **Space Required** | 2640 Sq. Ft. |

### SOURCE AND USE OF CAPITAL

| Capital Source | | Capital Use | |
|---|---|---|---|
| **Owner's Equity** | $100,250 | **Working Capital** | $ 89,750 |
| **Long Term Debt** | $ 30,500 | **Long Term Assets** | $ 41,000 |
| **Total Capital Requ'd** | $130,750 | **Total Capital Used** | $130,750 |

### SALES AND INCOME

| | Upper Quartile | Median | Lower Quartile |
|---|---|---|---|
| **Sales** | 750,000 | 600,000 | 450,000 |
| **Officer's Salary*** | 48,750 | 25,800 | 12,150 |
| **Net Profit*** | 27,750 | 16,250 | 6,500 |
| **Total Income*** | 76,500 | 42,050 | 18,650 |

*Before Tax

### PROFITABILITY VS ASSETS

| **Assets** | 0-250$K | 250-1,000$K | 1-10$M |
|---|---|---|---|
| **Profitability** | 42.1% | 32.2% | 21.2% |

**COMMENTS:**   *Average risk and good potential.*

| | |
|---|---|
| Total Assets | $250,000 |
| Profitability | 32.1% |
| Trend | +3.2% |
| Downside Risk | 48.4% |
| Upside Potential | 60.0% |
| Space Required | 6120 Sq. Ft. |

## SOURCE AND USE OF CAPITAL

| Capital Source | | Capital Use | |
|---|---|---|---|
| Owner's Equity | $118,500 | Working Capital | $ 99,750 |
| Long Term Debt | $ 26,250 | Long Term Assets | $ 45,000 |
| Total Capital Requ'd | $144,750 | Total Capital Used | $144,750 |

## SALES AND INCOME

| | Upper Quartile | Median | Lower Quartile |
|---|---|---|---|
| Sales | 700,000 | 600,000 | 500,000 |
| Officer's Salary* | 46,500 | 30,000 | 16,000 |
| Net Profit* | 27,500 | 16,500 | 8,000 |
| Total Income* | 74,000 | 46,000 | 24,000 |

*Before Tax

## PROFITABILITY VS ASSETS

| Assets | 0-250$K | 250-1,000$K | 1-10$M |
|---|---|---|---|
| Profitability | 53.8% | 32.1% | 24.7% |

**COMMENTS:** *Good uptrend. Average risk and good potential.*




| | |
|---|---|
| Total Assets | $250,000 |
| Profitability | 32.0% |
| Trend | -3.7% |
| Downside Risk | 43.4% |
| Upside Potential | 104.5% |
| Space Required | 1.955 Sq. Ft. |

## SOURCE AND USE OF CAPITAL

| Capital Source | | Capital Use | |
|---|---|---|---|
| Owner's Equity | $ 98,000 | Working Capital | $ 63,250 |
| Long Term Debt | $ 44,000 | Long Term Assets | $ 78,750 |
| Total Capital Requ'd | $142,000 | Total Capital Used | $142,000 |

## SALES AND INCOME

| | Upper Quartile | Median | Lower Quartile |
|---|---|---|---|
| Sales | 725,000 | 575,000 | 450,000 |
| Officer's Salary* | 56,550 | 23,000 | 13,500 |
| Net Profit* | 36,500 | 22,500 | 12,250 |
| Total Income* | 93,050 | 45,500 | 25,750 |

*Before Tax

## PROFITABILITY VS ASSETS

| Assets | 0-250$K | 250-1,000$K | 1-10$M |
|---|---|---|---|
| Profitability | N/A | 32.0% | 22.2% |

**COMMENTS:** *Strong down trend. Lower than average risk and excellent potential.*

# #137 KNITTING CLOTH, OUTERWEAR & UNDERWEAR (MFG)

| | | |
|---|---|---|
| Total Assets | $250,000 | SIC:2253,54,57,58 |
| Profitability | 31.9% | |
| Trend | 0.9% | |
| Downside Risk | 62.3% | |
| Upside Potential | 140.7% | |
| Space Required | 2755 Sq. Ft. | |

## SOURCE AND USE OF CAPITAL

| Capital Source | | Capital Use | |
|---|---|---|---|
| Owner's Equity | $121,500 | Working Capital | $ 63,750 |
| Long Term Debt | $ 18,000 | Long Term Assets | $ 75,750 |
| Total Capital Requ'd | $139,500 | Total Capital Used | $139,500 |

## SALES AND INCOME

| | Upper Quartile | Median | Lower Quartile |
|---|---|---|---|
| Sales | 1,000,000 | 725,000 | 550,000 |
| Officer's Salary* | 75,000 | 30,450 | 11,000 |
| Net Profit* | 32,000 | 14,000 | 5,750 |
| Total Income* | 107,000 | 44,450 | 16,750 |

*Before Tax

## PROFITABILITY VS ASSETS

| Assets | 0-250$K | 250-1,000$K | 1-10$M |
|---|---|---|---|
| Profitability | N/A | 31.9% | 23.4% |

**COMMENTS:** *High downside risk and excellent potential.*


# #138 PULP, PAPER & PAPERBOARD (MFG) SIC:2621,31

| | |
|---|---|
| Total Assets | $250,000 |
| Profitability | 31.9% |
| Trend | -0.1% |
| Downside Risk | 49.7% |
| Upside Potential | 91.3% |
| Space Required | 1400 Sq. Ft. |

## SOURCE AND USE OF CAPITAL

| Capital Source | | Capital Use | |
|---|---|---|---|
| Owner's Equity | $ 95,250 | Working Capital | $ 49,750 |
| Long Term Debt | $ 38,250 | Long Term Assets | $ 83,750 |
| Total Capital Requ'd | $133,500 | Total Capital Used | $133,500 |

## SALES AND INCOME

| | Upper Quartile | Median | Lower Quartile |
|---|---|---|---|
| Sales | 850,000 | 700,000 | 575,000 |
| Officer's Salary* | 46,750 | 23,100 | 10,925 |
| Net Profit* | 34,750 | 19,500 | 10,500 |
| Total Income* | 81,500 | 42,600 | 21,425 |

*Before Tax

## PROFITABILITY VS ASSETS

| Assets | 0-250$K | 250-1,000$K | 1-10$M |
|---|---|---|---|
| Profitability | N/A | 31.9% | 20.7% |

**COMMENTS:** *Average downside risk and good potential.*

# RESTAURANTS (RTL)                SIC:5812

| | |
|---|---|
| Total Assets | $250,000 |
| Profitability | 31.8% |
| Trend | -2.1% |
| Downside Risk | 65.9% |
| Upside Potential | 109.9% |
| Space Required | 6630 Sq. Ft. |

## SOURCE AND USE OF CAPITAL

| Capital Source | | Capital Use | |
|---|---|---|---|
| Owner's Equity | $ 78,500 | Working Capital | $ (28,250) |
| Long Term Debt | $ 85,750 | Long Term Assets | $192,500 |
| Total Capital Requ'd | $164,250 | Total Capital Used | $164,250 |

## SALES AND INCOME

| | Upper Quartile | Median | Lower Quartile |
|---|---|---|---|
| Sales | 875,000 | 650,000 | 425,000 |
| Officer's Salary* | 68,250 | 33,150 | 14,025 |
| Net Profit* | 41,250 | 19,000 | 3,750 |
| Total Income* | 109,500 | 52,150 | 17,775 |

*Before Tax

## PROFITABILITY VS ASSETS

| Assets | 0-250$K | 250-1,000$K | 1-10$M |
|---|---|---|---|
| Profitability | 58.1% | 31.8% | 21.9% |

**COMMENTS:** *Down trend. High risk and excellent potential. The negative working capital help finance the business - restaurant receives cash for food before it, itself, has paid for it.*



# AUTO REPAIR (SVE)                SIC:7538

| | |
|---|---|
| Total Assets | $250,000 |
| Profitability | 31.7% |
| Trend | -3.7% |
| Downside Risk | 46.5% |
| Upside Potential | 82.0% |
| Space Required | 2125 Sq. Ft. |

## SOURCE AND USE OF CAPITAL

| Capital Source | | Capital Use | |
|---|---|---|---|
| Owner's Equity | $ 93,000 | Working Capital | $ 53,000 |
| Long Term Debt | $ 56,750 | Long Term Assets | $ 96,750 |
| Total Capital Requ'd | $149,750 | Total Capital Used | $149,750 |

## SALES AND INCOME

| | Upper Quartile | Median | Lower Quartile |
|---|---|---|---|
| Sales | 800,000 | 625,000 | 425,000 |
| Officer's Salary* | 51,200 | 26,250 | 11,900 |
| Net Profit* | 35,250 | 21,250 | 13,500 |
| Total Income* | 86,450 | 47,500 | 25,400 |

*Before Tax

## PROFITABILITY VS ASSETS

| Assets | 0-250$K | 250-1,000$K | 1-10$M |
|---|---|---|---|
| Profitability | 61.8% | 31.7% | N/A |

**COMMENTS:** *Strong down trend, average risk and good potential.*

# SPORTING GOODS (MFG)          SIC:3949

| | |
|---|---|
| Total Assets | $250,000 |
| Profitability | 31.6% |
| Trend | -3.5% |
| Downside Risk | 66.2% |
| Upside Potential | 116.2% |
| Space Required | 1300 Sq. Ft. |

## SOURCE AND USE OF CAPITAL

| Capital Source | | Capital Use | |
|---|---|---|---|
| Owner's Equity | $111,750 | Working Capital | $ 94,000 |
| Long Term Debt | $ 37,750 | Long Term Assets | $ 55,500 |
| Total Capital Requ'd | $149,500 | Total Capital Used | $149,500 |

## SALES AND INCOME

| | Upper Quartile | Median | Lower Quartile |
|---|---|---|---|
| Sales | 650,000 | 500,000 | 400,000 |
| Officer's Salary* | 49,400 | 32,000 | 11,200 |
| Net Profit* | 52,750 | 15,250 | 4,750 |
| Total Income* | 102,150 | 47,250 | 15,950 |

*Before Tax

## PROFITABILITY VS ASSETS

| Assets | 0-250$K | 250-1,000$K | 1-10$M |
|---|---|---|---|
| Profitability | N/A | 31.6% | 25.3% |

**COMMENTS:** *Strong down trend. Higher than average risk and excellent potential.*

---



# BOAT DEALERS (RTL)          SIC:5551

| | |
|---|---|
| Total Assets | $250,000 |
| Profitability | 31.6% |
| Trend | +0.8% |
| Downside Risk | 56.1% |
| Upside Potential | 98.4% |
| Space Required | 1755 Sq. Ft. |

## SOURCE AND USE OF CAPITAL

| Capital Source | | Capital Use | |
|---|---|---|---|
| Owner's Equity | $ 69,250 | Working Capital | $ 57,750 |
| Long Term Debt | $ 35,750 | Long Term Assets | $ 47,250 |
| Total Capital Requ'd | $105,000 | Total Capital Used | $105,000 |

## SALES AND INCOME

| | Upper Quartile | Median | Lower Quartile |
|---|---|---|---|
| Sales | 875,000 | 675,000 | 475,000 |
| Officer's Salary* | 40,250 | 18,225 | 8,075 |
| Net Profit* | 25,750 | 15,000 | 6,500 |
| Total Income* | 66,000 | 33,225 | 14,575 |

*Before Tax

## PROFITABILITY VS ASSETS

| Assets | 0-250$K | 250-1,000$K | 1-10$M |
|---|---|---|---|
| Profitability | 34.4% | 31.6% | 20.7% |

**COMMENTS:** *Average risk and good - excellent potential.*

| | |
|---|---|
| Total Assets | $250,000 |
| Profitability | 31.5% |
| Trend | -0.8% |
| Downside Risk | 65.6% |
| Upside Potential | 180.5% |
| Space Required | 2340 Sq. Ft. |

## SOURCE AND USE OF CAPITAL

| Capital Source | | Capital Use | |
|---|---|---|---|
| Owner's Equity | $118,000 | Working Capital | $ 54,750 |
| Long Term Debt | $ 25,500 | Long Term Assets | $ 88,750 |
| Total Capital Requ'd | $143,500 | Total Capital Used | $143,500 |

## SALES AND INCOME

| | Upper Quartile | Median | Lower Quartile |
|---|---|---|---|
| Sales | 1,950,000 | 900,000 | 650,000 |
| Officer's Salary* | 101,400 | 27,900 | 11,050 |
| Net Profit* | 25,250 | 17,250 | 4,500 |
| Total Income* | 126,650 | 45,150 | 15,550 |

*Before Tax

## PROFITABILITY VS ASSETS

| Assets | 0-250$K | 250-1,000$K | 1-10$M |
|---|---|---|---|
| Profitability | N/A | 31.5% | 18.3% |

**COMMENTS:** *High risk, but excellent potential.*


#144    COATING, ENGRAVING (SVE)    SIC:3471,79

| | |
|---|---|
| Total Assets | $250,000 |
| Profitability | 31.5% |
| Trend | +1.9% |
| Downside Risk | 46.4% |
| Upside Potential | 97.2% |
| Space Required | 2400 Sq. Ft. |

## SOURCE AND USE OF CAPITAL

| Capital Source | | Capital Use | |
|---|---|---|---|
| Owner's Equity | $108,000 | Working Capital | $ 33,500 |
| Long Term Debt | $ 47,750 | Long Term Assets | $122,250 |
| Total Capital Requ'd | $155,750 | Total Capital Used | $155,750 |

## SALES AND INCOME

| | Upper Quartile | Median | Lower Quartile |
|---|---|---|---|
| Sales | 725,000 | 600,000 | 425,000 |
| Officer's Salary* | 62,350 | 30,600 | 16,575 |
| Net Profit* | 34,500 | 18,500 | 9,750 |
| Total Income* | 96,850 | 49,100 | 26,325 |

*Before Tax

## PROFITABILITY VS ASSETS

| Assets | 0-250$K | 250-1,000$K | 1-10$M |
|---|---|---|---|
| Profitability | 86.9% | 31.5% | 31.0% |

**COMMENTS:** *Uptrend. Average risk and good - excellent potential.*

# FARM MACHINERY (MFG)                    SIC:3523

| | |
|---|---|
| Total Assets | $250,000 |
| Profitability | 31.4% |
| Trend | -2.7% |
| Downside Risk | 59.1% |
| Upside Potential | 107.2% |
| Space Required | 1470 Sq. Ft. |

## SOURCE AND USE OF CAPITAL

| Capital Source | | Capital Use | |
|---|---|---|---|
| Owner's Equity | $ 81,250 | Working Capital | $ 51,250 |
| Long Term Debt | $ 55,250 | Long Term Assets | $ 85,250 |
| Total Capital Requ'd | $136,500 | Total Capital Used | $136,500 |

## SALES AND INCOME

| | Upper Quartile | Median | Lower Quartile |
|---|---|---|---|
| Sales | 600,000 | 525,000 | 400,000 |
| Officer's Salary* | 63,000 | 33,075 | 14,000 |
| Net Profit* | 25,750 | 9,750 | 3,500 |
| Total Income* | 88,750 | 42,825 | 17,500 |

*Before Tax

## PROFITABILITY VS ASSETS

| Assets | 0-250$K | 250-1,000$K | 1-10$M |
|---|---|---|---|
| Profitability | N/A | 31.4% | 16.0% |

**COMMENTS:**  *Down trend.  Above average risk and excellent potential.*




# CANDY (MFG)                    SIC:2065

| | |
|---|---|
| Total Assets | $250,000 |
| Profitability | 31.4% |
| Trend | -2.8% |
| Downside Risk | 44.9% |
| Upside Potential | 58.5% |
| Space Required | 1550 Sq. Ft. |

## SOURCE AND USE OF CAPITAL

| Capital Source | | Capital Use | |
|---|---|---|---|
| Owner's Equity | $122,500 | Working Capital | $ 70,000 |
| Long Term Debt | $ 35,000 | Long Term Assets | $ 87,500 |
| Total Capital Requ'd | $157,500 | Total Capital Used | $157,500 |

## SALES AND INCOME

| | Upper Quartile | Median | Lower Quartile |
|---|---|---|---|
| Sales | 1,075,000 | 775,000 | 600,000 |
| Officer's Salary* | 50,525 | 27,900 | 13,200 |
| Net Profit* | 27,750 | 21,500 | 14,000 |
| Total Income* | 78,275 | 49,400 | 27,200 |

*Before Tax

## PROFITABILITY VS ASSETS

| Assets | 0-250$K | 250-1,000$K | 1-10$M |
|---|---|---|---|
| Profitability | N/A | 31.4% | 17.6% |

**COMMENTS:**  *Down trend.  Lower than average risk, average potential.*

# #147  LOCAL TRUCKING-WITHOUT STORAGE (SVE)  SIC:4241

| | |
|---|---|
| Total Assets | $250,000 |
| Profitability | 31.3% |
| Trend | +0.4% |
| Downside Risk | 62.9% |
| Upside Potential | 92,4% |
| Space Required | 1380 Sq. Ft. |

## SOURCE AND USE OF CAPITAL

| Capital Source | | Capital Use | |
|---|---|---|---|
| Owner's Equity | $ 73,750 | Working Capital | $ (8,000) |
| Long Term Debt | $ 80,250 | Long Term Assets | $162,000 |
| Total Capital Requ'd | $154,000 | Total Capital Used | $154,000 |

## SALES AND INCOME

| | Upper Quartile | Median | Lower Quartile |
|---|---|---|---|
| Sales | 700,000 | 575,000 | 375,000 |
| Officer's Salary* | 53,900 | 29,900 | 10,875 |
| Net Profit* | 38,750 | 18,250 | 7,000 |
| Total Income* | 92,650 | 48,150 | 17,875 |

*Before Tax

## PROFITABILITY VS ASSETS

| Assets | 0-250$K | 250-1,000$K | 1-10$M |
|---|---|---|---|
| Profitability | 66.5% | 31.3% | 14.9% |

**COMMENTS:**   *Above average risk and good potential.  Effect of negative working capital see #141.*


# #148  MOVIE THEATERS (EXCEPT DRIVE-INS)(SVE)  SIC:7832

| | |
|---|---|
| Total Assets | $250,000 |
| Profitability | 31.2% |
| Trend | N/A |
| Downside Risk | 75.6% |
| Upside Potential | 157.1% |
| Space Required | 3705 Sq. Ft. |

## SOURCE AND USE OF CAPITAL

| Capital Source | | Capital Use | |
|---|---|---|---|
| Owner's Equity | $ 87,250 | Working Capital | $ (19,000) |
| Long Term Debt | $ 67,000 | Long Term Assets | $173,250 |
| Total Capital Requ'd | $154,250 | Total Capital Used | $154,250 |

## SALES AND INCOME

| | Upper Quartile | Median | Lower Quartile |
|---|---|---|---|
| Sales | 700,000 | 475,000 | 300,000 |
| Officer's Salary* | 78,400 | 21,850 | 1,500 |
| Net Profit* | 45,250 | 26,250 | 10,250 |
| Total Income* | 123,650 | 48,100 | 11,750 |

*Before Tax

## PROFITABILITY VS ASSETS

| Assets | 0-250$K | 250-1,000$K | 1-10$M |
|---|---|---|---|
| Profitability | N/A | 31.2% | N/A |

**COMMENTS:**   *High risk and excellent potential.*

| | |
|---|---|
| Total Assets | $250,000 |
| Profitability | 31.2% |
| Trend | -6.0% |
| Downside Risk | 82.9% |
| Upside Potential | 72.3% |
| Space Required | 1485 Sq. Ft. |

### SOURCE AND USE OF CAPITAL

| Capital Source | | Capital Use | |
|---|---|---|---|
| Owner's Equity | $ 89,000 | Working Capital | $ 34,000 |
| Long Term Debt | $ 47,000 | Long Term Assets | $102,000 |
| Total Capital Requ'd | $136,000 | Total Capital Used | $136,000 |

### SALES AND INCOME

| | Upper Quartile | Median | Lower Quartile |
|---|---|---|---|
| Sales | 875,000 | 825,000 | 575,000 |
| Officer's Salary* | 35,000 | 20,625 | 11,500 |
| Net Profit* | 38,000 | 21,750 | (4,250) |
| Total Income* | 73,000 | 42,375 | 7,250 |

*Before Tax

### PROFITABILITY VS ASSETS

| Assets | 0-250$K | 250-1,000$K | 1-10$M |
|---|---|---|---|
| Profitability | N/A | 31.2% | N/A |

**COMMENTS:** *Severe down trend.  Very high risk and good potential.*

---



| | |
|---|---|
| Total Assets | $250,000 |
| Profitability | 31.1% |
| Trend | +1.6% |
| Downside Risk | 75.1% |
| Upside Potential | 111.0% |
| Space Required | 1155 Sq. Ft. |

### SOURCE AND USE OF CAPITAL

| Capital Source | | Capital Use | |
|---|---|---|---|
| Owner's Equity | $ 80,250 | Working Capital | $ 60,750 |
| Long Term Debt | $ 30,500 | Long Term Assets | $ 50,000 |
| Total Capital Requ'd | $110,750 | Total Capital Used | $110,750 |

### SALES AND INCOME

| | Upper Quartile | Median | Lower Quartile |
|---|---|---|---|
| Sales | 1,250,000 | 825,000 | 575,000 |
| Officer's Salary* | 42,500 | 18,975 | 6,325 |
| Net Profit* | 30,250 | 15,500 | 2,250 |
| Total Income* | 72,750 | 34,475 | 8,575 |

*Before Tax

### PROFITABILITY VS ASSETS

| Assets | 0-250$K | 250-1,000$K | 1-10$M |
|---|---|---|---|
| Profitability | N/A | 31.1% | 26.9% |

**COMMENTS:** *Uptrend.  High risk and excellent potential.*

| Total Assets | $250,000 |
|---|---|
| Profitability | 31.1% |
| Trend | -0.1% |
| Downside Risk | 62.9% |
| Upside Potential | 77.3% |
| Space Required | 690 Sq. Ft. |

## SOURCE AND USE OF CAPITAL

| Capital Source | | Capital Use | |
|---|---|---|---|
| Owner's Equity | $106,500 | Working Capital | $ 87,250 |
| Long Term Debt | $ 29,250 | Long Term Assets | $ 48,500 |
| Total Capital Requ'd | $135,750 | Total Capital Used | $135,750 |

## SALES AND INCOME

| | Upper Quartile | Median | Lower Quartile |
|---|---|---|---|
| Sales | 775,000 | 575,000 | 475,000 |
| Officer's Salary* | 37,200 | 21,275 | 10,450 |
| Net Profit* | 37,750 | 21,000 | 5,250 |
| Total Income* | 74,950 | 42,275 | 15,700 |

*Before Tax

## PROFITABILITY VS ASSETS

| Assets | 0-250$K | 250-1,000$K | 1-10$M |
|---|---|---|---|
| Profitability | N/A | 31.1% | 33.4% |

**COMMENTS:**  *High risk and good potential.*


#152            **PAINT, GLASS & WALLPAPER (RTL) SIC:5231**

| Total Assets | $250,000 |
|---|---|
| Profitability | 30.9% |
| Trend | +1.7% |
| Downside Risk | 42.8% |
| Upside Potential | 119.9% |
| Space Required | 3190 Sq. Ft. |

## SOURCE AND USE OF CAPITAL

| Capital Source | | Capital Use | |
|---|---|---|---|
| Owner's Equity | $113,000 | Working Capital | $ 75,500 |
| Long Term Debt | $ 26,750 | Long Term Assets | $ 64,250 |
| Total Capital Requ'd | $139,750 | Total Capital Used | $139,750 |

## SALES AND INCOME

| | Upper Quartile | Median | Lower Quartile |
|---|---|---|---|
| Sales | 825,000 | 725,000 | 500,000 |
| Officer's Salary* | 70,950 | 28,275 | 14,000 |
| Net Profit* | 24,250 | 15,000 | 10,750 |
| Total Income* | 95,200 | 43,275 | 24,750 |

*Before Tax

## PROFITABILITY VS ASSETS

| Assets | 0-250$K | 250-1,000$K | 1-10$M |
|---|---|---|---|
| Profitability | 54.6% | 30.9% | N/A |

**COMMENTS:**  *Uptrend.  Low risk and excellent potential.*

| Total Assets | $250,000 |
|---|---|
| Profitability | 30.9% |
| Trend | +2.3% |
| Downside Risk | 49.5% |
| Upside Potential | 110.2% |
| Space Required | 1530 Sq. Ft. |

### SOURCE AND USE OF CAPITAL

| Capital Source | | Capital Use | |
|---|---|---|---|
| Owner's Equity | $106,250 | Working Capital | $ 80,750 |
| Long Term Debt | $ 21,750 | Long Term Assets | $ 47,250 |
| Total Capital Requ'd | $128,000 | Total Capital Used | $128,000 |

### SALES AND INCOME

| | Upper Quartile | Median | Lower Quartile |
|---|---|---|---|
| Sales | 1,000,000 | 850,000 | 675,000 |
| Officer's Salary* | 60,000 | 26,350 | 13,500 |
| Net Profit* | 23,250 | 13,250 | 6,500 |
| Total Income* | 83,250 | 39,600 | 20,000 |

*Before Tax

### PROFITABILITY VS ASSETS

| Assets | 0-250$K | 250-1,000$K | 1-10$M |
|---|---|---|---|
| Profitability | N/A | 30.9% | 30.2% |

**COMMENTS:**   *Uptrend.  Average risk and excellent potential.*

---

#154                 **LUGGAGE & GIFTS (RTL)**                SIC:5947,48

| Total Assets | $250,000 |
|---|---|
| Profitability | 30.9% |
| Trend | +0.1% |
| Downside Risk | 42.2% |
| Upside Potential | 55.3% |
| Space Required | 5415 Sq. Ft. |

### SOURCE AND USE OF CAPITAL

| Capital Source | | Capital Use | |
|---|---|---|---|
| Owner's Equity | $ 84,000 | Working Capital | $ 84,000 |
| Long Term Debt | $ 71,500 | Long Term Assets | $ 71,500 |
| Total Capital Requ'd | $155,500 | Total Capital Used | $155,500 |

### SALES AND INCOME

| | Upper Quartile | Median | Lower Quartile |
|---|---|---|---|
| Sales | 575,000 | 475,000 | 350,000 |
| Officer's Salary* | 37,950 | 26,600 | 15,050 |
| Net Profit* | 36,750 | 21,500 | 12,750 |
| Total Income* | 74,700 | 48,100 | 27,800 |

*Before Tax

### PROFITABILITY VS ASSETS

| Assets | 0-250$K | 250-1,000$K | 1-10$M |
|---|---|---|---|
| Profitability | 58.7% | 30.9% | N/A |

**COMMENTS:**   *Average risk and potential.*

# #155   DRY GOODS & GENERAL MERCHANDISE (RTL)   SIC:5399

| | |
|---|---|
| Total Assets | $250,000 |
| Profitability | 30.8% |
| Trend | -0.1% |
| Downside Risk | 60.5% |
| Upside Potential | 113.4% |
| Space Required | 2880 Sq. Ft. |

## SOURCE AND USE OF CAPITAL

| Capital Source | | Capital Use | |
|---|---|---|---|
| Owner's Equity | $125,250 | Working Capital | $102,750 |
| Long Term Debt | $ 36,000 | Long Term Assets | $ 58,500 |
| Total Capital Requ'd | $161,250 | Total Capital Used | $161,250 |

## SALES AND INCOME

| | Upper Quartile | Median | Lower Quartile |
|---|---|---|---|
| Sales | 825,000 | 600,000 | 475,000 |
| Officer's Salary* | 75,075 | 30,600 | 17,100 |
| Net Profit* | 30,750 | 19,000 | 2,500 |
| Total Income* | 105,825 | 49,600 | 19,600 |

*Before Tax

## PROFITABILITY VS ASSETS

| Assets | 0-250$K | 250-1,000$K | 1-10$M |
|---|---|---|---|
| Profitability | 37.1% | 30.8% | 18.7% |

**COMMENTS:**   *Above average risk and excellent potential.*


# #156   BUILDING MATERIALS (RTL)   SIC:5211

| | |
|---|---|
| Total Assets | $250,000 |
| Profitability | 30.8% |
| Trend | +2.3% |
| Downside Risk | 51.7% |
| Upside Potential | 73.6% |
| Space Required | 980 Sq. Ft. |

## SOURCE AND USE OF CAPITAL

| Capital Source | | Capital Use | |
|---|---|---|---|
| Owner's Equity | $114,750 | Working Capital | $ 84,250 |
| Long Term Debt | $ 31,750 | Long Term Assets | $ 62,250 |
| Total Capital Requ'd | $146,500 | Total Capital Used | $146,500 |

## SALES AND INCOME

| | Upper Quartile | Median | Lower Quartile |
|---|---|---|---|
| Sales | 825,000 | 700,000 | 525,000 |
| Officer's Salary* | 44,550 | 23,100 | 11,025 |
| Net Profit* | 33,750 | 22,000 | 10,750 |
| Total Income* | 78,300 | 45,100 | 21,775 |

*Before Tax

## PROFITABILITY VS ASSETS

| Assets | 0-250$K | 250-1,000$K | 1-10$M |
|---|---|---|---|
| Profitability | 43.1% | 30.8% | 27.1% |

**COMMENTS:**   *Uptrend.  Average risk and good potential.*

# #157    LUGGAGE & LEATHER GOODS (MFG)    SIC:3161,71,72

| | |
|---|---|
| Total Assets | $250,000 |
| Profitability | 30.5% |
| Trend | 1.8% |
| Downside Risk | 52.4% |
| Upside Potential | 108.9% |
| Space Required | 1430 Sq. Ft. |

## SOURCE AND USE OF CAPITAL

| Capital Source | | Capital Use | |
|---|---|---|---|
| Owner's Equity | $110,500 | Working Capital | $ 91,500 |
| Long Term Debt | $ 23,250 | Long Term Assets | $ 42,250 |
| Total Capital Requ'd | $133,750 | Total Capital Used | $133,750 |

## SALES AND INCOME

| | Upper Quartile | Median | Lower Quartile |
|---|---|---|---|
| Sales | 775,000 | 650,000 | 550,000 |
| Officer's Salary* | 44,175 | 26,650 | 13,200 |
| Net Profit* | 41,250 | 14,250 | 6,250 |
| Total Income* | 85,425 | 40,900 | 19,450 |

*Before Tax

## PROFITABILITY VS ASSETS

| Assets | 0-250$K | 250-1,000$K | 1-10$M |
|---|---|---|---|
| Profitability | N/A | 30.5% | 34.5% |

**COMMENTS:** *Uptrend. Average risk and excellent potential.*


# #158    MATTRESSES & BEDSPRINGS (MFG)    SIC:2515

| | |
|---|---|
| Total Assets | $250,000 |
| Profitability | 30.5% |
| Trend | -0.1% |
| Downside Risk | 49.4% |
| Upside Potential | 95.6% |
| Space Required | 2170 Sq. Ft. |

## SOURCE AND USE OF CAPITAL

| Capital Source | | Capital Use | |
|---|---|---|---|
| Owner's Equity | $107,500 | Working Capital | $ 79,750 |
| Long Term Debt | $ 26,250 | Long Term Assets | $ 54,000 |
| Total Capital Requ'd | $133,750 | Total Capital Used | $133,750 |

## SALES AND INCOME

| | Upper Quartile | Median | Lower Quartile |
|---|---|---|---|
| Sales | 975,000 | 775,000 | 525,000 |
| Officer's Salary* | 54,600 | 23,250 | 7,300 |
| Net Profit* | 25,500 | 17,500 | 13,250 |
| Total Income* | 80,100 | 40,750 | 20,600 |

*Before Tax

## PROFITABILITY VS ASSETS

| Assets | 0-250$K | 250-1,000$K | 1-10$M |
|---|---|---|---|
| Profitability | N/A | 30.5% | 24.2% |

**COMMENTS:** *Average risk and good potential.*

## MOTORCYCLES (RTL)                    SIC:5571

| | |
|---|---|
| Total Assets | $250,000 |
| Profitability | 30.5% |
| Trend | +2.4% |
| Downside Risk | 64.4% |
| Upside Potential | 79.8% |
| Space Required | 1680 Sq. Ft. |

### SOURCE AND USE OF CAPITAL

| Capital Source | | Capital Use | |
|---|---|---|---|
| Owner's Equity | $ 82,250 | Working Capital | $ 60,000 |
| Long Term Debt | $ 39,250 | Long Term Assets | $ 61,500 |
| Total Capital Requ'd | $121,500 | Total Capital Used | $121,500 |

### SALES AND INCOME

| | Upper Quartile | Median | Lower Quartile |
|---|---|---|---|
| Sales | 875,000 | 600,000 | 45,000 |
| Officer's Salary* | 39,375 | 19,800 | 7,200 |
| Net Profit* | 27,250 | 17,250 | 6,000 |
| Total Income* | 66,625 | 37,050 | 13,200 |

*Before Tax

### PROFITABILITY VS ASSETS

| Assets | 0-250$K | 250-1,000$K | 1-10$M |
|---|---|---|---|
| Profitability | 43.4% | 30.5% | N/A |

**COMMENTS:** *High risk and good potential.*



## HOUSEHOLD APPLIANCES (RTL)          SIC:5722

| | |
|---|---|
| Total Assets | $250,000 |
| Profitability | 30.4% |
| Trend | +0.1% |
| Downside Risk | 55.4% |
| Upside Potential | 81.4% |
| Space Required | 2000 Sq. Ft. |

### SOURCE AND USE OF CAPITAL

| Capital Source | | Capital Use | |
|---|---|---|---|
| Owner's Equity | $104,500 | Working Capital | $ 88,250 |
| Long Term Debt | $ 25,250 | Long Term Assets | $ 41,500 |
| Total Capital Requ'd | $129,750 | Total Capital Used | $129,750 |

### SALES AND INCOME

| | Upper Quartile | Median | Lower Quartile |
|---|---|---|---|
| Sales | 800,000 | 625,000 | 450,000 |
| Officer's Salary* | 42,400 | 23,750 | 10,350 |
| Net Profit* | 29,250 | 15,750 | 7,250 |
| Total Income* | 71,650 | 39,500 | 17,600 |

*Before Tax

### PROFITABILITY VS ASSETS

| Assets | 0-250$K | 250-1,000$K | 1-10$M |
|---|---|---|---|
| Profitability | 40.0% | 30.4% | 26.0% |

**COMMENTS:** *Average risk and good potential.*

## SCHOOL BUSES (SVE)          SIC:4151

| Total Assets | $250,000 |
| Profitability | 30.3% |
| Trend | N/A |
| Downside Risk | 57.3% |
| Upside Potential | 71.5% |
| Space Required | 1600 Sq. Ft. |

### SOURCE AND USE OF CAPITAL

| Capital Source | | Capital Use | |
|---|---|---|---|
| Owner's Equity | $116,500 | Working Capital | $ (5,750) |
| Long Term Debt | $ 59,000 | Long Term Assets | $181,250 |
| Total Capital Requ'd | $175,500 | Total Capital Used | $175,500 |

### SALES AND INCOME

| | Upper Quartile | Median | Lower Quartile |
|---|---|---|---|
| Sales | 525,000 | 400,000 | 350,000 |
| Officer's Salary* | 45,150 | 28,400 | 16,450 |
| Net Profit* | 46,000 | 24,750 | 6,250 |
| Total Income* | 91,150 | 53,150 | 22,700 |

*Before Tax

### PROFITABILITY VS ASSETS

| Assets | 0-250$K | 250-1,000$K | 1-10$M |
|---|---|---|---|
| Profitability | N/A | 30.3% | N/A |

**COMMENTS:**  *Average risk and good potential.*




## BOOKBINDING (MFG)          SIC:2789

| Total Assets | $250,000 |
| Profitability | 30.0% |
| Trend | +1.7% |
| Downside Risk | 49.1% |
| Upside Potential | 132.9% |
| Space Required | 3750 Sq. Ft. |

### SOURCE AND USE OF CAPITAL

| Capital Source | | Capital Use | |
|---|---|---|---|
| Owner's Equity | $118,500 | Working Capital | $ 60,500 |
| Long Term Debt | $ 50,000 | Long Term Assets | $108,000 |
| Total Capital Requ'd | $168,500 | Total Capital Used | $168,500 |

### SALES AND INCOME

| | Upper Quartile | Median | Lower Quartile |
|---|---|---|---|
| Sales | 775,000 | 625,000 | 425,000 |
| Officer's Salary* | 75,950 | 36,875 | 17,000 |
| Net Profit* | 42,000 | 13,750 | 8,750 |
| Total Income* | 117,950 | 50,625 | 25,750 |

*Before Tax

### PROFITABILITY VS ASSETS

| Assets | 0-250$K | 250-1,000$K | 1-10$M |
|---|---|---|---|
| Profitability | N/A | 30.0% | N/A |

**COMMENTS:**  *Average risk and excellent potential.*

 **JEWELRY (WSLE)** SIC:5094

| | |
|---|---|
| Total Assets | $250,000 |
| Profitability | 30.0% |
| Trend | -1.2% |
| Downside Risk | 54.4% |
| Upside Potential | 86.5% |
| Space Required | 900 Sq. Ft. |

## SOURCE AND USE OF CAPITAL

| Capital Source | | Capital Use | |
|---|---|---|---|
| Owner's Equity | $102,500 | Working Capital | $101,750 |
| Long Term Debt | $ 23,500 | Long Term Assets | $ 24,250 |
| Total Capital Requ'd | $126,000 | Total Capital Used | $126,000 |

## SALES AND INCOME

| | Upper Quartile | Median | Lower Quartile |
|---|---|---|---|
| Sales | 700,000 | 500,000 | 400,000 |
| Officer's Salary* | 36,400 | 18,500 | 7,200 |
| Net Profit* | 34,000 | 19,250 | 10,000 |
| Total Income* | 70,400 | 37,750 | 17,200 |

*Before Tax

## PROFITABILITY VS ASSETS

| Assets | 0-250$K | 250-1,000$K | 1-10$M |
|---|---|---|---|
| Profitability | 49.3% | 30.0% | N/A |

**COMMENTS:** *Some down trend. Average risk and good potential.*


 **IRON & STEEL FORGINGS (MFG)** SIC:3462

| | |
|---|---|
| Total Assets | $250,000 |
| Profitability | 30.0% |
| Trend | +1.7% |
| Downside Risk | 39.7% |
| Upside Potential | 78.7% |
| Space Required | 1210 Sq. Ft. |

## SOURCE AND USE OF CAPITAL

| Capital Source | | Capital Use | |
|---|---|---|---|
| Owner's Equity | $137,250 | Working Capital | $ 73,750 |
| Long Term Debt | $ 28,500 | Long Term Assets | $ 92,000 |
| Total Capital Requ'd | $165,750 | Total Capital Used | $165,750 |

## SALES AND INCOME

| | Upper Quartile | Median | Lower Quartile |
|---|---|---|---|
| Sales | 650,000 | 550,000 | 450,000 |
| Officer's Salary* | 47,450 | 26,400 | 16,200 |
| Net Profit* | 41,250 | 23,250 | 13,750 |
| Total Income* | 88,700 | 49,650 | 29,950 |

*Before Tax

## PROFITABILITY VS ASSETS

| Assets | 0-250$K | 250-1,000$K | 1-10$M |
|---|---|---|---|
| Profitability | N/A | 30.0% | 24.9% |

**COMMENTS:** *Low risk and good potential.*

| | |
|---|---|
| Total Assets | $250,000 |
| Profitability | 29.9% |
| Trend | +3.0% |
| Downside Risk | 62.5% |
| Upside Potential | 113.2% |
| Space Required | 1885 Sq. Ft. |

## SOURCE AND USE OF CAPITAL

| Capital Source | | Capital Use | |
|---|---|---|---|
| Owner's Equity | $ 49,000 | Working Capital | $ 24,500 |
| Long Term Debt | $ 43,000 | Long Term Assets | $ 67,500 |
| Total Capital Requ'd | $ 92,000 | Total Capital Used | $ 92,000 |

## SALES AND INCOME

| | Upper Quartile | Median | Lower Quartile |
|---|---|---|---|
| Sales | 875,000 | 725,000 | 525,000 |
| Officer's Salary* | 32,375 | 14,500 | 6,825 |
| Net Profit* | 26,250 | 13,000 | 3,500 |
| Total Income* | 58,625 | 27,500 | 10,325 |

*Before Tax

## PROFITABILITY VS ASSETS

| Assets | 0-250$K | 250-1,000$K | 1-10$M |
|---|---|---|---|
| Profitability | N/A | 29.9% | 23.9% |

**COMMENTS:**   *Uptrend. Above average risk and good potential.*




| | |
|---|---|
| Total Assets | $250,000 |
| Profitability | 29.9% |
| Trend | -0.1% |
| Downside Risk | 64.5% |
| Upside Potential | 73.7% |
| Space Required | 1035 Sq. Ft. |

## SOURCE AND USE OF CAPITAL

| Capital Source | | Capital Use | |
|---|---|---|---|
| Owner's Equity | $ 86,500 | Working Capital | $ 74,250 |
| Long Term Debt | $ 26,500 | Long Term Assets | $ 38,750 |
| Total Capital Requ'd | $113,000 | Total Capital Used | $113,000 |

## SALES AND INCOME

| | Upper Quartile | Median | Lower Quartile |
|---|---|---|---|
| Sales | 750,000 | 575,000 | 450,000 |
| Officer's Salary* | 33,750 | 17,825 | 6,750 |
| Net Profit* | 25,000 | 16,000 | 5,250 |
| Total Income* | 58,750 | 33,825 | 12,000 |

*Before Tax

## PROFITABILITY VS ASSETS

| Assets | 0-250$K | 250-1,000$K | 1-10$M |
|---|---|---|---|
| Profitability | N/A | 29.9% | 20.9% |

**COMMENTS:**   *Above average risk and good potential.*

| | |
|---|---|
| Total Assets | $250,000 |
| Profitability | 29.9% |
| Trend | -0.1% |
| Downside Risk | 48.3% |
| Upside Potential | 66.9% |
| Space Required | 1375 Sq. Ft. |

## SOURCE AND USE OF CAPITAL

| Capital Source | | Capital Use | |
|---|---|---|---|
| Owner's Equity | $101,000 | Working Capital | $ 93,500 |
| Long Term Debt | $ 25,500 | Long Term Assets | $ 33,000 |
| Total Capital Requ'd | $126,500 | Total Capital Used | $126,500 |

## SALES AND INCOME

| | Upper Quartile | Median | Lower Quartile |
|---|---|---|---|
| Sales | 800,000 | 625,000 | 450,000 |
| Officer's Salary* | 35,200 | 21,875 | 12,600 |
| Net Profit* | 28,000 | 16,000 | 7,000 |
| Total Income* | 63,200 | 37,875 | 19,600 |

*Before Tax

## PROFITABILITY VS ASSETS

| Assets | 0-250$K | 250-1,000$K | 1-10$M |
|---|---|---|---|
| Profitability | N/A | 29.9% | 27.6% |

**COMMENTS:** *Average risk and good potential.*


#168     **HARDWARE (RTL)**     SIC:5251

| | |
|---|---|
| Total Assets | $250,000 |
| Profitability | 29.8% |
| Trend | +2.3% |
| Downside Risk | 43.8% |
| Upside Potential | 90.2% |
| Space Required | 1920 Sq. Ft. |

## SOURCE AND USE OF CAPITAL

| Capital Source | | Capital Use | |
|---|---|---|---|
| Owner's Equity | $115,750 | Working Capital | $100,500 |
| Long Term Debt | $ 42,250 | Long Term Assets | $ 57,500 |
| Total Capital Requ'd | $158,000 | Total Capital Used | $158,000 |

## SALES AND INCOME

| | Upper Quartile | Median | Lower Quartile |
|---|---|---|---|
| Sales | 775,000 | 600,000 | 475,000 |
| Officer's Salary* | 59,675 | 26,400 | 14,250 |
| Net Profit* | 30,000 | 20,750 | 12,250 |
| Total Income* | 89,675 | 47,150 | 26,500 |

*Before Tax

## PROFITABILITY VS ASSETS

| Assets | 0-250$K | 250-1,000$K | 1-10$M |
|---|---|---|---|
| Profitability | 43.1% | 29.8% | 27.1% |

**COMMENTS:** *Below average risk and good potential.*

 **FROZEN GOODS (WSLE)**     SIC:5142

| | |
|---|---|
| Total Assets | $250,000 |
| Profitability | 29.7% |
| Trend | -1.3% |
| Downside Risk | 58.6% |
| Upside Potential | 148.0% |
| Space Required | 1275 Sq. Ft. |

## SOURCE AND USE OF CAPITAL

| Capital Source | | Capital Use | |
|---|---|---|---|
| Owner's Equity | $ 91,000 | Working Capital | $ 61,250 |
| Long Term Debt | $ 41,750 | Long Term Assets | $ 71,500 |
| Total Capital Requ'd | $132,750 | Total Capital Used | $132,750 |

## SALES AND INCOME

| | Upper Quartile | Median | Lower Quartile |
|---|---|---|---|
| Sales | 1,725,000 | 1,275,000 | 975,000 |
| Officer's Salary* | 67,275 | 26,775 | 15,600 |
| Net Profit* | 30,750 | 12,750 | 750 |
| Total Income* | 98,025 | 39,525 | 16,350 |

*Before Tax

## PROFITABILITY VS ASSETS

| Assets | 0-250$K | 250-1,000$K | 1-10$M |
|---|---|---|---|
| Profitability | N/A | 29.7% | 23.0% |

**COMMENTS:** *Average risk and good potential.*


 **PLAIN WOODEN FURNITURE (MFG)**     SIC:2511

| | |
|---|---|
| Total Assets | $250,000 |
| Profitability | 29.7% |
| Trend | -2.6% |
| Downside Risk | 70.4% |
| Upside Potential | 82.5% |
| Space Required | 1750 Sq. Ft. |

## SOURCE AND USE OF CAPITAL

| Capital Source | | Capital Use | |
|---|---|---|---|
| Owner's Equity | $103,250 | Working Capital | $ 80,000 |
| Long Term Debt | $ 42,750 | Long Term Assets | $ 66,000 |
| Total Capital Requ'd | $146,000 | Total Capital Used | $146,000 |

## SALES AND INCOME

| | Upper Quartile | Median | Lower Quartile |
|---|---|---|---|
| Sales | 725,000 | 625,000 | 400,000 |
| Officer's Salary* | 45,675 | 24,375 | 7,600 |
| Net Profit* | 33,500 | 19,000 | 5,250 |
| Total Income* | 79,175 | 43,375 | 12,850 |

*Before Tax

## PROFITABILITY VS ASSETS

| Assets | 0-250$K | 250-1,000$K | 1-10$M |
|---|---|---|---|
| Profitability | N/A | 29.7% | 18.3% |

**COMMENTS:** *Down trend.  High risk and good potential.*

| | |
|---|---|
| Total Assets | $250,000 |
| Profitability | 29.7% |
| Trend | -2.4% |
| Downside Risk | 65.3% |
| Upside Potential | 75.2% |
| Space Required | 3240 Sq. Ft. |

## SOURCE AND USE OF CAPITAL

| Capital Source | | Capital Use | |
|---|---|---|---|
| Owner's Equity | $114,250 | Working Capital | $ 4,750 |
| Long Term Debt | $ 50,000 | Long Term Assets | $159,500 |
| Total Capital Requ'd | $164,250 | Total Capital Used | $164,250 |

## SALES AND INCOME

| | Upper Quartile | Median | Lower Quartile |
|---|---|---|---|
| Sales | 775,000 | 600,000 | 350,000 |
| Officer's Salary* | 56,575 | 33,600 | 12,950 |
| Net Profit* | 29,000 | 15,250 | 4,000 |
| Total Income* | 85,575 | 48,850 | 16,950 |

*Before Tax

## PROFITABILITY VS ASSETS

| Assets | 0-250$K | 250-1,000$K | 1-10$M |
|---|---|---|---|
| Profitability | 63.4% | 29.7% | N/A |

**COMMENTS:** *Downtrend. High risk. Moderate Potential.*




| | |
|---|---|
| Total Assets | $250,000 |
| Profitability | 29.6% |
| Trend | +2.2% |
| Downside Risk | 49.1% |
| Upside Potential | 68.9% |
| Space Required | 810 Sq. Ft. |

## SOURCE AND USE OF CAPITAL

| Capital Source | | Capital Use | |
|---|---|---|---|
| Owner's Equity | $118,750 | Working Capital | $ 91,750 |
| Long Term Debt | $ 28,750 | Long Term Assets | $ 55,750 |
| Total Capital Requ'd | $147,500 | Total Capital Used | $147,500 |

## SALES AND INCOME

| | Upper Quartile | Median | Lower Quartile |
|---|---|---|---|
| Sales | 850,000 | 675,000 | 500,000 |
| Officer's Salary* | 39,100 | 22,950 | 11,000 |
| Net Profit* | 34,750 | 20,750 | 11,250 |
| Total Income* | 73,850 | 43,700 | 22,250 |

*Before Tax

## PROFITABILITY VS ASSETS

| Assets | 0-250$K | 250-1,000$K | 1-10$M |
|---|---|---|---|
| Profitability | 44.4% | 29.6% | 27.4% |

**COMMENTS:** *Average risk and potential.*

# #173　PHOTOGRAPHIC EQUIPMENT (MFG)　SIC:3861

| | |
|---|---|
| **Total Assets** | $250,000 |
| **Profitability** | 29.6% |
| **Trend** | -6.0% |
| **Downside Risk** | 69.4% |
| **Upside Potential** | 113.9% |
| **Space Required** | 1980 Sq. Ft. |

### SOURCE AND USE OF CAPITAL

| Capital Source | | Capital Use | |
|---|---|---|---|
| Owner's Equity | $112,750 | Working Capital | $ 92,750 |
| Long Term Debt | $ 50,750 | Long Term Assets | $ 70,750 |
| Total Capital Requ'd | $163,500 | Total Capital Used | $163,500 |

### SALES AND INCOME

| | Upper Quartile | Median | Lower Quartile |
|---|---|---|---|
| Sales | 825,000 | 550,000 | 375,000 |
| Officer's Salary* | 54,450 | 25,850 | 10,500 |
| Net Profit* | 49,000 | 22,500 | 4,250 |
| Total Income* | 103,450 | 48,350 | 14,750 |

*Before Tax

### PROFITABILITY VS ASSETS

| Assets | 0-250$K | 250-1,000$K | 1-10$M |
|---|---|---|---|
| Profitability | N/A | 29.6% | N/A |

**COMMENTS:**　*Strong down trend.  High risk and good potential.*


# #174　CAMPERS & TRAILERS (RTL)　SIC:5561

| | |
|---|---|
| **Total Assets** | $250,000 |
| **Profitability** | 29.5% |
| **Trend** | -7.5% |
| **Downside Risk** | 60.8% |
| **Upside Potential** | 98.6% |
| **Space Required** | 1395 Sq. Ft. |

### SOURCE AND USE OF CAPITAL

| Capital Source | | Capital Use | |
|---|---|---|---|
| Owner's Equity | $ 65,000 | Working Capital | $ 48,000 |
| Long Term Debt | $ 29,750 | Long Term Assets | $ 46,750 |
| Total Capital Requ'd | $ 94,750 | Total Capital Used | $ 94,750 |

### SALES AND INCOME

| | Upper Quartile | Median | Lower Quartile |
|---|---|---|---|
| Sales | 1,025,000 | 775,000 | 575,000 |
| Officer's Salary* | 32,800 | 14,750 | 7,475 |
| Net Profit* | 22,750 | 13,250 | 3,500 |
| Total Income* | 55,550 | 27,975 | 10,975 |

*Before Tax

### PROFITABILITY VS ASSETS

| Assets | 0-250$K | 250-1,000$K | 1-10$M |
|---|---|---|---|
| Profitability | 38.1% | 29.5% | 32.4% |

**COMMENTS:**　*High than average risk and good potential.*

          # CAMERAS (RTL)          SIC:5946

| | |
|---|---|
| Total Assets | $250,000 |
| Profitability | 29.3% |
| Trend | +1.8% |
| Downside Risk | 48.9% |
| Upside Potential | 63.6% |
| Space Required | 3000 Sq. Ft. |

## SOURCE AND USE OF CAPITAL

| Capital Source | | Capital Use | |
|---|---|---|---|
| Owner's Equity | $ 96,000 | Working Capital | $ 91,000 |
| Long Term Debt | $ 26,000 | Long Term Assets | $ 31,000 |
| Total Capital Requ'd | $122,000 | Total Capital Used | $122,000 |

## SALES AND INCOME

| | Upper Quartile | Median | Lower Quartile |
|---|---|---|---|
| Sales | 850,000 | 750,000 | 625,000 |
| Officer's Salary* | 34,000 | 21,000 | 13,750 |
| Net Profit* | 24,500 | 14,750 | 4,500 |
| Total Income* | 58,500 | 35,750 | 18,250 |

*Before Tax

## PROFITABILITY VS ASSETS

| Assets | 0-250$K | 250-1,000$K | 1-10$M |
|---|---|---|---|
| Profitability | 65.4% | 29.3% | 23.7% |

**COMMENTS:** *Average risk and average potential.*


      # MISC HOME FURNISHINGS (RTL)      SIC:5719

| | |
|---|---|
| Total Assets | $250,000 |
| Profitability | 29.0% |
| Trend | N/A |
| Downside Risk | 60.4% |
| Upside Potential | 94.7% |
| Space Required | 3480 Sq. Ft. |

## SOURCE AND USE OF CAPITAL

| Capital Source | | Capital Use | |
|---|---|---|---|
| Owner's Equity | $ 88,750 | Working Capital | $ 80,750 |
| Long Term Debt | $ 47,250 | Long Term Assets | $ 55,250 |
| Total Capital Requ'd | $136,000 | Total Capital Used | $136,000 |

## SALES AND INCOME

| | Upper Quartile | Median | Lower Quartile |
|---|---|---|---|
| Sales | 700,000 | 600,000 | 375,000 |
| Officer's Salary* | 37,800 | 25,200 | 12,375 |
| Net Profit* | 39,000 | 14,200 | 3,250 |
| Total Income* | 76,800 | 39,400 | 15,625 |

*Before Tax

## PROFITABILITY VS ASSETS

| Assets | 0-250$K | 250-1,000$K | 1-10$M |
|---|---|---|---|
| Profitability | 54.6% | 29.0% | N/A |

**COMMENTS:** *Above average risk and good potential.*

# #177 VENDING MACHINE OPERATORS (RTL)    SIC:5962

| | |
|---|---|
| Total Assets | $250,000 |
| Profitability | 29.0% |
| Trend | +2.0% |
| Downside Risk | 44.2% |
| Upside Potential | 75.2% |
| Space Required | 1485 Sq. Ft. |

## SOURCE AND USE OF CAPITAL

| Capital Source | | Capital Use | |
|---|---|---|---|
| Owner's Equity | $117,250 | Working Capital | $ 3,000 |
| Long Term Debt | $ 45,750 | Long Term Assets | $160,000 |
| Total Capital Requ'd | $163,000 | Total Capital Used | $163,000 |

## SALES AND INCOME

| | Upper Quartile | Median | Lower Quartile |
|---|---|---|---|
| Sales | 850,000 | 675,000 | 525,000 |
| Officer's Salary* | 51,000 | 24,975 | 12,600 |
| Net Profit* | 31,750 | 22,250 | 13,750 |
| Total Income* | 82,750 | 47,225 | 26,350 |

*Before Tax

## PROFITABILITY VS ASSETS

| Assets | 0-250$K | 250-1,000$K | 1-10$M |
|---|---|---|---|
| Profitability | 48.2% | 29.0% | 31.8% |

**COMMENTS:**  *Average risk and good potential.*


# #178 MUSICAL INSTRUMENTS (RTL)    SIC:5733

| | |
|---|---|
| Total Assets | $250,000 |
| Profitability | 28.9% |
| Trend | +0.3% |
| Downside Risk | 46.9% |
| Upside Potential | 98.5% |
| Space Required | 2160 Sq. Ft. |

## SOURCE AND USE OF CAPITAL

| Capital Source | | Capital Use | |
|---|---|---|---|
| Owner's Equity | $107,250 | Working Capital | $ 97,250 |
| Long Term Debt | $ 29,000 | Long Term Assets | $ 39,000 |
| Total Capital Requ'd | $136,250 | Total Capital Used | $136,250 |

## SALES AND INCOME

| | Upper Quartile | Median | Lower Quartile |
|---|---|---|---|
| Sales | 625,000 | 450,000 | 350,000 |
| Officer's Salary* | 40,625 | 21,600 | 11,900 |
| Net Profit* | 37,500 | 17,750 | 9,000 |
| Total Income* | 78,125 | 39,350 | 20,900 |

*Before Tax

## PROFITABILITY VS ASSETS

| Assets | 0-250$K | 250-1,000$K | 1-10$M |
|---|---|---|---|
| Profitability | 60.4% | 28.9% | 28.1% |

**COMMENTS:**  *Average risk and good potential.*

## CITRUS FRUIT GROWER

SIC:0174

| | |
|---|---|
| Total Assets | $250,000 |
| Profitability | 28.85% |
| Trend | N/A |
| Downside Risk | 56.5% |
| Upside Potential | 172.6% |
| Space Required | 1020 Sq. Ft. |

### SOURCE AND USE OF CAPITAL

| Capital Source | | Capital Use | |
|---|---|---|---|
| Owner's Equity | $117,500 | Working Capital | $ 11,750 |
| Long Term Debt | $ 50,250 | Long Term Assets | $156,000 |
| Total Capital Requ'd | $167,750 | Total Capital Used | $167,750 |

### SALES AND INCOME

| | Upper Quartile | Median | Lower Quartile |
|---|---|---|---|
| Sales | 525,000 | 300,000 | 150,000 |
| Officer's Salary* | 72,450 | 18,900 | 6,300 |
| Net Profit* | 59,500 | 29,500 | 14,750 |
| Total Income* | 131,950 | 48,400 | 21,050 |

*Before Tax

### PROFITABILITY VS ASSETS

| Assets | 0-250$K | 250-1,000$K | 1-10$M |
|---|---|---|---|
| Profitability | N/A | 28.8% | N/A |

**COMMENTS:** *Excellent potential.  Average risk.*


# #180 TRANSPORTATION EQUIPMENT (EXCEPT MOTOR VEHICLES)

SIC:5088

| | |
|---|---|
| Total Assets | $250,000 |
| Profitability | 28.8% |
| Trend | -1.2% |
| Downside Risk | 64.3% |
| Upside Potential | 107.8% |
| Space Required | 1320 Sq. Ft. |

### SOURCE AND USE OF CAPITAL

| Capital Source | | Capital Use | |
|---|---|---|---|
| Owner's Equity | $ 94,750 | Working Capital | $ 76,500 |
| Long Term Debt | $ 34,250 | Long Term Assets | $ 52,500 |
| Total Capital Requ'd | $129,000 | Total Capital Used | $129,000 |

### SALES AND INCOME

| | Upper Quartile | Median | Lower Quartile |
|---|---|---|---|
| Sales | 800,000 | 550,000 | 425,000 |
| Officer's Salary* | 36,800 | 18,700 | 9,775 |
| Net Profit* | 40,500 | 18,500 | 3,500 |
| Total Income* | 77,300 | 37,200 | 13,275 |

*Before Tax

### PROFITABILITY VS ASSETS

| Assets | 0-250$K | 250-1,000$K | 1-10$M |
|---|---|---|---|
| Profitability | N/A | 28.8% | 24.2% |

**COMMENTS:** *High risk and good potential.*

# #181 CANNED & DRIED FRUITS & VEGETABLES (MFG)

SIC:2033,34

| | |
|---|---|
| Total Assets | $250,000 |
| Profitability | 28.8% |
| Trend | +0.3% |
| Downside Risk | 79.3% |
| Upside Potential | 68.8% |
| Space Required | 2320 Sq. Ft. |

## SOURCE AND USE OF CAPITAL

| Capital Source | | Capital Use | |
|---|---|---|---|
| Owner's Equity | $107,500 | Working Capital | $ 47,500 |
| Long Term Debt | $ 37,750 | Long Term Assets | $ 97,750 |
| Total Capital Requ'd | $145,250 | Total Capital Used | $145,250 |

## SALES AND INCOME

| | Upper Quartile | Median | Lower Quartile |
|---|---|---|---|
| Sales | 875,000 | 725,000 | 350,000 |
| Officer's Salary* | 39,375 | 26,825 | 10,150 |
| Net Profit* | 31,250 | 15,000 | (1,500) |
| Total Income* | 70,625 | 41,825 | 8,650 |

*Before Tax

## PROFITABILITY VS ASSETS

| Assets | 0-250$K | 250-1,000$K | 1-10$M |
|---|---|---|---|
| Profitability | N/A | 28.8% | 19.0% |

**COMMENTS:** *Very high risk and good potential*


# #182 MEN'S & BOYS CLOTHING (RTL)

SIC:5611

| | |
|---|---|
| Total Assets | $250,000 |
| Profitability | 28.7% |
| Trend | +0.1% |
| Downside Risk | 60.0% |
| Upside Potential | 65.8% |
| Space Required | 4950 Sq. Ft. |

## SOURCE AND USE OF CAPITAL

| Capital Source | | Capital Use | |
|---|---|---|---|
| Owner's Equity | $117,250 | Working Capital | $103,750 |
| Long Term Debt | $ 35,750 | Long Term Assets | $ 49,250 |
| Total Capital Requ'd | $153,000 | Total Capital Used | $153,000 |

## SALES AND INCOME

| | Upper Quartile | Median | Lower Quartile |
|---|---|---|---|
| Sales | 650,000 | 550,000 | 425,000 |
| Officer's Salary* | 50,050 | 31,900 | 15,300 |
| Net Profit* | 22,750 | 12,000 | 2,250 |
| Total Income* | 72,800 | 43,900 | 17,550 |

*Before Tax

## PROFITABILITY VS ASSETS

| Assets | 0-250$K | 250-1,000$K | 1-10$M |
|---|---|---|---|
| Profitability | 44.1% | 28.6% | 29.1% |

**COMMENTS:** *High risk and good potential.*

| Total Assets | $250,000 |
|---|---|
| Profitability | 28.7% |
| Trend | +3.6% |
| Downside Risk | 43.9% |
| Upside Potential | 65.5% |
| Space Required | 1620 Sq. Ft. |

## SOURCE AND USE OF CAPITAL

| Capital Source | | Capital Use | |
|---|---|---|---|
| Owner's Equity | $109,500 | Working Capital | $ 97,250 |
| Long Term Debt | $ 37,750 | Long Term Assets | $ 50,000 |
| Total Capital Requ'd | $147,250 | Total Capital Used | $147,250 |

## SALES AND INCOME

| | Upper Quartile | Median | Lower Quartile |
|---|---|---|---|
| Sales | 850,000 | 675,000 | 600,000 |
| Officer's Salary* | 42,500 | 24,300 | 12,000 |
| Net Profit* | 27,500 | 18,000 | 11,750 |
| Total Income* | 70,000 | 42,300 | 23,750 |

*Before Tax

## PROFITABILITY VS ASSETS

| Assets | 0-250$K | 250-1,000$K | 1-10$M |
|---|---|---|---|
| Profitability | N/A | 28.7% | 23.5% |

**COMMENTS:**  *Good uptrend.  Average risk and good potential.*


#184     **HARDWOOD VENEER & PLYWOOD(MFG)**     SIC:2435

| Total Assets | $250,000 |
|---|---|
| Profitability | 28.5% |
| Trend | +0.3% |
| Downside Risk | 61.7% |
| Upside Potential | 198.2% |
| Space Required | 945 Sq. Ft. |

## SOURCE AND USE OF CAPITAL

| Capital Source | | Capital Use | |
|---|---|---|---|
| Owner's Equity | $121,000 | Working Capital | $ 65,000 |
| Long Term Debt | $ 34,000 | Long Term Assets | $ 90,000 |
| Total Capital Requ'd | $155,000 | Total Capital Used | $155,000 |

## SALES AND INCOME

| | Upper Quartile | Median | Lower Quartile |
|---|---|---|---|
| Sales | 1,075,000 | 675,000 | 550,000 |
| Officer's Salary* | 65,575 | 16,200 | 7,700 |
| Net Profit* | 66,250 | 28,000 | 9,250 |
| Total Income* | 131,825 | 44,200 | 16,950 |

*Before Tax

## PROFITABILITY VS ASSETS

| Assets | 0-250$K | 250-1,000$K | 1-10$M |
|---|---|---|---|
| Profitability | N/A | 28.5% | 19.9 |

**COMMENTS:**  *High risk but excellent potential.*

# #185    BARBER & BEAUTY SHOP SUPPLIES (WSLE) SIC:5087

| | |
|---|---|
| Total Assets | $250,000 |
| Profitability | 28.4% |
| Trend | -2.6% |
| Downside Risk | 44.0% |
| Upside Potential | 167.6% |
| Space Required | 1875 Sq. Ft. |

## SOURCE AND USE OF CAPITAL

| Capital Source | | Capital Use | |
|---|---|---|---|
| Owner's Equity | $115,750 | Working Capital | $ 86,000 |
| Long Term Debt | $ 11,750 | Long Term Assets | $ 41,500 |
| Total Capital Requ'd | $127,500 | Total Capital Used | $127,500 |

## SALES AND INCOME

| | Upper Quartile | Median | Lower Quartile |
|---|---|---|---|
| Sales | 900,000 | 625,000 | 550,000 |
| Officer's Salary* | 63,000 | 22,500 | 14,300 |
| Net Profit* | 34,000 | 13,750 | 6,000 |
| Total Income* | 97,000 | 36,250 | 20,300 |

*Before Tax

## PROFITABILITY VS ASSETS

| Assets | 0-250$K | 250-1,000$K | 1-10$M |
|---|---|---|---|
| Profitability | N/A | 28.4% | N/A |

**COMMENTS:** *Average risk but excellent potential. Some down trend.*


# #186    WOMAN'S DRESSES (MFG)    SIC:2335

| | |
|---|---|
| Total Assets | $250,000 |
| Profitability | 28.3% |
| Trend | -0.8% |
| Downside Risk | 49.4% |
| Upside Potential | 121.9% |
| Space Required | 1920 Sq. Ft. |

## SOURCE AND USE OF CAPITAL

| Capital Source | | Capital Use | |
|---|---|---|---|
| Owner's Equity | $108,500 | Working Capital | $ 98,500 |
| Long Term Debt | $ 20,750 | Long Term Assets | $ 30,750 |
| Total Capital Requ'd | $129,250 | Total Capital Used | $129,250 |

## SALES AND INCOME

| | Upper Quartile | Median | Lower Quartile |
|---|---|---|---|
| Sales | 1,075,000 | 800,000 | 625,000 |
| Officer's Salary* | 51,600 | 24,800 | 16,250 |
| Net Profit* | 29,500 | 11,750 | 2,250 |
| Total Income* | 81,100 | 36,550 | 18,500 |

*Before Tax

## PROFITABILITY VS ASSETS

| Assets | 0-250$K | 250-1,000$K | 1-10$M |
|---|---|---|---|
| Profitability | N/A | 28.3% | 19.6% |

**COMMENTS:** *Above average risk - debt is 10 times lower quartile profit. Good potential.*

# SOAP & DETERGENTS (MFG)　　　SIC:2841

| | |
|---|---|
| Total Assets | $250,000 |
| Profitability | 28.1% |
| Trend | -5.5% |
| Downside Risk | 43.2% |
| Upside Potential | 157.7% |
| Space Required | 1560 Sq. Ft. |

## SOURCE AND USE OF CAPITAL

| Capital Source | | Capital Use | |
|---|---|---|---|
| Owner's Equity | $125,750 | Working Capital | $ 78,000 |
| Long Term Debt | $ 35,000 | Long Term Assets | $ 82,750 |
| Total Capital Requ'd | $160,750 | Total Capital Used | $160,750 |

## SALES AND INCOME

| | Upper Quartile | Median | Lower Quartile |
|---|---|---|---|
| Sales | 875,000 | 650,000 | 500,000 |
| Officer's Salary* | 71,750 | 24,050 | 14,500 |
| Net Profit* | 45,000 | 21,250 | 11,250 |
| Total Income* | 116,750 | 45,300 | 25,750 |

*Before Tax

## PROFITABILITY VS ASSETS

| Assets | 0-250$K | 250-1,000$K | 1-10$M |
|---|---|---|---|
| Profitability | N/A | 28.1% | N/A |

**COMMENTS:**　*Strong downturn. Average risk and excellent potential.*




# CONFECTIONERY (WSLE)　　　SIC:5145

| | |
|---|---|
| Total Assets | $250,000 |
| Profitability | 27.8% |
| Trend | - 2.9% |
| Downside Risk | 55.9% |
| Upside Potential | 139.2% |
| Space Required | 1260 Sq. Ft. |

## SOURCE AND USE OF CAPITAL

| Capital Source | | Capital Use | |
|---|---|---|---|
| Owner's Equity | $105,500 | Working Capital | $ 82,000 |
| Long Term Debt | $ 40,000 | Long Term Assets | $ 63,500 |
| Total Capital Requ'd | $145,500 | Total Capital Used | $145,500 |

## SALES AND INCOME

| | Upper Quartile | Median | Lower Quartile |
|---|---|---|---|
| Sales | 1,600,000 | 1,050,000 | 650,000 |
| Officer's Salary* | 64,000 | 19,950 | 9,100 |
| Net Profit* | 32,750 | 20,500 | 8,750 |
| Total Income* | 96,750 | 40,450 | 17,850 |

*Before Tax

## PROFITABILITY VS ASSETS

| Assets | 0-250$K | 250-1,000$K | 1-10$M |
|---|---|---|---|
| Profitability | N/A | 27.8% | 17.0% |

**COMMENTS:**　*Down trend. High risk and good potential.*

| | |
|---|---|
| Total Assets | $250,000 |
| Profitability | 27.8% |
| Trend | +0.9% |
| Downside Risk | 55.5% |
| Upside Potential | 92.1% |
| Space Required | 1680 Sq. Ft. |

### SOURCE AND USE OF CAPITAL

| Capital Source | | Capital Use | |
|---|---|---|---|
| Owner's Equity | $122,250 | Working Capital | $105,500 |
| Long Term Debt | $ 16,500 | Long Term Assets | $ 33,250 |
| Total Capital Requ'd | $138,750 | Total Capital Used | $138,750 |

### SALES AND INCOME

| | Upper Quartile | Median | Lower Quartile |
|---|---|---|---|
| Sales | 850,000 | 700,000 | 425,000 |
| Officer's Salary* | 50,150 | 26,600 | 11,900 |
| Net Profit* | 24,000 | 12,000 | 5,250 |
| Total Income* | 74,150 | 38,600 | 17,150 |

*Before Tax

### PROFITABILITY VS ASSETS

| Assets | 0-250$K | 250-1,000$K | 1-10$M |
|---|---|---|---|
| Profitability | N/A | 27.8% | 27.0% |

**COMMENTS:**　*Above average risk and good potential.*



| | |
|---|---|
| Total Assets | $250,000 |
| Profitability | 27.8% |
| Trend | +4.9% |
| Downside Risk | 48.4% |
| Upside Potential | 67.1% |
| Space Required | 1425 Sq. Ft. |

### SOURCE AND USE OF CAPITAL

| Capital Source | | Capital Use | |
|---|---|---|---|
| Owner's Equity | $101,750 | Working Capital | $ 63,750 |
| Long Term Debt | $ 46,750 | Long Term Assets | $ 84,750 |
| Total Capital Requ'd | $148,500 | Total Capital Used | $148,500 |

### SALES AND INCOME

| | Upper Quartile | Median | Lower Quartile |
|---|---|---|---|
| Sales | 600,000 | 475,000 | 400,000 |
| Officer's Salary* | 31,200 | 18,525 | 12,800 |
| Net Profit* | 37,750 | 22,750 | 8,500 |
| Total Income* | 68,950 | 41,275 | 21,300 |

*Before Tax

### PROFITABILITY VS ASSETS

| Assets | 0-250$K | 250-1,000$K | 1-10$M |
|---|---|---|---|
| Profitability | N/A | 27.8% | N/A |

**COMMENTS:**　*Above average risk, average potential.  Good uptrend.*

# #191     SCRAP METAL (WSLE)     SIC:5093

| | |
|---|---|
| Total Assets | $250,000 |
| Profitability | 27.6% |
| Trend | +1.5% |
| Downside Risk | 61.7% |
| Upside Potential | 140.0% |
| Space Required | 1450 Sq. Ft. |

## SOURCE AND USE OF CAPITAL

| Capital Source | | Capital Use | |
|---|---|---|---|
| Owner's Equity | $111,500 | Working Capital | $ 51,750 |
| Long Term Debt | $ 40,000 | Long Term Assets | $ 99,750 |
| Total Capital Requ'd | $151,500 | Total Capital Used | $151,500 |

## SALES AND INCOME

| | Upper Quartile | Median | Lower Quartile |
|---|---|---|---|
| Sales | 925,000 | 725,000 | 500,000 |
| Officer's Salary* | 72,150 | 26,825 | 11,000 |
| Net Profit* | 28,250 | 15,000 | 5,000 |
| Total Income* | 100,400 | 41,825 | 16,000 |

*Before Tax

## PROFITABILITY VS ASSETS

| Assets | 0-250$K | 250-1,000$K | 1-10$M |
|---|---|---|---|
| Profitability | 57.1% | 27.6% | 17.8% |

**COMMENTS:** *High risk and good potential.*


# #192     WOMENS DRESSES (RTL)     SIC:5621

| | |
|---|---|
| Total Assets | $250,000 |
| Profitability | 27.6% |
| Trend | -2.7% |
| Downside Risk | 51.4% |
| Upside Potential | 105.6% |
| Space Required | 6125 Sq. Ft. |

## SOURCE AND USE OF CAPITAL

| Capital Source | | Capital Use | |
|---|---|---|---|
| Owner's Equity | $116,000 | Working Capital | $ 92,250 |
| Long Term Debt | $ 31,500 | Long Term Assets | $ 55,250 |
| Total Capital Requ'd | $147,500 | Total Capital Used | $147,500 |

## SALES AND INCOME

| | Upper Quartile | Median | Lower Quartile |
|---|---|---|---|
| Sales | 775,000 | 625,000 | 475,000 |
| Officer's Salary* | 55,025 | 25,000 | 13,300 |
| Net Profit* | 28,750 | 15,750 | 6,500 |
| Total Income* | 83,775 | 40,750 | 19,800 |

*Before Tax

## PROFITABILITY VS ASSETS

| Assets | 0-250$K | 250-1,000$K | 1-10$M |
|---|---|---|---|
| Profitability | 44.6% | 27.6% | 23.4% |

**COMMENTS:** *Above average risk and good potential. Moderately high down trend.*

| Total Assets | $250,000 |
|---|---|
| Profitability | 27.5% |
| Trend | +1.4% |
| Downside Risk | 52.2% |
| Upside Potential | 104.9% |
| Space Required | 1330 Sq. Ft. |

### SOURCE AND USE OF CAPITAL

| Capital Source | | Capital Use | |
|---|---|---|---|
| Owner's Equity | $ 75,750 | Working Capital | $ 58,250 |
| Long Term Debt | $ 28,750 | Long Term Assets | $ 46,250 |
| Total Capital Requ'd | $104,500 | Total Capital Used | $104,500 |

### SALES AND INCOME

| | Upper Quartile | Median | Lower Quartile |
|---|---|---|---|
| Sales | 1,275,000 | 950,000 | 675,000 |
| Officer's Salary* | 33,150 | 14,250 | 6,750 |
| Net Profit* | 25,750 | 14,500 | 7,000 |
| Total Income* | 58,900 | 28,750 | 13,750 |

*Before Tax

### PROFITABILITY VS ASSETS

| Assets | 0-250$K | 250-1,000$K | 1-10$M |
|---|---|---|---|
| Profitability | N/A | 27.5% | 25.4% |

**COMMENTS:** *Above average risk and good potential.*




| Total Assets | $250,000 |
|---|---|
| Profitability | 27.5% |
| Trend | +0.7% |
| Downside Risk | 55.6% |
| Upside Potential | 89.4% |
| Space Required | 1935 Sq. Ft. |

### SOURCE AND USE OF CAPITAL

| Capital Source | | Capital Use | |
|---|---|---|---|
| Owner's Equity | $ 78,250 | Working Capital | $ 60,250 |
| Long Term Debt | $ 20,500 | Long Term Assets | $ 38,500 |
| Total Capital Requ'd | $ 98,750 | Total Capital Used | $ 98,750 |

### SALES AND INCOME

| | Upper Quartile | Median | Lower Quartile |
|---|---|---|---|
| Sales | 1,325,000 | 1,075,000 | 850,000 |
| Officer's Salary* | 25,175 | 12,900 | 6,800 |
| Net Profit* | 26,250 | 14,250 | 5,250 |
| Total Income* | 51,425 | 27,150 | 12,050 |

*Before Tax

### PROFITABILITY VS ASSETS

| Assets | 0-250$K | 250-1,000$K | 1-10$M |
|---|---|---|---|
| Profitability | 42.1% | 27.5% | 26.8% |

**COMMENTS:** *High risk and fair potential.*

| | |
|---|---|
| **Total Assets** | $250,000 |
| **Profitability** | 27.5% |
| **Trend** | +2.7% |
| **Downside Risk** | 52.1% |
| **Upside Potential** | 64.0% |
| **Space Required** | 900 Sq. Ft. |

## SOURCE AND USE OF CAPITAL

| Capital Source | | Capital Use | |
|---|---|---|---|
| Owner's Equity | $104,000 | Working Capital | $ 45,500 |
| Long Term Debt | $ 49,750 | Long Term Assets | $108,250 |
| Total Capital Requ'd | $153,750 | Total Capital Used | $153,750 |

## SALES AND INCOME

| | Upper Quartile | Median | Lower Quartile |
|---|---|---|---|
| Sales | 675,000 | 500,000 | 400,000 |
| Officer's Salary* | 31,050 | 17,000 | 8,000 |
| Net Profit* | 38,250 | 25,250 | 12,250 |
| Total Income* | 69,300 | 42,250 | 20,250 |

*Before Tax

## PROFITABILITY VS ASSETS

| Assets | 0-250$K | 250-1,000$K | 1-10$M |
|---|---|---|---|
| Profitability | N/A | 27.5% | 23.5% |

**COMMENTS:**  *Above average risk and average potential.  Good uptrend.*




| | |
|---|---|
| **Total Assets** | $250,000 |
| **Profitability** | 27.4% |
| **Trend** | +2.8% |
| **Downside Risk** | 69.1% |
| **Upside Potential** | 78.4% |
| **Space Required** | 1045 Sq. Ft. |

## SOURCE AND USE OF CAPITAL

| Capital Source | | Capital Use | |
|---|---|---|---|
| Owner's Equity | $ 93,250 | Working Capital | $(16,000) |
| Long Term Debt | $ 67,750 | Long Term Assets | $177,000 |
| Total Capital Requ'd | $161,000 | Total Capital Used | $161,000 |

## SALES AND INCOME

| | Upper Quartile | Median | Lower Quartile |
|---|---|---|---|
| Sales | 400,000 | 275,000 | 150,000 |
| Officer's Salary* | 40,800 | 21,175 | 5,400 |
| Net Profit* | 38,000 | 23,000 | 8,250 |
| Total Income* | 78,800 | 44,175 | 13,650 |

*Before Tax

## PROFITABILITY VS ASSETS

| Assets | 0-250$K | 250-1,000$K | 1-10$M |
|---|---|---|---|
| Profitability | 44.7% | 27.4% | 17.8% |

**COMMENTS:**  *Very high risk; negative working capital helps (see #141).  Average potential.  Good uptrend.*

# FURNITURE (RTL)  SIC:5712

| | |
|---|---|
| Total Assets | $250,000 |
| Profitability | 27.3% |
| Trend | +1.3% |
| Downside Risk | 51.2% |
| Upside Potential | 92.3% |
| Space Required | 3100 Sq. Ft. |

## SOURCE AND USE OF CAPITAL

| Capital Source | | Capital Use | |
|---|---|---|---|
| Owner's Equity | $110,000 | Working Capital | $104,000 |
| Long Term Debt | $ 39,500 | Long Term Assets | $ 45,500 |
| Total Capital Requ'd | $149,500 | Total Capital Used | $149,500 |

## SALES AND INCOME

| | Upper Quartile | Median | Lower Quartile |
|---|---|---|---|
| Sales | 675,000 | 500,000 | 375,000 |
| Officer's Salary* | 50,625 | 24,500 | 13,125 |
| Net Profit* | 27,750 | 16,250 | 6,750 |
| Total Income* | 78,375 | 40,750 | 19,875 |

*Before Tax

## PROFITABILITY VS ASSETS

| Assets | 0-250$K | 250-1,000$K | 1-10$M |
|---|---|---|---|
| Profitability | 45.7% | 27.3% | 19.9% |

**COMMENTS:**  *Above average risk and average potential.*




# COFFEE, TEA & SPICES (WSLE)  SIC:5149

| | |
|---|---|
| Total Assets | $250,000 |
| Profitability | 27.2% |
| Trend | +2.3% |
| Downside Risk | 46.6% |
| Upside Potential | 100.9% |
| Space Required | 1750 Sq. Ft. |

## SOURCE AND USE OF CAPITAL

| Capital Source | | Capital Use | |
|---|---|---|---|
| Owner's Equity | $117,000 | Working Capital | $ 79,750 |
| Long Term Debt | $ 24,000 | Long Term Assets | $ 61,250 |
| Total Capital Requ'd | $141,000 | Total Capital Used | $141,000 |

## SALES AND INCOME

| | Upper Quartile | Median | Lower Quartile |
|---|---|---|---|
| Sales | 1,225,000 | 875,000 | 700,000 |
| Officer's Salary* | 42,875 | 16,625 | 10,500 |
| Net Profit* | 34,250 | 21,750 | 10,000 |
| Total Income* | 77,125 | 38,375 | 20,500 |

*Before Tax

## PROFITABILITY VS ASSETS

| Assets | 0-250$K | 250-1,000$K | 1-10$M |
|---|---|---|---|
| Profitability | N/A | N/A | 35.1% |

**COMMENTS:**  *Good uptrend.  Above average risk and average potential.*

# #199  REAL ESTATE AGENTS & BROKERS (SVE) SIC:6531

| | |
|---|---|
| Total Assets | $250,000 |
| Profitability | 26.9% |
| Trend | +6.6% |
| Downside Risk | 85.5% |
| Upside Potential | 253.4% |
| Space Required | 1320 Sq. Ft. |

### SOURCE AND USE OF CAPITAL

| Capital Source | | Capital Use | |
|---|---|---|---|
| Owner's Equity | $ 89,750 | Working Capital | $ 14,750 |
| Long Term Debt | $ 57,750 | Long Term Assets | $132,750 |
| Total Capital Requ'd | $147,500 | Total Capital Used | $147,500 |

### SALES AND INCOME

| | Upper Quartile | Median | Lower Quartile |
|---|---|---|---|
| Sales | 600,000 | 275,000 | 50,000 |
| Officer's Salary* | 106,200 | 26,675 | 2,250 |
| Net Profit* | 34,000 | 13,000 | 3,500 |
| Total Income* | 140,200 | 39,675 | 5,750 |

*Before Tax

### PROFITABILITY VS ASSETS

| Assets | 0-250$K | 250-1,000$K | 1-10$M |
|---|---|---|---|
| Profitability | 175.6% | 26.9% | 14.6% |

**COMMENTS:**  *This business is a special case.  Depreciation of property owned by agents and brokers shields true income.  Otherwise lower quartile could not support such high L. T. debt.*

# #200  SPECIAL INDUSTRIAL MACHINERY (MFG) SIC:3551-55,59

| | |
|---|---|
| Total Assets | $250,000 |
| Profitability | 26.8% |
| Trend | +0.1% |
| Downside Risk | 44.6% |
| Upside Potential | 143.4% |
| Space Required | 1500 Sq. Ft. |

### SOURCE AND USE OF CAPITAL

| Capital Source | | Capital Use | |
|---|---|---|---|
| Owner's Equity | $111,250 | Working Capital | $ 73,500 |
| Long Term Debt | $ 44,500 | Long Term Assets | $ 82,250 |
| Total Capital Requ'd | $155,750 | Total Capital Used | $155,750 |

### SALES AND INCOME

| | Upper Quartile | Median | Lower Quartile |
|---|---|---|---|
| Sales | 700,000 | 500,000 | 400,000 |
| Officer's Salary* | 54,600 | 21,500 | 10,400 |
| Net Profit* | 47,000 | 20,250 | 12,750 |
| Total Income* | 101,600 | 41,750 | 23,150 |

*Before Tax

### PROFITABILITY VS ASSETS

| Assets | 0-250$K | 250-1,000$K | 1-10$M |
|---|---|---|---|
| Profitability | 47.4% | 26.8% | 28.8% |

**COMMENTS:**  *Above average risk, but excellent potential.*

# #201    ENAMELED PLUMBING FIXTURES (MFG) SIC:3431,32

|                 |               |
|-----------------|---------------|
| Total Assets    | $250,000      |
| Profitability   | 26.8%         |
| Trend           | -2.4%         |
| Downside Risk   | 58.9%         |
| Upside Potential| 87.9%         |
| Space Required  | 1235 Sq. Ft.  |

## SOURCE AND USE OF CAPITAL

| Capital Source      |           | Capital Use        |           |
|---------------------|-----------|--------------------|-----------|
| Owner's Equity      | $123,750  | Working Capital    | $ 84,000  |
| Long Term Debt      | $ 36,000  | Long Term Assets   | $ 75,750  |
| Total Capital Requ'd| $159,750  | Total Capital Used | $159,750  |

## SALES AND INCOME

|                  | Upper Quartile | Median  | Lower Quartile |
|------------------|----------------|---------|----------------|
| Sales            | 625,000        | 475,000 | 400,000        |
| Officer's Salary*| 34,375         | 13,775  | 7,600          |
| Net Profit*      | 46,000         | 29,000  | 10,000         |
| Total Income*    | 80,375         | 42,775  | 17,600         |

*Before Tax

## PROFITABILITY VS ASSETS

| Assets        | 0-250$K | 250-1,000$K | 1-10$M |
|---------------|---------|-------------|--------|
| Profitability | N/A     | 26.8%       | N/A    |

COMMENTS: *Down trend. Very high risk and good potential.*


# #202    LOCAL TRUCKING & STORAGE (SVE)   SIC:4214

|                 |               |
|-----------------|---------------|
| Total Assets    | $250,000      |
| Profitability   | 26.7%         |
| Trend           | +0.7%         |
| Downside Risk   | 55.3%         |
| Upside Potential| 112.9%        |
| Space Required  | 4620 Sq. Ft.  |

## SOURCE AND USE OF CAPITAL

| Capital Source      |           | Capital Use        |           |
|---------------------|-----------|--------------------|-----------|
| Owner's Equity      | $103,250  | Working Capital    | $ 14,500  |
| Long Term Debt      | $ 53,500  | Long Term Assets   | $142,250  |
| Total Capital Requ'd| $156,750  | Total Capital Used | $156,750  |

## SALES AND INCOME

|                  | Upper Quartile | Median  | Lower Quartile |
|------------------|----------------|---------|----------------|
| Sales            | 750,000        | 500,000 | 400,000        |
| Officer's Salary*| 57,750         | 28,050  | 15,200         |
| Net Profit*      | 31,250         | 13,750  | 3,500          |
| Total Income*    | 89,000         | 41,800  | 18,700         |

*Before Tax

## PROFITABILITY VS ASSETS

| Assets        | 0-250$K | 250-1,000$K | 1-10$M |
|---------------|---------|-------------|--------|
| Profitability | 28.0%   | 26.7%       | N/A    |

COMMENTS: *Above average risk and good potential.*

# #203  SOFT DRINK BOTTLER (MFG) SIC:2086,5149,5812

| | |
|---|---|
| Total Assets | $250,000 |
| Profitability | 26.7% |
| Trend | -3.3% |
| Downside Risk | 57.9% |
| Upside Potential | 77.9% |
| Space Required | 840 Sq. Ft. |

## SOURCE AND USE OF CAPITAL

| Capital Source | | Capital Use | |
|---|---|---|---|
| Owner's Equity | $127,250 | Working Capital | $ 48,250 |
| Long Term Debt | $ 46,250 | Long Term Assets | $125,250 |
| Total Capital Requ'd | $173,500 | Total Capital Used | $173,500 |

## SALES AND INCOME

| | Upper Quartile | Median | Lower Quartile |
|---|---|---|---|
| Sales | 875,000 | 700,000 | 500,000 |
| Officer's Salary* | 35,875 | 16,800 | 7,500 |
| Net Profit* | 46,500 | 29,500 | 12,000 |
| Total Income* | 82,375 | 46,300 | 19,500 |

*Before Tax

## PROFITABILITY VS ASSETS

| Assets | 0-250$K | 250-1,000$K | 1-10$M |
|---|---|---|---|
| Profitability | N/A | 26.7% | 22.3% |

**COMMENTS:**  *Moderately high down trend.  High risk and good potential.*


# #204  LIQUOR (RTL)  SIC:5921

| | |
|---|---|
| Total Assets | $250,000 |
| Profitability | 26.5% |
| Trend | +2.5% |
| Downside Risk | 60.3% |
| Upside Potential | 157.2% |
| Space Required | 2145 Sq. Ft. |

## SOURCE AND USE OF CAPITAL

| Capital Source | | Capital Use | |
|---|---|---|---|
| Owner's Equity | $ 90,500 | Working Capital | $ 58,000 |
| Long Term Debt | $ 54,500 | Long Term Assets | $ 87,000 |
| Total Capital Requ'd | $145,000 | Total Capital Used | $145,000 |

## SALES AND INCOME

| | Upper Quartile | Median | Lower Quartile |
|---|---|---|---|
| Sales | 1,450,000 | 975,000 | 750,000 |
| Officer's Salary* | 53,650 | 21,450 | 10,500 |
| Net Profit* | 45,250 | 17,000 | 4,750 |
| Total Income* | 98,900 | 38,450 | 15,250 |

*Before Tax

## PROFITABILITY VS ASSETS

| Assets | 0-250$K | 250-1,000$K | 1-10$M |
|---|---|---|---|
| Profitability | 44.2% | 26.5% | 26.1% |

**COMMENTS:**  *Up trend.  High risk but good potential.*

# #205     AM RADIO STATION (SVE)     SIC:4832

| | |
|---|---|
| Total Assets | $250,000 |
| Profitability | 26.4% |
| Trend | +3.2% |
| Downside Risk | 41.8% |
| Upside Potential | 130.8% |
| Space Required | 1100 Sq. Ft. |

## SOURCE AND USE OF CAPITAL

| Capital Source | | Capital Use | |
|---|---|---|---|
| Owner's Equity | $100,000 | Working Capital | $ 34,000 |
| Long Term Debt | $ 99,500 | Long Term Assets | $165,500 |
| Total Capital Requ'd | $199,500 | Total Capital Used | $199,500 |

## SALES AND INCOME

| | Upper Quartile | Median | Lower Quartile |
|---|---|---|---|
| Sales | 450,000 | 275,000 | 225,000 |
| Officer's Salary* | 66,150 | 25,850 | 17,100 |
| Net Profit* | 55,250 | 26,750 | 13,500 |
| Total Income* | 121,400 | 52,600 | 30,600 |

*Before Tax

## PROFITABILITY VS ASSETS

| Assets | 0-250$K | 250-1,000$K | 1-10$M |
|---|---|---|---|
| Profitability | N/A | 26.4% | N/A |

COMMENTS: *High risk but excellent potential.*


# #206     OUTDOOR ADVERTISING (SVE)     SIC:7312

| | |
|---|---|
| Total Assets | $250,000 |
| Profitability | 26.3% |
| Trend | +3.3% |
| Downside Risk | 77.2% |
| Upside Potential | 113.1% |
| Space Required | 4680 Sq. Ft. |

## SOURCE AND USE OF CAPITAL

| Capital Source | | Capital Use | |
|---|---|---|---|
| Owner's Equity | $105,500 | Working Capital | $ 5,750 |
| Long Term Debt | $ 68,750 | Long Term Assets | $168,500 |
| Total Capital Requ'd | $174,250 | Total Capital Used | $174,250 |

## SALES AND INCOME

| | Upper Quartile | Median | Lower Quartile |
|---|---|---|---|
| Sales | 425,000 | 325,000 | 225,000 |
| Officer's Salary* | 53,550 | 23,400 | 7,200 |
| Net Profit* | 44,250 | 22,500 | 3,250 |
| Total Income* | 97,800 | 45,900 | 10,450 |

*Before Tax

## PROFITABILITY VS ASSETS

| Assets | 0-250$K | 250-1,000$K | 1-10$M |
|---|---|---|---|
| Profitability | N/A | 26.3% | N/A |

COMMENTS: *Very high risk but good potential. Good uptrend.*

## #207  FLOWERS & SUPPLIES (WSLE)  SIC:5199

| | |
|---|---|
| Total Assets | $250,000 |
| Profitability | 26.1% |
| Trend | -1.3% |
| Downside Risk | 53.5% |
| Upside Potential | 95.8% |
| Space Required | 2250 Sq. Ft. |

### SOURCE AND USE OF CAPITAL

| Capital Source | | Capital Use | |
|---|---|---|---|
| Owner's Equity | $108,250 | Working Capital | $ 76,750 |
| Long Term Debt | $ 50,250 | Long Term Assets | $ 81,750 |
| Total Capital Requ'd | $158,500 | Total Capital Used | $158,500 |

### SALES AND INCOME

| | Upper Quartile | Median | Lower Quartile |
|---|---|---|---|
| Sales | 825,000 | 625,000 | 475,000 |
| Officer's Salary* | 57,750 | 25,625 | 14,250 |
| Net Profit* | 23,250 | 15,750 | 5,000 |
| Total Income* | 81,000 | 41,375 | 19,250 |

*Before Tax

### PROFITABILITY VS ASSETS

| Assets | 0-250$K | 250-1,000$K | 1-10$M |
|---|---|---|---|
| Profitability | N/A | 26.1% | 24.0% |

**COMMENTS:** *Very high risk and good potential.*


## #208  FAMILY CLOTHING (RTL)  SIC:5651

| | |
|---|---|
| Total Assets | $250,000 |
| Profitability | 26.0% |
| Trend | -0.1% |
| Downside Risk | 54.3% |
| Upside Potential | 97.9% |
| Space Required | 3520 Sq. Ft. |

### SOURCE AND USE OF CAPITAL

| Capital Source | | Capital Use | |
|---|---|---|---|
| Owner's Equity | $109,250 | Working Capital | $ 97,000 |
| Long Term Debt | $ 43,000 | Long Term Assets | $ 55,250 |
| Total Capital Requ'd | $152,250 | Total Capital Used | $152,250 |

### SALES AND INCOME

| | Upper Quartile | Median | Lower Quartile |
|---|---|---|---|
| Sales | 725,000 | 550,000 | 425,000 |
| Officer's Salary* | 48,575 | 24,200 | 11,900 |
| Net Profit* | 30,000 | 15,500 | 6,250 |
| Total Income* | 78,575 | 39,700 | 18,150 |

*Before Tax

### PROFITABILITY VS ASSETS

| Assets | 0-250$K | 250-1,000$K | 1-10$M |
|---|---|---|---|
| Profitability | 36.4% | 26.0% | 20.2% |

**COMMENTS:** *Very high risk and good potential.*

| Total Assets | $250,000 |
| Profitability | 25.8% |
| Trend | +1.0% |
| Downside Risk | 77.1% |
| Upside Potential | 116.8% |
| Space Required | 1540 Sq. Ft. |

### SOURCE AND USE OF CAPITAL

| Capital Source | | Capital Use | |
|---|---|---|---|
| Owner's Equity | $ 93,500 | Working Capital | $ 39,750 |
| Long Term Debt | $ 52,250 | Long Term Assets | $106,000 |
| Total Capital Requ'd | $145,750 | Total Capital Used | $145,750 |

### SALES AND INCOME

| | Upper Quartile | Median | Lower Quartile |
|---|---|---|---|
| Sales | 725,000 | 550,000 | 425,000 |
| Officer's Salary* | 50,750 | 17,600 | 6,375 |
| Net Profit* | 30,750 | 20,000 | 2,250 |
| Total Income* | 81,500 | 37,600 | 8,625 |

*Before Tax

### PROFITABILITY VS ASSETS

| Assets | 0-250$K | 250-1,000$K | 1-10$M |
|---|---|---|---|
| Profitability | N/A | 25.8% | 25.5% |

**COMMENTS:**  *Excessively high risk and good potential.*


#210  WOMEN'S UNDERGARMENTS & SLEEPWEAR (MFG)

| Total Assets | $250,000 |
| Profitability | 25.7% |
| Trend | -2.9% |
| Downside Risk | 50.0% |
| Upside Potential | 135.3% |
| Space Required | 1035 Sq. Ft. |

SIC:2341

### SOURCE AND USE OF CAPITAL

| Capital Source | | Capital Use | |
|---|---|---|---|
| Owner's Equity | $109,500 | Working Capital | $ 83,500 |
| Long Term Debt | $ 28,500 | Long Term Assets | $ 54,500 |
| Total Capital Requ'd | $138,000 | Total Capital Used | $138,000 |

### SALES AND INCOME

| | Upper Quartile | Median | Lower Quartile |
|---|---|---|---|
| Sales | 675,000 | 575,000 | 500,000 |
| Officer's Salary* | 42,525 | 11,500 | 5,500 |
| Net Profit* | 41,000 | 24,000 | 12,250 |
| Total Income* | 83,525 | 35,500 | 17,750 |

*Before Tax

### PROFITABILITY VS ASSETS

| Assets | 0-250$K | 250-1,000$K | 1-10$M |
|---|---|---|---|
| Profitability | N/A | 25.7% | 22.1% |

**COMMENTS:**  *High risk and good potential.*

## #211      REFUSE SYSTEMS (SVE)      SIC:4953

| | |
|---|---|
| Total Assets | $250,000 |
| Profitability | 25.5% |
| Trend | +0.5% |
| Downside Risk | 42.1% |
| Upside Potential | 122.3% |
| Space Required | 1120 Sq. Ft. |

### SOURCE AND USE OF CAPITAL

| Capital Source | | Capital Use | |
|---|---|---|---|
| Owner's Equity | $ 76,000 | Working Capital | $ (20,250) |
| Long Term Debt | $ 90,500 | Long Term Assets | $186,750 |
| Total Capital Requ'd | $166,500 | Total Capital Used | $166,500 |

### SALES AND INCOME

| | Upper Quartile | Median | Lower Quartile |
|---|---|---|---|
| Sales | 525,000 | 350,000 | 300,000 |
| Officer's Salary* | 42,000 | 13,650 | 7,800 |
| Net Profit* | 52,250 | 28,750 | 16,750 |
| Total Income* | 94,250 | 42,400 | 24,550 |

*Before Tax

### PROFITABILITY VS ASSETS

| Assets | 0-250$K | 250-1,000$K | 1-10$M |
|---|---|---|---|
| Profitability | N/A | 25.5% | N/A |

**COMMENTS:** *Very high risk, although negative working capital helps (see #139). Good potential.*

## #212      FUEL OIL (WSLE)      SIC:5172

| | |
|---|---|
| Total Assets | $250,000 |
| Profitability | 25.5% |
| Trend | +0.2% |
| Downside Risk | 57.3% |
| Upside Potential | 104.5% |
| Space Required | 1350 Sq. Ft. |

### SOURCE AND USE OF CAPITAL

| Capital Source | | Capital Use | |
|---|---|---|---|
| Owner's Equity | $ 87,000 | Working Capital | $ 25,750 |
| Long Term Debt | $ 39,750 | Long Term Assets | $101,000 |
| Total Capital Requ'd | $126,750 | Total Capital Used | $126,750 |

### SALES AND INCOME

| | Upper Quartile | Median | Lower Quartile |
|---|---|---|---|
| Sales | 1,575,000 | 1,125,000 | 825,000 |
| Officer's Salary* | 40,950 | 16,875 | 9,075 |
| Net Profit* | 25,250 | 15,500 | 4,750 |
| Total Income* | 66,200 | 32,375 | 13,825 |

*Before Tax

### PROFITABILITY VS ASSETS

| Assets | 0-250$K | 250-1,000$K | 1-10$M |
|---|---|---|---|
| Profitability | 52.3% | 25.5% | 20.9% |

**COMMENTS:** *High risk and average potential.*

| | |
|---|---|
| **Total Assets** | $250,000 |
| **Profitability** | 25.3% |
| **Trend** | N/A |
| **Downside Risk** | 42.7% |
| **Upside Potential** | 89.5% |
| **Space Required** | 500 Sq. Ft. |

## SOURCE AND USE OF CAPITAL

| Capital Source | | Capital Use | |
|---|---|---|---|
| Owner's Equity | $104,250 | Working Capital | $ 67,250 |
| Long Term Debt | $ 36,000 | Long Term Assets | $ 73,000 |
| Total Capital Requ'd | $140,250 | Total Capital Used | $140,250 |

## SALES AND INCOME

| | Upper Quartile | Median | Lower Quartile |
|---|---|---|---|
| Sales | 825,000 | 625,000 | 475,000 |
| Officer's Salary* | 38,775 | 17,500 | 8,075 |
| Net Profit* | 28,500 | 18,000 | 12,250 |
| Total Income* | 67,275 | 35,500 | 20,325 |

*Before Tax

## PROFITABILITY VS ASSETS

| Assets | 0-250$K | 250-1,000$K | 1-10$M |
|---|---|---|---|
| Profitability | N/A | 25.3% | N/A |

**COMMENTS:**   *High risk and average potential.*

#214        **NARROW FABRICS (MFG)**                **SIC:2241**

| | |
|---|---|
| **Total Assets** | $250,000 |
| **Profitability** | 25.3% |
| **Trend** | -0.3% |
| **Downside Risk** | 50.8% |
| **Upside Potential** | 64.1% |
| **Space Required** | 880 Sq. Ft. |

## SOURCE AND USE OF CAPITAL

| Capital Source | | Capital Use | |
|---|---|---|---|
| Owner's Equity | $134,500 | Working Capital | $ 88,000 |
| Long Term Debt | $ 31,000 | Long Term Assets | $ 77,500 |
| Total Capital Requ'd | $165,500 | Total Capital Used | $165,500 |

## SALES AND INCOME

| | Upper Quartile | Median | Lower Quartile |
|---|---|---|---|
| Sales | 700,000 | 550,000 | 425,000 |
| Officer's Salary* | 28,000 | 15,400 | 6,375 |
| Net Profit* | 40,750 | 26,500 | 14,250 |
| Total Income* | 68,750 | 41,900 | 20,625 |

*Before Tax

## PROFITABILITY VS ASSETS

| Assets | 0-250$K | 250-1,000$K | 1-10$M |
|---|---|---|---|
| Profitability | N/A | 25.3% | 26.1% |

**COMMENTS:**   *High risk and low potential.*

| | |
|---|---|
| Total Assets | $250,000 |
| Profitability | 25.1% |
| Trend | +2.2% |
| Downside Risk | 89.5% |
| Upside Potential | 184.9% |
| Space Required | 2070 Sq. Ft. |

## SOURCE AND USE OF CAPITAL

| Capital Source | | Capital Use | |
|---|---|---|---|
| Owner's Equity | $ 79,000 | Working Capital | $ 5,250 |
| Long Term Debt | $ 67,500 | Long Term Assets | $141,250 |
| Total Capital Requ'd | $146,500 | Total Capital Used | $146,500 |

## SALES AND INCOME

| | Upper Quartile | Median | Lower Quartile |
|---|---|---|---|
| Sales | 1,825,000 | 1,150,000 | 700,000 |
| Officer's Salary* | 74,825 | 20,700 | 5,600 |
| Net Profit* | 29,750 | 16,000 | (1,750) |
| Total Income* | 104,575 | 36,700 | 3,850 |

*Before Tax

## PROFITABILITY VS ASSETS

| Assets | 0-250$K | 250-1,000$K | 1-10$M |
|---|---|---|---|
| Profitability | 80.3% | 25.1% | 16.6% |

**COMMENTS:** *Very, very high risk, but excellent potential.*



| | |
|---|---|
| Total Assets | $250,000 |
| Profitability | 25.0% |
| Trend | +0.4% |
| Downside Risk | 57.6% |
| Upside Potential | 204.2% |
| Space Required | 1750 Sq. Ft. |

## SOURCE AND USE OF CAPITAL

| Capital Source | | Capital Use | |
|---|---|---|---|
| Owner's Equity | $116,250 | Working Capital | $ 69,750 |
| Long Term Debt | $ 27,500 | Long Term Assets | $ 74,000 |
| Total Capital Requ'd | $143,750 | Total Capital Used | $143,750 |

## SALES AND INCOME

| | Upper Quartile | Median | Lower Quartile |
|---|---|---|---|
| Sales | 850,000 | 625,000 | 450,000 |
| Officer's Salary* | 72,250 | 21,250 | 11,250 |
| Net Profit* | 37,250 | 14,750 | 4,000 |
| Total Income* | 109,500 | 36,000 | 15,250 |

*Before Tax

## PROFITABILITY VS ASSETS

| Assets | 0-250$K | 250-1,000$K | 1-10$M |
|---|---|---|---|
| Profitability | N/A | 25.0% | N/A |

**COMMENTS:** *High risk but excellent potential.*

## #217    TOBACCO (EXCEPT LEAF) (WSLE)    SIC:5194

| | |
|---|---|
| Total Assets | $250,000 |
| Profitability | 25.0% |
| Trend | -1.3% |
| Downside Risk | 62.3% |
| Upside Potential | 76.7% |
| Space Required | 1125 Sq. Ft. |

### SOURCE AND USE OF CAPITAL

| Capital Source | | Capital Use | |
|---|---|---|---|
| Owner's Equity | $116,750 | Working Capital | $ 99,250 |
| Long Term Debt | $ 25,250 | Long Term Assets | $ 42,750 |
| Total Capital Requ'd | $142,000 | Total Capital Used | $142,000 |

### SALES AND INCOME

| | Upper Quartile | Median | Lower Quartile |
|---|---|---|---|
| Sales | 2,375,000 | 1,875,000 | 1,325,000 |
| Officer's Salary* | 33,250 | 18,750 | 6,625 |
| Net Profit* | 29,500 | 16,750 | 6,750 |
| Total Income* | 62,750 | 35,500 | 13,375 |

*Before Tax

### PROFITABILITY VS ASSETS

| Assets | 0-250$K | 250-1,000$K | 1-10$M |
|---|---|---|---|
| Profitability | N/A | 25.0% | 21.4% |

**COMMENTS:**  *Very high risk, average potential.*


## #218    READY MIXED CONCRETE (MFG)    SIC:3273

| | |
|---|---|
| Total Assets | $250,000 |
| Profitability | 24.9% |
| Trend | +2.8% |
| Downside Risk | 44.9% |
| Upside Potential | 87.0% |
| Space Required | 1050 Sq. Ft. |

### SOURCE AND USE OF CAPITAL

| Capital Source | | Capital Use | |
|---|---|---|---|
| Owner's Equity | $106,500 | Working Capital | $ 24,750 |
| Long Term Debt | $ 50,250 | Long Term Assets | $132,000 |
| Total Capital Requ'd | $156,750 | Total Capital Used | $156,750 |

### SALES AND INCOME

| | Upper Quartile | Median | Lower Quartile |
|---|---|---|---|
| Sales | 725,000 | 525,000 | 450,000 |
| Officer's Salary* | 36,975 | 16,275 | 9,000 |
| Net Profit* | 36,000 | 22,750 | 12,500 |
| Total Income* | 72,975 | 39,025 | 21,500 |

*Before Tax

### PROFITABILITY VS ASSETS

| Assets | 0-250$K | 250-1,000$K | 1-10$M |
|---|---|---|---|
| Profitability | N/A | 24.9% | 24.2% |

**COMMENTS:**  *Uptrend. High risk and average potential.*

# #219 WOMEN'S SUITS,SKIRTS,COATS & SPORTSWEAR (MFG)

| | | SIC:2337,39 |
|---|---|---|
| Total Assets | $250,000 | |
| Profitability | 24.7% | |
| Trend | -1.5% | |
| Downside Risk | 60.7% | |
| Upside Potential | 116.6% | |
| Space Required | 1755 Sq. Ft. | |

## SOURCE AND USE OF CAPITAL

| Capital Source | | Capital Use | |
|---|---|---|---|
| Owner's Equity | $109,250 | Working Capital | $ 92,750 |
| Long Term Debt | $ 25,750 | Long Term Assets | $ 42,250 |
| Total Capital Requ'd | $135,000 | Total Capital Used | $135,000 |

## SALES AND INCOME

| | Upper Quartile | Median | Lower Quartile |
|---|---|---|---|
| Sales | 800,000 | 675,000 | 525,000 |
| Officer's Salary* | 48,800 | 23,625 | 12,600 |
| Net Profit* | 23,500 | 9,750 | 500 |
| Total Income* | 72,300 | 33,375 | 13,100 |

*Before Tax

## PROFITABILITY VS ASSETS

| Assets | 0-250$K | 250-1,000$K | 1-10$M |
|---|---|---|---|
| Profitability | 57.1% | 24.7% | 31.9% |

**COMMENTS:** *Very high risk and average potential.*


# #220 BEEF CATTLE FEEDLOTS (SVE)

| | | SIC:0211 |
|---|---|---|
| Total Assets | $250,000 | |
| Profitability | 24.6% | |
| Trend | +4.9% | |
| Downside Risk | 73.6% | |
| Upside Potential | 75.4% | |
| Space Required | 285 Sq. Ft. | |

## SOURCE AND USE OF CAPITAL

| Capital Source | | Capital Use | |
|---|---|---|---|
| Owner's Equity | $ 79,000 | Working Capital | $ 31,250 |
| Long Term Debt | $ 42,500 | Long Term Assets | $ 90,250 |
| Total Capital Requ'd | $121,500 | Total Capital Used | $121,500 |

## SALES AND INCOME

| | Upper Quartile | Median | Lower Quartile |
|---|---|---|---|
| Sales | 675,000 | 475,000 | 225,000 |
| Officer's Salary* | 18,900 | 7,125 | 1,125 |
| Net Profit* | 33,500 | 22,750 | 6,750 |
| Total Income* | 52,400 | 29,875 | 7,875 |

*Before Tax

## PROFITABILITY VS ASSETS

| Assets | 0-250$K | 250-1,000$K | 1-10$M |
|---|---|---|---|
| Profitability | N/A | 24.6% | 23.0% |

**COMMENTS:** *Good uptrend. Very, very high risk and poor potential.*

## LONG DISTANCE TRUCKING (SVE)  SIC:4213

| | |
|---|---|
| Total Assets | $250,000 |
| Profitability | 24.5% |
| Trend | -0.3% |
| Downside Risk | 55.7% |
| Upside Potential | 113.3% |
| Space Required | 1495 Sq. Ft. |

### SOURCE AND USE OF CAPITAL

| Capital Source | | Capital Use | |
|---|---|---|---|
| Owner's Equity | $ 87,750 | Working Capital | $ (9,750) |
| Long Term Debt | $ 60,750 | Long Term Assets | $158,250 |
| Total Capital Requ'd | $148,500 | Total Capital Used | $148,500 |

### SALES AND INCOME

| | Upper Quartile | Median | Lower Quartile |
|---|---|---|---|
| Sales | 750,000 | 575,000 | 450,000 |
| Officer's Salary* | 47,250 | 20,700 | 9,900 |
| Net Profit* | 30,500 | 15,750 | 6,250 |
| Total Income* | 77,750 | 36,450 | 16,150 |

*Before Tax

### PROFITABILITY VS ASSETS

| Assets | 0-250$K | 250-1,000$K | 1-10$M |
|---|---|---|---|
| Profitability | 48.7% | 24.5% | 22.6% |

**COMMENTS:**  *High risk and average potential.*




## FEED & SEED SUPPLY (RTL)  SIC:5261

| | |
|---|---|
| Total Assets | $250,000 |
| Profitability | 24.4% |
| Trend | -1.3% |
| Downside Risk | 63.4% |
| Upside Potential | 134.6% |
| Space Required | 1170 Sq. Ft. |

### SOURCE AND USE OF CAPITAL

| Capital Source | | Capital Use | |
|---|---|---|---|
| Owner's Equity | $ 92,500 | Working Capital | $ 61,000 |
| Long Term Debt | $ 54,250 | Long Term Assets | $ 85,750 |
| Total Capital Requ'd | $146,750 | Total Capital Used | $146,750 |

### SALES AND INCOME

| | Upper Quartile | Median | Lower Quartile |
|---|---|---|---|
| Sales | 875,000 | 650,000 | 450,000 |
| Officer's Salary* | 53,375 | 22,750 | 10,350 |
| Net Profit* | 30,500 | 13,000 | 2,750 |
| Total Income* | 83,875 | 35,750 | 13,100 |

*Before Tax

### PROFITABILITY VS ASSETS

| Assets | 0-250$K | 250-1,000$K | 1-10$M |
|---|---|---|---|
| Profitability | 42.5% | 24.4% | 18.0% |

**COMMENTS:**  *Down trend.  Very, very high risk and good potential.*

# FUNERAL SERVICES (SVE)                SIC:7261

| | |
|---|---|
| Total Assets | $250,000 |
| Profitability | 24.4% |
| Trend | -1.7% |
| Downside Risk | 56.1% |
| Upside Potential | 121.7% |
| Space Required | 2000 Sq. Ft. |

## SOURCE AND USE OF CAPITAL

| Capital Source | | Capital Use | |
|---|---|---|---|
| Owner's Equity | $108,500 | Working Capital | $ 11,000 |
| Long Term Debt | $ 80,250 | Long Term Assets | $177,750 |
| Total Capital Requ'd | $188,750 | Total Capital Used | $188,750 |

## SALES AND INCOME

| | Upper Quartile | Median | Lower Quartile |
|---|---|---|---|
| Sales | 350,000 | 250,000 | 175,000 |
| Officer's Salary* | 75,250 | 34,500 | 17,675 |
| Net Profit* | 26,750 | 11,500 | 2,500 |
| Total Income* | 102,000 | 46,000 | 20,175 |

*Before Tax

## PROFITABILITY VS ASSETS

| Assets | 0-250$K | 250-1,000$K | 1-10$M |
|---|---|---|---|
| Profitability | 41.9% | 24.4% | N/A |

**COMMENTS:**   *Down trend.  Above average risk and excellent potential.*




# METAL HOUSEHOLD FURNITURE (MFG)          SIC:2514

| | |
|---|---|
| Total Assets | $250,000 |
| Profitability | 24.1% |
| Trend | -0.7% |
| Downside Risk | 62.6% |
| Upside Potential | 157.8% |
| Space Required | 660 Sq. Ft. |

## SOURCE AND USE OF CAPITAL

| Capital Source | | Capital Use | |
|---|---|---|---|
| Owner's Equity | $ 98,500 | Working Capital | $ 65,750 |
| Long Term Debt | $ 41,000 | Long Term Assets | $ 73,750 |
| Total Capital Requ'd | $139,500 | Total Capital Used | $139,500 |

## SALES AND INCOME

| | Upper Quartile | Median | Lower Quartile |
|---|---|---|---|
| Sales | 750,000 | 550,000 | 450,000 |
| Officer's Salary* | 49,500 | 15,400 | 5,850 |
| Net Profit* | 37,250 | 18,250 | 6,750 |
| Total Income* | 86,750 | 33,650 | 12,600 |

*Before Tax

## PROFITABILITY VS ASSETS

| Assets | 0-250$K | 250-1,000$K | 1-10$M |
|---|---|---|---|
| Profitability | N/A | 24.1% | N/A |

**COMMENTS:**   *Very, very high risk and good potential.*

| | |
|---|---|
| Total Assets | $250,000 |
| Profitability | 24.0% |
| Trend | -5.2% |
| Downside Risk | 45.9% |
| Upside Potential | 105.8% |
| Space Required | 3240 Sq. Ft. |

## SOURCE AND USE OF CAPITAL

| Capital Source | | Capital Use | |
|---|---|---|---|
| Owner's Equity | $ 87,500 | Working Capital | $ 26,000 |
| Long Term Debt | $ 58,750 | Long Term Assets | $120,250 |
| Total Capital Requ'd | $146,250 | Total Capital Used | $146,250 |

## SALES AND INCOME

| | Upper Quartile | Median | Lower Quartile |
|---|---|---|---|
| Sales | 2,125,000 | 1,350,000 | 950,000 |
| Officer's Salary* | 51,000 | 21,600 | 9,500 |
| Net Profit* | 21,250 | 13,500 | 9,500 |
| Total Income* | 72,250 | 35,100 | 19,000 |

*Before Tax

## PROFITABILITY VS ASSETS

| Assets | 0-250$K | 250-1,000$K | 1-10$M |
|---|---|---|---|
| Profitability | 53.4% | 24.0% | N/A |

**COMMENTS:**  *Strong down trend.  High risk and good potential.*


#226    **FLAVORING EXTRACTS & SYRUPS (MFG)**   SIC:2087

| | |
|---|---|
| Total Assets | $250,000 |
| Profitability | 23.8% |
| Trend | -4.7% |
| Downside Risk | 42.4% |
| Upside Potential | 206.2% |
| Space Required | 1000 Sq. Ft. |

## SOURCE AND USE OF CAPITAL

| Capital Source | | Capital Use | |
|---|---|---|---|
| Owner's Equity | $146,250 | Working Capital | $ 90,250 |
| Long Term Debt | $ 43,250 | Long Term Assets | $ 99,250 |
| Total Capital Requ'd | $189,500 | Total Capital Used | $189,500 |

## SALES AND INCOME

| | Upper Quartile | Median | Lower Quartile |
|---|---|---|---|
| Sales | 675,000 | 525,000 | 400,000 |
| Officer's Salary* | 62,750 | 17,850 | 8,000 |
| Net Profit* | 75,250 | 27,250 | 18,000 |
| Total Income* | 138,000 | 45,100 | 26,000 |

*Before Tax

## PROFITABILITY VS ASSETS

| Assets | 0-250$K | 250-1,000$K | 1-10$M |
|---|---|---|---|
| Profitability | N/A | 23.8% | N/A |

**COMMENTS:**  *Strong down trend.  Above average risk but excellent potential.*

## MOTOR VEHICLES (MFG)                SIC:3711

| | |
|---|---|
| Total Assets | $250,000 |
| Profitability | 23.6% |
| Trend | -0.2% |
| Downside Risk | 56.5% |
| Upside Potential | 156.6% |
| Space Required | 2000 Sq. Ft. |

### SOURCE AND USE OF CAPITAL

| Capital Source | | Capital Use | |
|---|---|---|---|
| Owner's Equity | $ 98,500 | Working Capital | $ 83,250 |
| Long Term Debt | $ 42,000 | Long Term Assets | $ 57,250 |
| Total Capital Requ'd | $140,500 | Total Capital Used | $140,500 |

### SALES AND INCOME

| | Upper Quartile | Median | Lower Quartile |
|---|---|---|---|
| Sales | 750,000 | 625,000 | 425,000 |
| Officer's Salary* | 30,000 | 16,875 | 7,650 |
| Net Profit* | 55,000 | 16,250 | 6,750 |
| Total Income* | 85,000 | 33,125 | 14,400 |

*Before Tax

### PROFITABILITY VS ASSETS

| Assets | 0-250$K | 250-1,000$K | 1-10$M |
|---|---|---|---|
| Profitability | N/A | 23.6% | N/A |

**COMMENTS:**   *Above average risk and good potential.*




## CANNED & CURED FISH (MFG)                SIC:2091

| | |
|---|---|
| Total Assets | $250,000 |
| Profitability | 23.6% |
| Trend | N/A |
| Downside Risk | 80.9% |
| Upside Potential | 122.1% |
| Space Required | 770 Sq. Ft. |

### SOURCE AND USE OF CAPITAL

| Capital Source | | Capital Use | |
|---|---|---|---|
| Owner's Equity | $ 86,000 | Working Capital | $ 40,000 |
| Long Term Debt | $ 36,750 | Long Term Assets | $ 82,750 |
| Total Capital Requ'd | $122,750 | Total Capital Used | $122,750 |

### SALES AND INCOME

| | Upper Quartile | Median | Lower Quartile |
|---|---|---|---|
| Sales | 975,000 | 550,000 | 325,000 |
| Officer's Salary* | 33,150 | 11,000 | 2,275 |
| Net Profit* | 31,250 | 18,000 | 3,250 |
| Total Income* | 64,400 | 29,000 | 5,525 |

*Before Tax

### PROFITABILITY VS ASSETS

| Assets | 0-250$K | 250-1,000$K | 1-10$M |
|---|---|---|---|
| Profitability | N/A | N/A | 26.3% |

**COMMENTS:**   *Very, very high risk and average potential.*

# #229 CONSTRUCTION & MINING EQUIPMENT (MFG) SIC:3531,32

| | |
|---|---|
| Total Assets | $250,000 |
| Profitability | 23.6% |
| Trend | +0.1% |
| Downside Risk | 63.6% |
| Upside Potential | 119.7% |
| Space Required | 760 Sq. Ft. |

## SOURCE AND USE OF CAPITAL

| Capital Source | | Capital Use | |
|---|---|---|---|
| Owner's Equity | $107,500 | Working Capital | $ 82,500 |
| Long Term Debt | $ 43,500 | Long Term Assets | $ 68,500 |
| Total Capital Requ'd | $151,000 | Total Capital Used | $151,000 |

## SALES AND INCOME

| | Upper Quartile | Median | Lower Quartile |
|---|---|---|---|
| Sales | 725,000 | 475,000 | 300,000 |
| Officer's Salary* | 34,075 | 11,400 | 4,200 |
| Net Profit* | 44,250 | 24,250 | 8,750 |
| Total Income* | 78,325 | 35,650 | 12,950 |

*Before Tax

## PROFITABILITY VS ASSETS

| Assets | 0-250$K | 250-1,000$K | 1-10$M |
|---|---|---|---|
| Profitability | N/A | 23.6% | 22.2% |

COMMENTS: *High risk and good potential.*


# #230 MEN'S & BOY'S SUITS COATS & OVERCOATS (MFG)

SIC:2311

| | |
|---|---|
| Total Assets | $250,000 |
| Profitability | 23.5% |
| Trend | +2.5% |
| Downside Risk | 69.1% |
| Upside Potential | 126.5% |
| Space Required | 2970 Sq. Ft. |

## SOURCE AND USE OF CAPITAL

| Capital Source | | Capital Use | |
|---|---|---|---|
| Owner's Equity | $120,250 | Working Capital | $112,750 |
| Long Term Debt | $ 23,500 | Long Term Assets | $ 31,000 |
| Total Capital Requ'd | $143,750 | Total Capital Used | $143,750 |

## SALES AND INCOME

| | Upper Quartile | Median | Lower Quartile |
|---|---|---|---|
| Sales | 875,000 | 675,000 | 450,000 |
| Officer's Salary* | 51,625 | 26,325 | 9,450 |
| Net Profit* | 25,000 | 7,500 | 1,000 |
| Total Income* | 76,625 | 33,825 | 10,450 |

*Before Tax

## PROFITABILITY VS ASSETS

| Assets | 0-250$K | 250-1,000$K | 1-10$M |
|---|---|---|---|
| Profitability | N/A | 23.5% | 28.3% |

COMMENTS: *Very high risk and average potential.*

**#231**   **SEED COS (MFG)**   **SIC:0181,5191,5261**

| | |
|---|---|
| Total Assets | $250,000 |
| Profitability | 23.1% |
| Trend | -2.4% |
| Downside Risk | 65.9% |
| Upside Potential | 144.6% |
| Space Required | 805 Sq. Ft. |

### SOURCE AND USE OF CAPITAL

| Capital Source | | Capital Use | |
|---|---|---|---|
| Owner's Equity | $ 98,000 | Working Capital | $ 55,250 |
| Long Term Debt | $ 43,250 | Long Term Assets | $ 86,000 |
| Total Capital Requ'd | $141,250 | Total Capital Used | $141,250 |

### SALES AND INCOME

| | Upper Quartile | Median | Lower Quartile |
|---|---|---|---|
| Sales | 750,000 | 575,000 | 425,000 |
| Officer's Salary* | 62,250 | 21,850 | 9,350 |
| Net Profit* | 17,500 | 10,750 | 1,750 |
| Total Income* | 79,750 | 32,600 | 11,100 |

*Before Tax

### PROFITABILITY VS ASSETS

| Assets | 0-250$K | 250-1,000$K | 1-10$M |
|---|---|---|---|
| Profitability | N/A | 23.1% | 18.0% |

**COMMENTS:** *Down trend. Very high risk and good potential.*


**#232**   **FLOUR & GRAIN PRODUCTS (MFG)**   **SIC:2041**

| | |
|---|---|
| Total Assets | $250,000 |
| Profitability | 23.0% |
| Trend | +1.8% |
| Downside Risk | 78.2% |
| Upside Potential | 163.9% |
| Space Required | 725 Sq. Ft. |

### SOURCE AND USE OF CAPITAL

| Capital Source | | Capital Use | |
|---|---|---|---|
| Owner's Equity | $116,750 | Working Capital | $ 75,000 |
| Long Term Debt | $ 44,000 | Long Term Assets | $ 85,750 |
| Total Capital Requ'd | $160,750 | Total Capital Used | $160,750 |

### SALES AND INCOME

| | Upper Quartile | Median | Lower Quartile |
|---|---|---|---|
| Sales | 900,000 | 725,000 | 475,000 |
| Officer's Salary* | 61,200 | 16,675 | 3,800 |
| Net Profit* | 36,250 | 20,250 | 4,250 |
| Total Income* | 97,450 | 36,925 | 8,050 |

*Before Tax

### PROFITABILITY VS ASSETS

| Assets | 0-250$K | 250-1,000$K | 1-10$M |
|---|---|---|---|
| Profitability | N/A | 23.0% | N/A |

**COMMENTS:** *Very, very high risk and good - excellent potential.*

| | |
|---|---|
| Total Assets | $250,000 |
| Profitability | 22.7% |
| Trend | -0.9% |
| Downside Risk | 56.0% |
| Upside Potential | 114.5% |
| Space Required | 1410 Sq. Ft. |

## SOURCE AND USE OF CAPITAL

| Capital Source | | Capital Use | |
|---|---|---|---|
| Owner's Equity | $ 84,250 | Working Capital | $ 30,250 |
| Long Term Debt | $ 44,750 | Long Term Assets | $ 98,750 |
| Total Capital Requ'd | $129,000 | Total Capital Used | $129,000 |

## SALES AND INCOME

| | Upper Quartile | Median | Lower Quartile |
|---|---|---|---|
| Sales | 1,525,000 | 1,175,000 | 825,000 |
| Officer's Salary* | 36,600 | 18,800 | 9,900 |
| Net Profit* | 26,250 | 10,500 | 3,000 |
| Total Income* | 62,850 | 29,300 | 12,900 |

*Before Tax

## PROFITABILITY VS ASSETS

| Assets | 0-250$K | 250-1,000$K | 1-10$M |
|---|---|---|---|
| Profitability | N/A | 22.7% | 17.7% |

**COMMENTS:**   *Very, very high risk and good potential.*


#234    **DEPARTMENT STORES (RTL)**      SIC:5311

| | |
|---|---|
| Total Assets | $250,000 |
| Profitability | 22.1% |
| Trend | +0.4% |
| Downside Risk | 46.9% |
| Upside Potential | 118.6% |
| Space Required | 3900 Sq. Ft. |

## SOURCE AND USE OF CAPITAL

| Capital Source | | Capital Use | |
|---|---|---|---|
| Owner's Equity | $134,500 | Working Capital | $106,000 |
| Long Term Debt | $ 27,500 | Long Term Assets | $ 56,000 |
| Total Capital Requ'd | $162,000 | Total Capital Used | $162,000 |

## SALES AND INCOME

| | Upper Quartile | Median | Lower Quartile |
|---|---|---|---|
| Sales | 750,000 | 650,000 | 500,000 |
| Officer's Salary* | 45,750 | 27,300 | 15,000 |
| Net Profit* | 32,500 | 8,500 | 4,000 |
| Total Income* | 78,250 | 35,800 | 19,000 |

*Before Tax

## PROFITABILITY VS ASSETS

| Assets | 0-250$K | 250-1,000$K | 1-10$M |
|---|---|---|---|
| Profitability | N/A | 22.1% | 13.0% |

**COMMENTS:**   *Above average risk and average potential.*

# DYEING & FINISHING (MFG)     SIC:2261,62

| | |
|---|---|
| Total Assets | $250,000 |
| Profitability | 21.9% |
| Trend | +1.3% |
| Downside Risk | 69.7% |
| Upside Potential | 213.7% |
| Space Required | 2790 Sq. Ft. |

## SOURCE AND USE OF CAPITAL

| Capital Source | | Capital Use | |
|---|---|---|---|
| Owner's Equity | $121,750 | Working Capital | $ 62,500 |
| Long Term Debt | $ 45,750 | Long Term Assets | $105,000 |
| Total Capital Requ'd | $167,500 | Total Capital Used | $167,500 |

## SALES AND INCOME

| | Upper Quartile | Median | Lower Quartile |
|---|---|---|---|
| Sales | 850,000 | 775,000 | 450,000 |
| Officer's Salary* | 56,100 | 16,275 | 5,400 |
| Net Profit* | 59,250 | 20,500 | 5,750 |
| Total Income* | 115,350 | 36,775 | 11,150 |

*Before Tax

## PROFITABILITY VS ASSETS

| Assets | 0-250$K | 250-1,000$K | 1-10$M |
|---|---|---|---|
| Profitability | N/A | 21.9% | 17.1% |

**COMMENTS:**  *Very high risk, but excellent potential.*




# FUEL OIL (RTL)     SIC:5982

| | |
|---|---|
| Total Assets | $250,000 |
| Profitability | 21.9% |
| Trend | +1.1% |
| Downside Risk | 57.1% |
| Upside Potential | 103.2% |
| Space Required | 740 Sq. Ft. |

## SOURCE AND USE OF CAPITAL

| Capital Source | | Capital Use | |
|---|---|---|---|
| Owner's Equity | $ 97,000 | Working Capital | $ 38,750 |
| Long Term Debt | $ 45,750 | Long Term Assets | $104,000 |
| Total Capital Requ'd | $142,750 | Total Capital Used | $142,750 |

## SALES AND INCOME

| | Upper Quartile | Median | Lower Quartile |
|---|---|---|---|
| Sales | 1,250,000 | 925,000 | 725,000 |
| Officer's Salary* | 41,250 | 18,500 | 10,150 |
| Net Profit* | 22,250 | 12,750 | 3,250 |
| Total Income* | 63,500 | 31,250 | 13,400 |

*Before Tax

## PROFITABILITY VS ASSETS

| Assets | 0-250$K | 250-1,000$K | 1-10$M |
|---|---|---|---|
| Profitability | 37.9% | 21.9% | 22.0% |

**COMMENTS:**  *Very high risk and low potential.*

## #237 GAMES & TOYS (EXCEPT DOLLS & BICYCLES) (MFG)

|                    |              |
|--------------------|--------------|
| Total Assets       | $250,000     |
| Profitability      | 21.7%        |
| Trend              | -1.4%        |
| Downside Risk      | 48.8%        |
| Upside Potential   | 84.4%        |
| Space Required     | 1540 Sq. Ft. |

SIC:3944

### SOURCE AND USE OF CAPITAL

| Capital Source | | Capital Use | |
|---|---|---|---|
| Owner's Equity | $116,250 | Working Capital | $101,500 |
| Long Term Debt | $ 32,500 | Long Term Assets | $ 47,250 |
| Total Capital Requ'd | $148,750 | Total Capital Used | $148,750 |

### SALES AND INCOME

|                   | Upper Quartile | Median  | Lower Quartile |
|-------------------|----------------|---------|----------------|
| Sales             | 775,000        | 700,000 | 475,000        |
| Officer's Salary* | 37,975         | 17,500  | 9,025          |
| Net Profit*       | 21,500         | 14,750  | 7,500          |
| Total Income*     | 59,475         | 32,250  | 16,525         |

*Before Tax

### PROFITABILITY VS ASSETS

| Assets        | 0-250$K | 250-1,000$K | 1-10$M |
|---------------|---------|-------------|--------|
| Profitability | N/A     | 21.7%       | 31.8%  |

**COMMENTS:**  *High risk and low potential.*


## #238  NURSING HOMES (SVE)

SIC:8051,59

|                    |              |
|--------------------|--------------|
| Total Assets       | $250,000     |
| Profitability      | 21.6%        |
| Trend              | -0.8%        |
| Downside Risk      | 56.2%        |
| Upside Potential   | 85.3%        |
| Space Required     | 4800 Sq. Ft. |

### SOURCE AND USE OF CAPITAL

| Capital Source | | Capital Use | |
|---|---|---|---|
| Owner's Equity | $ 77,250 | Working Capital | $  6,250 |
| Long Term Debt | $101,500 | Long Term Assets | $172,500 |
| Total Capital Requ'd | $178,750 | Total Capital Used | $178,750 |

### SALES AND INCOME

|                   | Upper Quartile | Median  | Lower Quartile |
|-------------------|----------------|---------|----------------|
| Sales             | 675,000        | 400,000 | 275,000        |
| Officer's Salary* | 36,450         | 18,800  | 9,900          |
| Net Profit*       | 35,000         | 19,750  | 7,000          |
| Total Income*     | 71,450         | 38,550  | 16,900         |

*Before Tax

### PROFITABILITY VS ASSETS

| Assets        | 0-250$K | 250-1,000$K | 1-10$M |
|---------------|---------|-------------|--------|
| Profitability | N/A     | 21.6%       | 11.0%  |

**COMMENTS:**  *High risk and average potential.*

**#239**    **LINEN SUPPLY (SVE)**    **SIC:7213**

| | |
|---|---|
| **Total Assets** | $250,000 |
| **Profitability** | 21.0% |
| **Trend** | -0.4% |
| **Downside Risk** | 61.8% |
| **Upside Potential** | 88.9% |
| **Space Required** | 1980 Sq. Ft. |

## SOURCE AND USE OF CAPITAL

| Capital Source | | Capital Use | |
|---|---|---|---|
| Owner's Equity | $112,250 | Working Capital | $ 43,750 |
| Long Term Debt | $ 60,750 | Long Term Assets | $129,250 |
| Total Capital Requ'd | $173,000 | Total Capital Used | $173,000 |

## SALES AND INCOME

| | Upper Quartile | Median | Lower Quartile |
|---|---|---|---|
| Sales | 600,000 | 450,000 | 350,000 |
| Officer's Salary* | 35,400 | 17,100 | 7,350 |
| Net Profit* | 33,250 | 19,250 | 6,500 |
| Total Income* | 68,650 | 36,350 | 13,850 |

*Before Tax

## PROFITABILITY VS ASSETS

| Assets | 0-250$K | 250-1,000$K | 1-10$M |
|---|---|---|---|
| Profitability | N/A | 21.0% | N/A |

**COMMENTS:** *Very high risk and low potential.*


**#240**    **FARM PRODUCE STORAGE (SVE)**    **SIC:4221**

| | |
|---|---|
| **Total Assets** | $250,000 |
| **Profitability** | 20.4% |
| **Trend** | +1.1% |
| **Downside Risk** | 79.1% |
| **Upside Potential** | 282.7% |
| **Space Required** | 450 Sq. Ft. |

## SOURCE AND USE OF CAPITAL

| Capital Source | | Capital Use | |
|---|---|---|---|
| Owner's Equity | $110,500 | Working Capital | $ 39,000 |
| Long Term Debt | $ 51,000 | Long Term Assets | $122,500 |
| Total Capital Requ'd | $161,500 | Total Capital Used | $161,500 |

## SALES AND INCOME

| | Upper Quartile | Median | Lower Quartile |
|---|---|---|---|
| Sales | 1,150,000 | 750,000 | 350,000 |
| Officer's Salary* | 88,550 | 18,000 | 3,150 |
| Net Profit* | 37,750 | 15,000 | 3,750 |
| Total Income* | 126,300 | 33,000 | 6,900 |

*Before Tax

## PROFITABILITY VS ASSETS

| Assets | 0-250$K | 250-1,000$K | 1-10$M |
|---|---|---|---|
| Profitability | N/A | 20.4% | N/A |

**COMMENTS:** *Very, very high risk, but excellent potential.*

# #241    MOTEL, HOTEL & TOURIST CAMPS (SVE)   SIC:7011

| | |
|---|---|
| Total Assets | $250,000 |
| Profitability | 20.3% |
| Trend | +1.5% |
| Downside Risk | 83.8% |
| Upside Potential | 327.5% |
| Space Required | 1980 Sq. Ft. |

### SOURCE AND USE OF CAPITAL

| Capital Source | | Capital Use | |
|---|---|---|---|
| Owner's Equity | $ 69,500 | Working Capital | $ (21,750) |
| Long Term Debt | $117,500 | Long Term Assets | $208,750 |
| Total Capital Requ'd | $187,000 | Total Capital Used | $187,000 |

### SALES AND INCOME

| | Upper Quartile | Median | Lower Quartile |
|---|---|---|---|
| Sales | 850,000 | 275,000 | 150,000 |
| Officer's Salary* | 115,600 | 24,475 | 5,400 |
| Net Profit* | 46,750 | 13,500 | 750 |
| Total Income* | 162,350 | 37,975 | 6,150 |

*Before Tax

### PROFITABILITY VS ASSETS

| Assets | 0-250$K | 250-1,000$K | 1-10$M |
|---|---|---|---|
| Profitability | N/A | 20.3% | 9.7% |

**COMMENTS:**   *Very, very high risk, but excellent potential helped by negative cash flow (see #139).*


# #242 NEWSPAPER PUBLISHING & PRINTING (MFG) SIC:2711

| | |
|---|---|
| Total Assets | $250,000 |
| Profitability | 20.1% |
| Trend | -1.5% |
| Downside Risk | 61.5% |
| Upside Potential | 167.2% |
| Space Required | 1470 Sq. Ft. |

### SOURCE AND USE OF CAPITAL

| Capital Source | | Capital Use | |
|---|---|---|---|
| Owner's Equity | $126,750 | Working Capital | $ 45,750 |
| Long Term Debt | $ 49,750 | Long Term Assets | $130,750 |
| Total Capital Requ'd | $176,500 | Total Capital Used | $176,500 |

### SALES AND INCOME

| | Upper Quartile | Median | Lower Quartile |
|---|---|---|---|
| Sales | 725,000 | 525,000 | 375,000 |
| Officer's Salary* | 60,900 | 19,425 | 7,875 |
| Net Profit* | 33,750 | 16,000 | 5,750 |
| Total Income* | 94,650 | 35,425 | 13,625 |

*Before Tax

### PROFITABILITY VS ASSETS

| Assets | 0-250$K | 250-1,000$K | 1-10$M |
|---|---|---|---|
| Profitability | N/A | 20.1% | N/A |

**COMMENTS:**   *Very, very high risk and average potential.*

| | |
|---|---|
| Total Assets | $250,000 |
| Profitability | 19.8% |
| Trend | +1.8% |
| Downside Risk | 57.9% |
| Upside Potential | 133.4% |
| Space Required | 740 Sq. Ft. |

### SOURCE AND USE OF CAPITAL

| Capital Source | | Capital Use | |
|---|---|---|---|
| Owner's Equity | $104,250 | Working Capital | $ 56,000 |
| Long Term Debt | $ 47,250 | Long Term Assets | $ 95,500 |
| Total Capital Requ'd | $151,500 | Total Capital Used | $151,500 |

### SALES AND INCOME

| | Upper Quartile | Median | Lower Quartile |
|---|---|---|---|
| Sales | 2,475,000 | 1,850,000 | 975,000 |
| Officer's Salary* | 37,125 | 14,800 | 4,875 |
| Net Profit* | 33,000 | 15,250 | 7,750 |
| Total Income* | 70,125 | 30,050 | 12,625 |

*Before Tax

### PROFITABILITY VS ASSETS

| Assets | 0-250$K | 250-1,000$K | 1-10$M |
|---|---|---|---|
| Profitability | N/A | 19.8% | 27.3% |

**COMMENTS:** *Very high risk and average potential.*

---

#244      **CASKETS & BURIEL SUPPLIES (MFG)**      SIC:3995

| | |
|---|---|
| Total Assets | $250,000 |
| Profitability | 19.7% |
| Trend | +0.7% |
| Downside Risk | 56.3% |
| Upside Potential | 135.0% |
| Space Required | 1000 Sq. Ft. |

### SOURCE AND USE OF CAPITAL

| Capital Source | | Capital Use | |
|---|---|---|---|
| Owner's Equity | $115,250 | Working Capital | $ 80,000 |
| Long Term Debt | $ 48,500 | Long Term Assets | $ 83,750 |
| Total Capital Requ'd | $163,750 | Total Capital Used | $163,750 |

### SALES AND INCOME

| | Upper Quartile | Median | Lower Quartile |
|---|---|---|---|
| Sales | 700,000 | 500,000 | 400,000 |
| Officer's Salary* | 51,800 | 18,000 | 9,600 |
| Net Profit* | 24,000 | 14,250 | 4,500 |
| Total Income* | 75,800 | 32,250 | 14,100 |

*Before Tax

### PROFITABILITY VS ASSETS

| Assets | 0-250$K | 250-1,000$K | 1-10$M |
|---|---|---|---|
| Profitability | N/A | 19.7 | N/A |

**COMMENTS:** *Very high risk, and average potential.*

 **CONSTRUCTION GRAVEL & SAND (MFG)**  SIC:1442

| | |
|---|---|
| Total Assets | $250,000 |
| Profitability | 19.7% |
| Trend | +2.4% |
| Downside Risk | 80.9% |
| Upside Potential | 79.3% |
| Space Required | 1150 Sq. Ft. |

## SOURCE AND USE OF CAPITAL

| Capital Source | | Capital Use | |
|---|---|---|---|
| Owner's Equity | $111,750 | Working Capital | $ 15,000 |
| Long Term Debt | $ 59,750 | Long Term Assets | $156,500 |
| Total Capital Requ'd | $171,500 | Total Capital Used | $171,500 |

## SALES AND INCOME

| | Upper Quartile | Median | Lower Quartile |
|---|---|---|---|
| Sales | 375,000 | 250,000 | 200,000 |
| Officer's Salary* | 25,500 | 10,000 | 5,200 |
| Net Profit* | 35,000 | 23,750 | 1,250 |
| Total Income* | 60,500 | 33,750 | 6,450 |

*Before Tax

## PROFITABILITY VS ASSETS

| Assets | 0-250$K | 250-1,000$K | 1-10$M |
|---|---|---|---|
| Profitability | N/A | 19.7% | 11.6% |

**COMMENTS:**  *Very, very high risk and below average potential.*


#246  **MEN'S WORK CLOTHING (MFG)**  SIC:2328

| | |
|---|---|
| Total Assets | $250,000 |
| Profitability | 19.6% |
| Trend | -2.1% |
| Downside Risk | 62.3% |
| Upside Potential | 116.6% |
| Space Required | 9000 Sq. Ft. |

## SOURCE AND USE OF CAPITAL

| Capital Source | | Capital Use | |
|---|---|---|---|
| Owner's Equity | $118,750 | Working Capital | $ 95,250 |
| Long Term Debt | $ 34,500 | Long Term Assets | $ 58,000 |
| Total Capital Requ'd | $153,250 | Total Capital Used | $153,250 |

## SALES AND INCOME

| | Upper Quartile | Median | Lower Quartile |
|---|---|---|---|
| Sales | 750,000 | 500,000 | 400,000 |
| Officer's Salary* | 25,500 | 12,500 | 2,800 |
| Net Profit* | 39,500 | 17,500 | 8,500 |
| Total Income* | 65,000 | 30,000 | 11,300 |

*Before Tax

## PROFITABILITY VS ASSETS

| Assets | 0-250$K | 250-1,000$K | 1-10$M |
|---|---|---|---|
| Profitability | N/A | 19.6% | N/A |

**COMMENTS:**  *Very, very high risk and below average potential.*

# #247 YARN-COTTON, SILK & SYNTHETIC (MFG)   SIC:2282

| | |
|---|---|
| Total Assets | $250,000 |
| Profitability | 19.3% |
| Trend | -0.1% |
| Downside Risk | 64.7% |
| Upside Potential | 158.2% |
| Space Required | 1125 Sq. Ft. |

## SOURCE AND USE OF CAPITAL

| Capital Source | | Capital Use | |
|---|---|---|---|
| Owner's Equity | $128,250 | Working Capital | $ 70,750 |
| Long Term Debt | $ 36,750 | Long Term Assets | $ 94,250 |
| Total Capital Requ'd | $165,000 | Total Capital Used | $165,000 |

## SALES AND INCOME

| | Upper Quartile | Median | Lower Quartile |
|---|---|---|---|
| Sales | 800,000 | 625,000 | 500,000 |
| Officer's Salary* | 36,800 | 9,375 | 5,000 |
| Net Profit* | 45,500 | 22,500 | 6,250 |
| Total Income* | 82,300 | 31,875 | 11,250 |

*Before Tax

## PROFITABILITY VS ASSETS

| Assets | 0-250$K | 250-1,000$K | 1-10$M |
|---|---|---|---|
| Profitability | N/A | 19.3% | N/A |

**COMMENTS:** *Below average risk and average potential.*

# #248   GRAIN (WSLE)   SIC:5153

| | |
|---|---|
| Total Assets | $250,000 |
| Profitability | 19.1% |
| Trend | -3.0% |
| Downside Risk | 69.4% |
| Upside Potential | 133.6% |
| Space Required | 540 Sq. Ft. |

## SOURCE AND USE OF CAPITAL

| Capital Source | | Capital Use | |
|---|---|---|---|
| Owner's Equity | $110,500 | Working Capital | $ 42,250 |
| Long Term Debt | $ 37,250 | Long Term Assets | $105,500 |
| Total Capital Requ'd | $147,750 | Total Capital Used | $147,750 |

## SALES AND INCOME

| | Upper Quartile | Median | Lower Quartile |
|---|---|---|---|
| Sales | 1,375,000 | 900,000 | 625,000 |
| Officer's Salary* | 39,875 | 16,200 | 5,625 |
| Net Profit* | 26,000 | 12,000 | 3,000 |
| Total Income* | 65,875 | 28,200 | 8,625 |

*Before Tax

## PROFITABILITY VS ASSETS

| Assets | 0-250$K | 250-1,000$K | 1-10$M |
|---|---|---|---|
| Profitability | N/A | 19.1% | 9.6% |

**COMMENTS:** *Strong down trend. Very, very high risk and below average potential.*

# BOWLING ALLEYS (SVE)

SIC:7933

| | |
|---|---|
| Total Assets | $250,000 |
| Profitability | 18.6% |
| Trend | -3.0% |
| Downside Risk | 62% |
| Upside Potential | 139.2% |
| Space Required | 3330 Sq. Ft. |

## SOURCE AND USE OF CAPITAL

| Capital Source | | Capital Use | |
|---|---|---|---|
| Owner's Equity | $ 68,750 | Working Capital | $ (37,500) |
| Long Term Debt | $113,500 | Long Term Assets | $219,750 |
| Total Capital Requ'd | $182,250 | Total Capital Used | $182,250 |

## SALES AND INCOME

| | Upper Quartile | Median | Lower Quartile |
|---|---|---|---|
| Sales | 425,000 | 225,000 | 175,000 |
| Officer's Salary* | 45,900 | 19,575 | 12,600 |
| Net Profit* | 35,000 | 14,250 | 250 |
| Total Income* | 80,900 | 33,825 | 12,850 |

*Before Tax

## PROFITABILITY VS ASSETS

| Assets | 0-250$K | 250-1,000$K | 1-10$M |
|---|---|---|---|
| Profitability | 64.7% | 18.6% | N/A |

**COMMENTS:** *High risk, moderate potential. Negative working capital helps to fund excessive long-term debt.*



# BITUMINOUS COAL MINING (MFG)

SIC:1211

| | |
|---|---|
| Total Assets | $250,000 |
| Profitability | 18.1% |
| Trend | N/A |
| Downside Risk | 88.3% |
| Upside Potential | 150% |
| Space Required | 780 Sq. Ft. |

## SOURCE AND USE OF CAPITAL

| Capital Source | | Capital Use | |
|---|---|---|---|
| Owner's Equity | $ 97,250 | Working Capital | $ (250) |
| Long Term Debt | $ 69,000 | Long Term Assets | $166,500 |
| Total Capital Requ'd | $166,250 | Total Capital Used | $166,250 |

## SALES AND INCOME

| | Upper Quartile | Median | Lower Quartile |
|---|---|---|---|
| Sales | 400,000 | 300,000 | 175,000 |
| Officer's Salary* | 35,600 | 14,400 | 4,025 |
| Net Profit* | 39,750 | 15,750 | (500) |
| Total Income* | 75,350 | 30,150 | 3,525 |

*Before Tax

## PROFITABILITY VS ASSETS

| Assets | 0-250$K | 250-1,000$K | 1-10$M |
|---|---|---|---|
| Profitability | N/A | 18.1% | 21.4% |

**COMMENTS:** *Extremely high risk; moderate potential.*

| | |
|---|---|
| **Total Assets** | $250,000 |
| **Profitability** | 17.8% |
| **Trend** | N/A |
| **Downside Risk** | 105.5% |
| **Upside Potential** | 241.9% |
| **Space Required** | 2520 Sq. Ft. |

### SOURCE AND USE OF CAPITAL

| Capital Source | | Capital Use | |
|---|---|---|---|
| Owner's Equity | $129,000 | Working Capital | $ 23,000 |
| Long Term Debt | $ 42,000 | Long Term Assets | $148,000 |
| Total Capital Requ'd | $171,000 | Total Capital Used | $171,000 |

### SALES AND INCOME

| | Upper Quartile | Median | Lower Quartile |
|---|---|---|---|
| Sales | 650,000 | 350,000 | 150,000 |
| Officer's Salary* | 66,950 | 15,400 | 3,300 |
| Net Profit* | 37,000 | 15,000 | (5,000 ) |
| Total Income* | 103,950 | 30,400 | (1,700 ) |

*Before Tax

### PROFITABILITY VS ASSETS

| Assets | 0-250$K | 250-1,000$K | 1-10$M |
|---|---|---|---|
| Profitability | N/A | 17.8% | 18.4% |

**COMMENTS:** *Exceptionally high risk, but also excellent potential.*


## #252   MEN'S & BOY'S SHIRTS & NIGHTWEAR (MFG) SIC:2321

| | |
|---|---|
| **Total Assets** | $250,000 |
| **Profitability** | 17.2% |
| **Trend** | -2.1% |
| **Downside Risk** | 40.4% |
| **Upside Potential** | 102.3% |
| **Space Required** | 945 Sq. Ft. |

### SOURCE AND USE OF CAPITAL

| Capital Source | | Capital Use | |
|---|---|---|---|
| Owner's Equity | $ 93,250 | Working Capital | $ 72,500 |
| Long Term Debt | $ 39,000 | Long Term Assets | $ 59,750 |
| Total Capital Requ'd | $132,250 | Total Capital Used | $132,250 |

### SALES AND INCOME

| | Upper Quartile | Median | Lower Quartile |
|---|---|---|---|
| Sales | 725,000 | 525,000 | 425,000 |
| Officer's Salary* | 29,750 | 12,600 | 6,375 |
| Net Profit* | 16,500 | 10,250 | 7,250 |
| Total Income* | 46,225 | 22,850 | 13,625 |

*Before Tax

### PROFITABILITY VS ASSETS

| Assets | 0-250$K | 250-1,000$K | 1-10$M |
|---|---|---|---|
| Profitability | N/A | N/A | 23.9% |

**COMMENTS:** *Very high risk and low potential.*

# #253 BUS TRANSPORTATION (SVE) SIC:4131

| | |
|---|---|
| Total Assets | $250,000 |
| Profitability | 16.8% |
| Trend | N/A |
| Downside Risk | 69.5% |
| Upside Potential | 108.7% |
| Space Required | 1430 Sq. Ft. |

## SOURCE AND USE OF CAPITAL

| Capital Source | | Capital Use | |
|---|---|---|---|
| Owner's Equity | $ 79,750 | Working Capital | $ (27,500) |
| Long Term Debt | $ 72,000 | Long Term Assets | $179,250 |
| Total Capital Requ'd | $151,750 | Total Capital Used | $151,750 |

## SALES AND INCOME

| | Upper Quartile | Median | Lower Quartile |
|---|---|---|---|
| Sales | 425,000 | 325,000 | 250,000 |
| Officer's Salary* | 36,125 | 14,950 | 6,000 |
| Net Profit* | 17,000 | 10,500 | 1,750 |
| Total Income* | 53,125 | 25,450 | 7,750 |

*Before Tax

## PROFITABILITY VS ASSETS

| Assets | 0-250$K | 250-1,000$K | 1-10$M |
|---|---|---|---|
| Profitability | N/A | 16.8% | N/A |

**COMMENTS:** *Very high risk and low potential.*


# #254 TELEPHONE SERVICE SIC:4811

| | |
|---|---|
| Total Assets | $250,000 |
| Profitability | 15.3% |
| Trend | +2.5% |
| Downside Risk | 50.3% |
| Upside Potential | 154.5% |
| Space Required | 425 Sq. Ft. |

## SOURCE AND USE OF CAPITAL

| Capital Source | | Capital Use | |
|---|---|---|---|
| Owner's Equity | $ 90,250 | Working Capital | $ 13,000 |
| Long Term Debt | $ 98,250 | Long Term Assets | $175,500 |
| Total Capital Requ'd | $188,500 | Total Capital Used | $188,500 |

## SALES AND INCOME

| | Upper Quartile | Median | Lower Quartile |
|---|---|---|---|
| Sales | 375,000 | 125,000 | 100,000 |
| Officer's Salary* | 40,500 | 7,375 | 3,600 |
| Net Profit* | 33,000 | 21,500 | 10,750 |
| Total Income* | 73,500 | 28,875 | 14,350 |

*Before Tax

## PROFITABILITY VS ASSETS

| Assets | 0-250$K | 250-1,000$K | 1-10$M |
|---|---|---|---|
| Profitability | N/A | 15.3% | N/A |

**COMMENTS:** *Very high risk and average potential.*

# DAIRY PRODUCTS (MFG)    SIC:2021-26

| | |
|---|---|
| Total Assets | $250,000 |
| Profitability | 15.1% |
| Trend | -2.2% |
| Downside Risk | 80.0% |
| Upside Potential | 191.1% |
| Space Required | 925 Sq. Ft. |

## SOURCE AND USE OF CAPITAL

| Capital Source | | Capital Use | |
|---|---|---|---|
| Owner's Equity | $ 85,750 | Working Capital | $ 31,750 |
| Long Term Debt | $ 42,500 | Long Term Assets | $ 96,500 |
| Total Capital Requ'd | $128,250 | Total Capital Used | $128,250 |

## SALES AND INCOME

| | Upper Quartile | Median | Lower Quartile |
|---|---|---|---|
| Sales | 1,725,000 | 925,000 | 625,000 |
| Officer's Salary* | 34,500 | 8,325 | 4,375 |
| Net Profit* | 21,750 | 11,000 | ( 500 ) |
| Total Income* | 56,250 | 19,325 | 3,875 |

*Before Tax

## PROFITABILITY VS ASSETS

| Assets | 0-250$K | 250-1,000$K | 1-10$M |
|---|---|---|---|
| Profitability | N/A | N/A | 15.8% |

**COMMENTS:**  *Very, very high risk, low potential, and down trend.*



# PREPARED FEEDS FOR ANIMALS (MFG)    SIC:2048

| | |
|---|---|
| Total Assets | $250,000 |
| Profitability | 13.3% |
| Trend | -5.7% |
| Downside Risk | 194.7% |
| Upside Potential | 114.0% |
| Space Required | 585 Sq. Ft. |

## SOURCE AND USE OF CAPITAL

| Capital Source | | Capital Use | |
|---|---|---|---|
| Owner's Equity | $ 83,250 | Working Capital | $ 38,750 |
| Long Term Debt | $ 58,000 | Long Term Assets | $102,500 |
| Total Capital Requ'd | $141,250 | Total Capital Used | $141,250 |

## SALES AND INCOME

| | Upper Quartile | Median | Lower Quartile |
|---|---|---|---|
| Sales | 1,125,000 | 975,000 | 750,000 |
| Officer's Salary* | 19,125 | 9,750 | 5,250 |
| Net Profit* | 21,000 | 9,000 | (23,000) |
| Total Income* | 40,125 | 18,750 | (17,750) |

*Before Tax

## PROFITABILITY VS ASSETS

| Assets | 0-250$K | 250-1,000$K | 1-10$M |
|---|---|---|---|
| Profitability | N/A | N/A | 16.5% |

**COMMENTS:**  *Strong down trend, exceptionally high risk and very low potential.*

| | |
|---|---|
| Total Assets | $250,000 |
| Profitability | 12.7% |
| Trend | -0.9% |
| Downside Risk | 53.2% |
| Upside Potential | 132.6% |
| Space Required | 660 Sq. Ft. |

### SOURCE AND USE OF CAPITAL

| Capital Source | | Capital Use | |
|---|---|---|---|
| Owner's Equity | $ 60,750 | Working Capital | $ (40,000) |
| Long Term Debt | $ 81,000 | Long Term Assets | $181,750 |
| Total Capital Requ'd | $141,750 | Total Capital Used | $141,750 |

### SALES AND INCOME

| | Upper Quartile | Median | Lower Quartile |
|---|---|---|---|
| Sales | 250,000 | 150,000 | 100,000 |
| Officer's Salary* | 22,750 | 8,700 | 3,900 |
| Net Profit* | 19,000 | 9,250 | 4,500 |
| Total Income* | 41,750 | 17,950 | 8,400 |

*Before Tax

### PROFITABILITY VS ASSETS

| Assets | 0-250$K | 250-1,000$K | 1-10$M |
|---|---|---|---|
| Profitability | N/A | 12.7% | 9.0% |

**COMMENTS:**  *Very, very high risk; relatively poor potential.*



| | |
|---|---|
| Total Assets | $250,000 |
| Profitability | 11.4% |
| Trend | N/A |
| Downside Risk | 60.9% |
| Upside Potential | 349.6% |
| Space Required | 1080 Sq. Ft. |

### SOURCE AND USE OF CAPITAL

| Capital Source | | Capital Use | |
|---|---|---|---|
| Owner's Equity | $ 76,500 | Working Capital | $ (3,250) |
| Long Term Debt | $ 97,250 | Long Term Assets | $178,000 |
| Total Capital Requ'd | $173,750 | Total Capital Used | $173,750 |

### SALES AND INCOME

| | Upper Quartile | Median | Lower Quartile |
|---|---|---|---|
| Sales | 375,000 | 225,000 | 150,000 |
| Officer's Salary* | 51,000 | 8,100 | 4,500 |
| Net Profit* | 38,250 | 11,750 | 3,250 |
| Total Income* | 89,250 | 19,850 | 7,750 |

*Before Tax

### PROFITABILITY VS ASSETS

| Assets | 0-250$K | 250-1,000$K | 1-10$M |
|---|---|---|---|
| Profitability | N/A | 11.4% | N/A |

**COMMENTS:**  *High risk and average potential.*

# CABLE TV (SVE)                    SIC:4899

| | |
|---|---|
| Total Assets | $250,000 |
| Profitability | 10.1% |
| Trend | N/A |
| Downside Risk | 111.2% |
| Upside Potential | 221.1% |
| Space Required | 1170 Sq. Ft. |

## SOURCE AND USE OF CAPITAL

| Capital Source | | Capital Use | |
|---|---|---|---|
| Owner's Equity | $ 29,000 | Working Capital | $(26,000) |
| Long Term Debt | $139,250 | Long Term Assets | $194,250 |
| Total Capital Requ'd | $168,250 | Total Capital Used | $168,250 |

## SALES AND INCOME

| | Upper Quartile | Median | Lower Quartile |
|---|---|---|---|
| Sales | 275,000 | 150,000 | 75,000 |
| Officer's Salary* | 25,850 | 9,000 | 3,600 |
| Net Profit* | 28,750 | 8,000 | (5,300) |
| Total Income* | 54,600 | 17,000 | (1,900) |

*Before Tax

## PROFITABILITY VS ASSETS

| Assets | 0-250$K | 250-1,000$K | 1-10$M |
|---|---|---|---|
| Profitability | N/A | 10.1% | N/A |

**COMMENTS:**  *Exceptionally high risk and low potential.  Future potential may be different.*


# #260 MEMBERSHIP SPORTS & RECREATION  CLUBS (SVE)

| | | |
|---|---|---|
| Total Assets | $250,000 | |
| Profitability | 8.3% | SIC:7997 |
| Trend | -1.4% | |
| Downside Risk | 115.3% | |
| Upside Potential | 185.0% | |
| Space Required | 735 Sq. Ft. | |

## SOURCE AND USE OF CAPITAL

| Capital Source | | Capital Use | |
|---|---|---|---|
| Owner's Equity | $ 97,750 | Working Capital | $( 9,750 ) |
| Long Term Debt | $ 96,500 | Long Term Assets | $204,000 |
| Total Capital Requ'd | $194,250 | Total Capital Used | $194,250 |

## SALES AND INCOME

| | Upper Quartile | Median | Lower Quartile |
|---|---|---|---|
| Sales | 250,000 | 175,000 | 100,000 |
| Officer's Salary* | 33,250 | 16,800 | 5,300 |
| Net Profit* | 12,500 | (750) | (7,750) |
| Total Income* | 45,750 | 16,050 | ( 2,450) |

*Before Tax

## PROFITABILITY VS ASSETS

| Assets | 0-250$K | 250-1,000$K | 1-10$M |
|---|---|---|---|
| Profitability | N/A | 8.3% | N/A |

**COMMENTS:**  *You have to be almost philanthropic to operate such a business.*